主编 郭继荣 白靖宇

研究生英语创新教育系列教材

学术论文写作与发表

本册主编 史文霞

副主编 王 华

编 者 （以姓氏笔画为序）

王 华 史文霞 李小棉

张蕾蕾 郭继荣

西安交通大学出版社

XI'AN JIAOTONG UNIVERSITY PRESS

图书在版编目(CIP)数据

学术论文写作与发表 / 郭继荣　白靖宇主编. —西安:西安交通大学
出版社,2012.5(2025.7重印)
　(研究生英语创新教育系列教材)
　ISBN 978 - 7 - 5605 - 4209 - 6

　Ⅰ.①学…　Ⅱ.①郭…　②白…　Ⅲ.①英语－论文－写作－高等学校－教材
Ⅳ.①H315

中国版本图书馆 CIP 数据核字(2012)第 025501 号

书　　名	学术论文写作与发表
主　　编	郭继荣　白靖宇
本册主编	史文霞
责任编辑	黄炜炜

出版发行	西安交通大学出版社
	(西安市兴庆南路 1 号　邮政编码 710048)
网　　址	http://www.xjtupress.com
电　　话	(029)82668357　82667874(市场营销中心)
	(029)82668315(总编办)
传　　真	(029)82668280
印　　刷	西安日报社印务中心

开　　本	787mm×1092mm　1/16　**印张** 16.125　**字数** 379 千字
版次印次	2012 年 5 月第 1 版　　2025 年 7 月第 10 次印刷
书　　号	ISBN 978 - 7 - 5605 - 4209 - 6
定　　价	38.00 元

如发现印装质量问题,请与本社市场营销中心联系。
订购热线:(029)82665248　(029)82667874
投稿热线:(029)82665371
读者信箱:xjtu_rw@163.com

研究生英语创新教育系列教材

编写委员会

学术顾问：何福胜

总　监　制：林　全　　　项目策划：陈　丽

主　　　编：郭继荣　白靖宇

编　　　委：（按姓氏笔画）

马志媛　王　芳　王宏俐　冯广宜

史文霞　白静宇　吉　乐　李雪梅

袁小陆　贾立平　班荣学　郭继荣

总 序
Preface

　　随着21世纪经济全球化、信息网络化和文化多元化的不断发展，世界各国的研究生教育正在面临着国际化创新能力教育的巨大压力与挑战。目前，我国的研究生教育也正处在从传统教育向现代教育转型的重要时期，正在实现由知识教育向创新教育的转变。在这一背景下，研究生英语教育必须改变传统观念，要"以研究生为本"，建立以"英语创新教育"为核心的新理念，融入培养创新型人才和建设创新型国家的时代潮流。为此，我们组织编写了这套"研究生英语创新教育"（Graduate English for Innovative Education）系列教材。

　　本系列教材是以教育部研究生创新教育计划西部研究生教育创新平台建设为依托，开发编写的一套全新的研究生英语系列教材，其宗旨是确立研究生英语创新教育的新理念，在研究生英语教学中实施自主学习的理论，激发研究生创新思维能力，提高研究生英语教学质量和水平，培养高层次创新型人才。

◎本系列教材的特点

　　1.建立"研究生英语创新教育"的新理念。现代教育强调教育教学过程是一个高度创造性的过程，以点拨、启发、引导、开发和训练学生的创造才能为基本目标。因此，研究生英语教育必须改变传统的教学观念和方式，确立新的教学目标，挖掘利用新的教学资源和手段，采取不同的教学评价体系。本系列教材的建设和编写符合当前研究生创新能力教育的理念，有助于研究生英语教育实现启发式和讨论式的教学，有利于研究生英语综合能力的提高和自主学习能力的培养，在开拓认知视野的同时激发研究生的创新思维。

　　2.实施"以研究生为本"的自主学习理论。语言学习自主性这一概念是当代语言教学理论中的一个热门问题，深刻地影响了世界范围内的教育改革，其理论基础为美国奈塞尔(U.Neisser)的认知心理学和马斯洛（A.Maslow）、罗杰斯（C.R.Rogers）

等人为代表的人本主义心理学。根据研究生的心理和学习特点，他们具有较为完整的知识结构、较强的独立意识和自主学习能力，因此自主学习的模式在研究生英语教育过程中是十分可行的，也是非常必要的。同时，我们倡导的"以研究生为本"的理念，就是强调在英语教学活动中要采取启发式、讨论式、研究式等各类方法，要求研究生主动参与，发挥他们在英语学习过程中的主体作用，突出对他们创新意识的培养和实践，使英语教育成为他们人生发展过程中的一个重要因素。另外，本系列教材是一种开放性、立体式的现代化教材，包括纸质教材、多媒体光盘和网络系统，以适应在现代信息技术条件下研究生英语自主学习的新需求。

3.语言材料具有思想性、真实性和时代感。选材在英语教材编写和教学中具有重要意义，是决定教材质量优劣的关键。本系列教材以研究生英语创新教育为理念，在语言材料选择中把文章内容的思想性放在第一位，注重选择思想性好和情感品位高的文章，激发和调动研究生思考问题的积极性，培养他们的创新思维能力和提高他们的思想素养。同时，本系列教材文章的选择非常注重语言材料的真实性和时代感。根据现代教材理论，真实材料指社会上流通和人们日常接触到的各种语言材料。本系列教材的文章均选自外国报刊、杂志、网络、书籍和辞典，保证了语言材料的"原汁原味"（in original），并以最新的语言材料为主，反映多学科发展的前沿信息和当前社会的精神面貌，具有强烈的时代感。

4.教材练习设计具有多样性和实践性。教材练习设计是英语教材编写和教学中的一个重要环节。一方面,对于学习者来说,它有利于巩固所学的知识,发展运用英语的能力和提高英语水平;另一方面,对于教师来讲,它有利于检查教学效果,帮助教师进一步改进教学和促进教学效率。据此,本系列教材练习根据不同种类的教材,设计了多种多样的练习形式,使研究生有足够的练习量来巩固和提高所学的语言知识。更重要的是，新的英语教学理念强调学习者要成为语言信息的加工主体和知识的构建者。这就要求研究生要从依靠教师课堂讲授中解脱出来，积极主动参与到语言实践中去，从一个被动的语言信息接受者转变成为一位语言学习的实践者，通过对本系列教材练习部分的多听多说多练，在大量反复的实践中巩固和掌握所学英语语言知识和技能，切实提高英语水平。

◎本系列教材的构成体系

根据当前研究生英语教学和学习的实际情况，本系列教材分为必修课教材和选修课教材两大类别、博士和硕士两个层次。

必修课教材

1.英语综合教程共3册：1册供博士使用，学习时间为半年；2册供硕士使用，学习时间为1年。该教程以课文和练习为核心，主要是培养综合运用英语的能力。每册共有10~12个单元，每单元课文分为A、B两篇。每册教材都配有教师用书和录音光盘。另外，《硕士英语综合教程》还配有一本学习指导书，供自主学习使用。

2.口语、听说教程共3册：1册供博士使用，学习时间为半年；2册供硕士使用，学习时间为1年。该教程以英语口语、听说训练为主，主要是培养口头运用英语的能力。每册共有16个单元，每单元分为课堂教学和自主学习两部分。每册教材后都配有练习答案、录音原文和光盘。

选修课教材

研究生英语创新教育的核心是改革研究生英语课程设置，在研究生英语课程体系中开设选修课是势在必行，也是这次研究生英语创新教育系列教材开发编写的重点，其目的主要是培养研究生的语言实际应用能力，推动研究生专业知识的学习，特别是提高研究生在本专业领域的国际学术交流能力，同时增强研究生的英语文化知识和培养研究生的人文素质。

选修课教材实行硕士、博士一体化设置，以实用性和通用性为基本原则，分为三大类8种：

1.英语文化知识类选修课教材，共2种：《西方文化简史》和《英美名著赏析》，主要涵盖英语国家文学、文化知识。

2.英语语言技能类选修课教材，共4种：《科技英语文献阅读》、《英语媒体时文选读》、《学术论文写作与发表》和《口译技能与实践》，主要包括英语阅读、写作技能等。

3.英语情景交流类选修课教材，共2种：《国际学术交流英语》和《经典影视赏析》，主要涉及英语在交流场合中的实际应用。

研究生英语选修课的开发与设置是一个十分复杂的问题，受到各校学科门类、专业设置、培养机制、师资力量和生源质量等条件的制约。所以，一种教材很难适合不同类别的研究生，各高校可以结合本校的学科专业，开发出具有本校特色的选修课教材，以满足教学的需求和研究生的实际需要。

　　本系列教材在编写和出版过程中汇集各方面的智慧和力量，是团结合作的结晶。本系列教材由陕西省学位与研究生教育学会研究生外语教学工作委员会统一协调，邀请清华大学研究生院副院长、英语教学和教材专家何福胜教授担任学术顾问，以在陕西的国家985、211工程高校、驻陕西的军队院校和省属重点大学的教授、博士为骨干力量，组织全省各研究生培养高校有丰富教学经验的教师合作编写。

　　本系列教材在教材编写出版过程中，西安交通大学出版社的各级领导和编辑人员给予了全力支持和积极配合，做了许多卓有成效的工作。同时，本系列教材的编写得到了陕西省教育厅和学位办的领导、各研究生培养单位的领导和广大研究生英语教师的大力支持，在此一并表示衷心的感谢。另外，本系列教材的编写参考了一些国外的报刊、杂志、图书和网站上的文章，也在此向原作者表示感谢。

　　由于我们水平有限，在编写中难免有疏漏和错误之处，希望广大师生和读者在使用中批评指正和提出宝贵意见，我们对此表示诚挚的欢迎和虚心的接受，使本系列教材在以后的出版中力求达到臻善臻美。

编　者
2012年

前 言

Foreword

英语已经成为国际科技领域的主流语言，各国学者主要通过在国际学术期刊上发表英文学术论文达到与国外学者交流和推广自己的科技成果的目的。在国际期刊上发表论文的档次和数量已成为衡量学者、研究机构乃至整个国家学术水平的一个重要指标。非英语专业研究生作为科技队伍的主要力量之一，其学术英语写作与发表能力的培养已经成为其进行国际学术交流不可或缺的一项基本能力和要求。学术英语写作与发表能力是研究生科研素质以及语言能力的综合体现，已经成为高校培养国际型、创新型人才的一个重要衡量标准。《学术论文写作与发表》正是在这样的需求背景下编写而成。本书作为学术论文写作的实用教材，既可供高校教师、研究生、高年级本科生以及相关科研人员学习使用，也可用于对国际学术会议参会人员的培训。

本书是在编者们长期教学实践的基础上，以教学讲义为蓝本，充分吸收和借鉴了近年来相关学术写作教学与研究的最新成果，按照国际学术论文写作与发表的基本流程来安排教材的相应体系，在结构安排上力求全面、简洁、合理、规范，在内容上充分体现实用和创新特色。全书共分为五篇。第一篇包括第一章，主要对研究性论文的基本概念及体裁特征等基本问题进行全面介绍和梳理。第二篇包括第二章和第三章，主要介绍文献阅读过程中所需的基本阅读策略及如何做阅读笔记等常规策略与方法。第三篇包括第四章、第五章、第六章、第七章、第八章、第九章和第十章，涵盖研究性论文的各个组成部分的写作策略，主要涉及标题、引言、研究方法、研究结果及结论等部分的修辞结构及主要语体特色。第四篇包括第十一章，主要介绍学术论文发表的流程和环节，涉及期刊杂志的选择、论文发表的过程、作者与编辑间的书信往来等问题。第五篇包括第十二章，对中国科技论文作者在研究性论文写作中容易出现的语言问题进行了详细的梳理和分析，并且给出了相应的修改策略。

本书以国家《非英语专业研究生英语教学大纲》为依据，以功能教学法、语类理论、跨文化交际理论、二语习得理论及语篇衔接和连贯理论为理论支撑，力图体现新的课程观、教材观、教学观和学习观：

在编写思路上体现科学性、系统性和合理性，突出教学方法的科学性，体现以学生为主体、以提高学生的学术写作与发表能力为目标。书中提供了大量的例文和训练材料，或拓展视野，或引发兴趣，或启迪思维，既便于教师采取灵活多变的教学方法组织教学，又便于学生在教师的指导下自学、研讨、练习，有利于调动学生的积极性，把学习的主动权交给学生，让学生在自主学习中掌握学术写作的方法和技巧，以培养学生的创新思维能力。

在教材内容的设计上体现教学内容的系统性、连贯性及趣味性，努力做到三个相结合：学术写作知识的教授与写作能力的培养相结合，学术写作能力的培养与跨文化交际能力的培养相结合，学术写作能力的培养与学生创新思维能力相结合。力图解决三个问题：一是进一步解决学生乐学、自主学习问题。二是解决学生学习学术写作的方法问题，促进学生学习方式的改变，为他们的终身学习和发展奠定坚实的基础。三是解决如何在重视基础写作学习的同时，引导学生大量阅读专业文献，加强写作实践，发展创新意识，培养学术写作的实践能力、创新思维能力，以全面提高学生的学术英语素养。

在本书编写的过程中，编者参阅并借鉴了大量国内外相关文献资料和同类教材，主要的参考教材和文献资料均已列在书后，在此向所有相关的作者表示深深的致谢！西安交通大学出版社的编辑们为本书的出版付出了大量的汗水和辛勤的劳动，在此一并向他们致以诚挚的谢意！本书虽经反复讨论和精心编写，但由于编者才疏学浅，加之时间仓促，书中的不妥之处和谬误可能在所难免，恳请学界各位专家、学者以及广大读者朋友提出宝贵的批评、修改意见和建议。

编者

2012年4月

目 录

Contents

Part I Preliminaries for Research Paper Writing

Chapter One General Introduction to Research Paper Writing

We live in a scientific age, and like to show, by the words we use, that we think in a scientific way.

—— *Pauline Perrin*

1.1 Research Paper: Definition

The research paper (hereinafter referred to as RP) naturally derives itself from the way in which it is written. In contemporary English, research means "careful, systematic, patient study and investigation in some field of knowledge, undertaken to discover or establish facts or principle."(See word entry of "research" in *Webster's New World Dictionary*. 3rd College Ed. New York: Simon & Schuster, 1998.) "Research Paper" usually conjures up images of hoards of books and journals piled on top of each other as one undertakes the unenviable task of scanning ideas and arguments from numerous different sources. Regardless of the picture that this term creates in our mind, it is almost certain that a research paper is a presentation of facts which are based upon reading or consulting several specified sources, presented according to a standard method of procedure, limited to a relatively narrow phase of a subject, and original in selection, evaluation, expression, and conclusion. What distinguishes a research paper from an ordinary review of a subject or a summarization of the various ideas related to a topic is its analytical and argumentative approach. No matter which field our paper focuses on, it ultimately highlights our own views on a particular subject that are supported by factual proofs derived from existing ideas and arguments. To draw a parallel, a lawyer writing a research paper on a specific case will read up case histories of similar nature to support his or her ideas; while a scientist may rummage through numerous case studies to establish his/her idea about a scientific principle. Thus, ideally we can define a research paper as an extended essay that represents or reflects the writers' own evaluation or interpretation of a specific facet of a subject.

A research paper shares many common characteristics with an ordinary essay. Like a good essay of any other type, a research paper is, first of all, united around a central point (often called the "thesis") that the author wants to make. It also begins with an introduction, and ends with a conclusion. Moreover, the ways of developing a research paper are more or less the same as those used in developing an ordinary essay. However, there are some important aspects in which a research paper differs from a standard essay.

First, while writing an ordinary essay we try to bring forward our own ideas and opinions about the topic in question; whereas in a research paper we attempt to develop our own knowledge about the topic in question and deliberately attempt to find out what other competent people know and feel about the subject, that is to say, we make our point by way of consulting available sources related to the topic we have chosen to discuss. The purpose of doing research on a certain topic is not simply to collect supporting evidences for our point of view. More important than that, doing research might help us find an appropriate position we should assume in the discussion of our chosen topic. In other words, it makes us fully and unmistakably informed of who have so far said what about this topic or problems related to it, so that we may proceed with a more mature approach to the topic and a better-informed basis for the establishment of our own point. Therefore, a research paper involves surveying a field of knowledge in order to find the best possible information in that field. And that survey can be orderly and focused, if we know how to approach it.

Another major difference between a research paper and an ordinary essay is that in writing a research paper we have to acknowledge our debt to the people who originally provided us with the facts or ideas we are using now for our purpose. This simply means that for each piece of borrowed information we are putting into our own paper, we have to make clear where we borrowed it. In the academic circle, this is commonly called documentation of the sources.

In one word, research is an evaluative, interpretive and selective process. In order to write a research paper, we have to find and evaluate a considerable amount of sources. But eventually, we will use only some of the sources we think appropriate either as starting points for our arguments or as supporting evidences for our points. Even so, we still benefit from the research process as a whole. This is because in completing the entire research process, not only have we made ourselves an "expert" on our particular chosen topic, but also acquainted ourselves with a series of practical research skills such as using library resources, evaluating and documenting sources, and establishing viewpoints with the help of relevant sources. These skills will sooner or later prove to be useful when you have to write longer papers in our future study or work.

1.2 Science of Research Paper Writing

Research paper is often hard to read. Most people assume that its difficulties are born out of necessity, out of the extreme complexity of professional concepts, data and analysis. We argue here that complexity of thought need not lead to impenetrability of expression; we demonstrate a number of rhetorical principles that can produce clarity in communication without oversimplifying professional issues. It is held that improving the quality of writing actually improves the quality of thought.

The fundamental purpose of academic discourse is not the mere presentation of information and thought, but rather its actual communication. It does not matter how pleased an author might be to have converted all the right data into sentences and paragraphs; it matters only whether a large majority of the reading audience accurately perceives what the author had in mind. Therefore, in order to understand how best to improve writing, we would do well to understand better how readers go about reading. Such an understanding

has recently become available through work done in the fields of rhetoric, linguistics and cognitive psychology. It has helped to produce a methodology based on the concept of reader expectation.

Readers do not simply read; they interpret. Any piece of prose, no matter how short, may "mean" in 10 (or more) different ways to 10 different readers. This methodology of reader expectations is founded on the recognition that readers make many of their most important interpretive decisions about the substance of prose based on clues they receive from its structure.

This interplay between substance and structure can be demonstrated by something as basic as a simple table. Let us say that in tracking the temperature of a liquid over a period of time, an investigator takes measurements every three minutes and records a list of temperatures. Those data could be presented by a number of written structures. Here are two possibilities:

[First Approach]

t (time) = 15', T (temperature) = 32℃; t = 0', T =25℃;

t = 6', T =29℃; t = 3' T =27℃; t = 12', T =32℃; t = 9', T =31℃

[Second Approach]

Time (min)	Temperature (℃)
0	25
3	27
6	29
9	31
12	32
15	32

Precisely the same information appears in both formats, yet most readers find the second easier to interpret. It may be that the very familiarity of the tabular structure makes it easier to use. But, more significantly, the structure of the second table provides the reader with an easily perceived context (time) in which the significant piece of information (temperature) can be interpreted. The contextual material appears on the left in a pattern that produces an expectation of regularity; the interesting results appear on the right in a less obvious pattern, the discovery of which is the point of the table. If the two sides of this simple table are reversed, it becomes much harder to read.

Temperature(℃)	Time(min)
25	0
27	3
29	6
31	9
32	12
32	15

Since we read from left to right, we prefer the context on the left, where it can more effectively familiarize the reader. We prefer the new, important information on the right, since its job is to intrigue the reader.

Information is interpreted more easily and more uniformly if it is placed where most readers expect to find it. These needs and expectations of readers affect the interpretation not only of tables and illustrations but also of paper itself. Readers have relatively fixed expectations about where in the structure of paper they will encounter particular items of its substance. If writers can become consciously aware of these locations, they can better control the degrees of recognition and emphasis a reader will give to the various pieces of information being presented. Good writers are intuitively aware of these expectations.

This underlying concept of reader expectation is perhaps most immediately evident at the level of larger units of discourse. A unit of discourse is defined as anything with a beginning and an end: a clause, a sentence, a section, an article, etc. A research paper, for example, is generally divided into recognizable sections, sometimes labeled Introduction, Experimental Methods, Results and Discussion. When the sections are confused—when too much experimental detail is found in the Results section, or when discussion and results intermingle—readers are often equally confused. In smaller units of discourse the functional divisions are not so explicitly labeled, but readers have definite expectations all the same, and they search for certain information in particular places. If these structural expectations are continually violated, readers are forced to divert energy from understanding the content of a passage to unraveling its structure. As the complexity of the context moderately increases,

the possibility of misinterpretation or non-interpretation dramatically increases.

Here are some principles derived from the study of reader expectation that could be a help to improve our academic writing.

Reader-expectation Principles

1. Information is interpreted more easily and more uniformly if it is placed where most readers expect.

2. Beginning with the exciting material and ending with a lack of luster often leaves us disappointed and destroys our sense of momentum.

3. We cannot succeed in making even a single sentence mean one and only one thing; we can only increase the odds that a large majority of readers will tend to interpret our discourse according to our intentions.

4. The information that begins a sentence establishes for the reader a perspective for viewing the sentence as a unit.

5. In our experience, the misplacement of old and new information turns out to be the No.1 problem in academic writing today.

6. Put in the topic position the old information that links backward; put in the stress position the new information we want the reader to emphasize.

7. As critical scientific readers, we would like to concentrate our energy on whether the experiments prove the hypotheses.

None of these reader-expectation principles should be considered "rules". Slavish adherence to them will succeed no better than has slavish adherence to avoiding split infinitives or to using the active voice instead of the passive. There can be no fixed algorithm for good writing, for two reasons.

First, too many reader expectations are functioning at any given moment for structural decisions to remain easily activated. Second, any reader expectation can be violated to good effect. Our best stylists turn out to be our most skillful violators; but in order to carry this off, they must fulfill expectations most of the time, causing the violations to be perceived as exceptional moments, worthy of note.

A writer's personal style is the sum of all the structural choices that person tends to make when facing the challenges of creating discourse. Writers who fail to put new information in the stress position of many sentences in one document are likely to repeat that unhelpful structural pattern in all other documents. But for the very reason that writers tend to be consistent in making such choices, they can learn to improve their writing style; they can permanently reverse those habitual structural decisions that mislead or burden readers.

The writing principles suggested here make conscious for the writer some of the interpretive clues readers derive from structures. Armed with this awareness, the writer can achieve far greater control (although never complete control) of the reader's interpretive process.

1.3 Stylistic Conventions of RP Writing

It is important to note that knowing about the process of RP writing and how to structure a paper is important; however, knowing about the appropriate style and conventions to use in our writing is equally important. Although there are distinct differences apparent in different types of writing in the various university disciplines (i.e. writing in the sciences as compared to writing in a humanities based discipline), concerning RP writing, some stylistic features could contribute to an appropriate academic style.

RP writing in English is generally linear, which means it has one central point or theme with every part contributing to the main line of argument, without digressions or repetitions. Its objective is to inform rather than entertain. It is in the standard written form of language. Six main stylistic features of academic writing that are often discussed are, more specifically, as follows: complexity, formality, objectivity, explicitness, hedging, and responsibility.

1.3.1 Complexity

1.3.1.1 Complex Formation of Words

Adding affixes to existing words (the base) to form new words is common in academic English. Prefixes are added to the front of the base (like→dislike), whereas suffixes are added to the end of the base (active→activate). Prefixes usually do not change the class of the base word, but suffixes usually do change the class of the word.

The most common prefixes used to form new verbs in academic English are: re-, dis-, over-, un-, mis-, out-. The most common suffixes are: -ise, -en, -ate, -(i)fy. By far the most common affix in academic English is -ise.

Verb + Prefix →Verb

Prefix	Meaning	Example
re-	again or back	restructure, revisit, reappear, rebuild, refinance
dis-	reverses the meaning of the verb	disappear, disallow, disarm, disconnect, discontinue
over-	too much	overbook, oversleep, overwork
un-	reverses the meaning of the verb	unbend, uncouple, unfasten
mis-	badly or wrongly	mislead, misinform, misidentify
out-	more or better than others	outperform, outbid
be-	make or cause	befriend, belittle
co-	together	co-exist, co-operate, co-own
de-	do the opposite of	devalue, deselect
fore-	earlier, before	foreclose, foresee
inter-	between	interact, intermix, interface
pre-	before	pre-expose, prejudge, pretest
sub-	under/below	subcontract, subdivide
trans-	across, over	transform, transcribe, transplant
under-	not enough	underfund, undersell, undervalue, underdevelop

Suffix Used to Form Verb with the Meaning "Cause to Be"

Suffix	Example
-ise	stabilise, characterise, symbolise, visualise, specialise
-ate	differentiate, liquidate, pollinate, duplicate, fabricate
-fy	classify, exemplify, simplify, justify
-en	awaken, fasten, shorten, moisten

The most common prefixes used to form new nouns in academic English are: co- and sub-. The most common suffixes are: -tion, -ity, -er, -ness, -ism, -ment, -ant, -ship, -age, -ery. By far the most common noun affix in academic English is -tion.

Noun + Prefix → Noun

Prefix	Meaning	Examples
anti-	against	anticlimax, antidote, antithesis
auto-	self	autobiography, automobile
bi-	two	bilingualism, biculturalism, bi-metalism
co-	joint	co-founder, co-owner, co-descendant
counter-	against	counter-argument, counter-example, counter-proposal
dis-	the converse of	discomfort, dislike
ex-	former	ex-chairman, ex-hunter
hyper-	extreme	hyperinflation, hypersurface
in-	the converse of	inattention, incoherence, incompatibility
in-	inside	inpatient
inter-	between	interaction, inter-change, interference
kilo-	thousand	kilobyte
mal-	bad	malfunction, maltreatment, malnutrition
mega-	million	megabyte
mis-	wrong	misconduct, misdeed, mismanagement
mini-	small	mini-publication, mini-theory

mono-	one	monosyllable, monograph, monogamy
neo-	new	neo-colonialism, neo-impressionism
out-	separate	outbuilding
poly-	many	polysyllable
pseudo-	false	pseudo-expert
re-	again	re-organisation, re-assessment, re-examination
semi-	half	semicircle, semi-darkness
sub-	below	subset, subdivision
super-	more than, above	superset, superimposition, superpowers
sur-	over and above	surtax
tele-	distant	telecommunications
tri-	three	tripartism
ultra-	beyond	ultrasound
under-	below, too little	underpayment, under-development, undergraduate
vice-	deputy	vice-president

Suffix Added to a Verb, Noun or Adjective→ Noun

Suffix	Meaning	Example
-tion	action/instance of V-ing	alteration, demonstration
-ity	state or quality of being A	ability, similarity, responsibility
-er	person who V-s something used for V-ing person	advertiser, driver, computer, silencer astronomer, geographer
-ness	state or quality of being A	darkness, preparedness, consciousness
-ism	doctrine of N	Marxism, Maoism, Thatcherism
-ment	action/instance of V-ing	development, punishment, unemployment

-ant/-ent	person who V-s	assistant, consultant, student
-ship	state of being N	friendship, citizenship, leadership
-age	collection of N action/ result of V	baggage, plumage, breakage, wastage, package
-ery/-ry	action/instance of V-ing place of V-ing	bribery, robbery, misery, refinery, bakery

Many adjectives are formed from a base of a different class with a suffix (e.g. -less, -ous). Adjectives can also be formed from other adjectives, especially by the negative prefixes (un-, in- and non-). The most common suffixes are -al, -ent, -ive, -ous, -ful, -less.

Suffix Added to Verbs or Nouns→Adjective

Suffix	Example
-al	central, political, national, optional, professional
-ent	different, dependent, excellent
-ive	attractive, effective, imaginative, repetitive
-ous	continuous, dangerous, famous
-ful	beautiful, peaceful, careful
-less	endless, homeless, careless, thoughtless
-able	drinkable, countable, avoidable

Negative + Adjective → Adjective

Prefix	Example
un-	unfortunate, uncomfortable, unjust
im-/in-/ir-/il-	immature, impatient, improbable, inconvenient, irreplaceable, illegal
non-	non-fiction, non-political, non-neutral
dis-	disloyal, dissimilar, dishonest

Base with Both Prefix and Suffix

	-able	-tion	-tive	-ment	-ar
un-	uncomfortable unavoidable unforgettable		unimaginative		
mis-		mis-information		misjudgement mismanagement	
re-	recoverable				
	reformulation	reproductive	realignment repayment		
in-		inattention	inactive inoperative		
dis-		disconnection		disappointment	
semi-			semiconductive		semi-circular

1.3.1.2 Technical Words and Semi-technical Words

Technical words and semi-technical words are widely used in research paper writing. Technical words are specialized vocabulary used just in one discipline or some limited areas. They, with precise and narrow meanings, are often derived from Latin and Greek roots or compounded from existing words, whose meaning is well-known and not very much changed. For instance, metallurgical(冶金工业), pharmaceutical(药物), turbine(涡轮机).

Besides technical words, semi-technical words are widely used in RP writing. Semi-technical words are words derived from ordinary English and have different specific meanings in their different technical fields. For instance, the word carrier in ordinary English means a person or business that carries goods or passengers from one place to another for payment. But in medicine it refers to a person or thing that carries and passes diseases to others without him-/herself or itself suffering from it; in military it refers to a vehicle or ship which carries soldiers, planes, weapons, etc.; in physics it refers to a hole or an electron capable of carrying an electric charge; in telecommunication it refers to an electric wave or alternating current; in mechanics it refers to a container for carrying; in chemistry it refers to a usually inactive accessory substance.

✖ 1.3.1.3 Nominalization

A nominalization is an action expressed as a noun. Any nominalization can be turned into a verb, and vice versa. Sometimes the two forms, the noun and the verb, are identical.

Verb	==>	Nominalization
help	==>	help
argue	==>	argument
analyze	==>	analysis
behave	==>	behavior
perform	==>	performance
try	==>	try
describe	==>	description
reveal	==>	revelation
act	==>	action
explain	==>	explanation
distort	==>	distortion
nominalize	==>	nominalization

As the last six examples above show, nominalizations very often end in -ion, and especially in -tion: abstract nouns like revolution, operation, abstraction, and speculation.

Nominalization (chiefly of predicate transitive verbs) is another way of making sentences compact, impersonal and formal. It is frequently associated with the occurrence of prepositional phrases, introduced by of . In RP writing, there are many examples of this. A comparison of the following sentences indicates the roles of nominalization in sentence construction.

[Everyday English]

If a potential is applied to gas at low pressure, ionization of the molecules will result.

[Academic English]

The application of a potential to gas at low pressure will result in ionization of the molecules.

[Everyday English]

The progress of the work will depend on how modern the equipment is.

[Academic English]

The progress of the work will depend on the modernization of the equipment.

✖ 1.3.1.4 Expanded Modification of Noun-phrases

Academic written English is lexically dense — there are a higher proportion of content words per clause. This can be done by modification of noun-phrases.

Premodifier	adjective	The use of this method of control unquestionably leads to *safer and faster* train running in the most adverse weather conditions.
	ed-participle	A *charged* body can attract small pieces of paper.
	ing-participle	Fig. 3 is a photograph of a freely *falling* body.
	noun	This alloy is 5 *parts* tin and 3 *parts* lead.
Postmodifier	relative clause	All *that one should do* is to adjust the resistance.
	to-clauses	The television camera scans the subject *to be transmitted*.
	ing-clauses	A direct current is a current *flowing always in the same direction*.
	ed-clauses	The results *obtained* must be checked.
	prepositional phrase	The device *with buttons on it* is called a keyboard.
	adverb (phrase)	The two equations *below* are very important.
	adjective (phrase)	The forces *due to friction* are called frictional forces.

✖ 1.3.1.5 Extensive Use of the Passive Voice

Voice is a property of transitive verbs that take direct objects. There are two kinds of voice, active and passive. In the active voice, the subject of the verb performs the action—it is active. In the passive voice, the subject receives the action—it is passive. The same transitive verb can be put into the active voice or the passive voice at the writer's choice. The active voice expresses actions in a straightforward fashion. The subject performs the action upon the direct object. In the passive voice, however, this is turned around. The subject, which is expressed as the direct object in the active voice, receives the action. This quality of the passive voice allows one to duck the question of who did something.

Sometimes the passive voice is a good, reasonable choice. It is probably a good choice when we do not know who did an action, do not care, or do not want our reader to know—in other words, when we want to put the focus on the thing receiving the action.

[Example]

1. Earthquakes are caused by the movement of plates over the earth's mantle.

2. The economic crisis was caused by the Prime Minister.

The passive voice can also prove useful if we want to put the doer of the action at the end of the sentence in order to create a bridge to the next sentence.

[Example]

1. The marathon was won by a runner from Kenya. This African nation has produced many world-class long-distance runners.

2. Saturn was created in 1985 by General Motors. GM, the world's largest auto maker, was trying to learn a new way to build and market cars.

Compared with other types of writing, RP writing tends to the passive voice. But active voice is still suggested to use for expressing an action, because the papers written in the passive voice is usually harder to read than the active voice.

学术论文写作与发表

1.3.2 Formality

When we write academic texts, we are expected to use formal language rather than the relaxed conversational language we use in everyday situations. One way in which we can make our language more formal is by using sophisticated or formal words in place of colloquial ones such as "stuff", "a lot of", "thing", "sort of".

Colloquial vocabulary includes words and expressions that are used in everyday spoken language. They do not provide the exactness needed in an academic setting. Compare the following sentences which might offer us some useful suggestions about how to write in a more formal style.

Informality	Formality
The analysis *didn't* yield any new results.	The analysis yielded no results.
These semiconductors can be used in robots, CD players, *etc.*	These semiconductors can be used in robots, and CD players.
You can see the results in Table 1.	The result can be seen in Table 1. or Table 1 presents the results.
What can be done to lower costs?	We now need to consider what can be done to lower costs.
Then the solution can be discarded.	The solution can then be discarded.
Researchers *looked at* the way strain accumulates.	Researchers observed the way strain accumulates.
We *got* encouraging results.	We obtained encouraging results.

1.3.3 Objectivity

RP writing is all about expressing opinion, yet this opinion needs to be presented as objective, educated position based on sound evidence. Our text should provide this supporting evidence. RP writing is in general objective rather than personal. It therefore has fewer words that refer to the writer or the reader. This means that the main emphasis should be on the information that we want to give and the arguments we want to make, rather than us.

Compare the following texts:

Text 1	Text 2
In this paper we are presenting our analysis of our assignment on teamwork development. The group we selected for this assignment (the survey team) is a group of people who work for Advance Tours. We used two questionnaires developed by Cacioppe (1998) to try to measure the performance of the team and the way the team members felt about it. We then tried to present an analysis of the findings and we made a few recommendations about what the team can do to improve the way they work. Our recommendations are based a lot on what we read in the journals etc., but we would also like to say something about our own life and work experiences.	This paper presents the findings of an analysis of teamwork development. The group selected for this assignment (the survey team) is a small team of four people working in a small department of Advance Tours. The performance of the team and the team members' attitudes to their team were measured using two questionnaires developed by Cacioppe (1998). An analysis of the findings is then presented and recommendations are made as to what measures can be employed to improve the overall teamwork and performance of the team. Recommendations are based largely on readings from the relevant literature, but also draw on the life/ work experiences of the three writers.

Text 2 is more objective while Text 1 is more personal because personal pronoun "we" and "our" are widely used, especially as sentence subject, in Text 1. This example indicates that there are indeed some personal language expressions that should be avoided for the purpose of objectivity in research paper writing. The use of impersonal language can ensure an objective tone, which requires us, as the writer, to avoid characteristics of personal language.

How to Avoid Personal Language

1. To avoid Using personal pronouns such as "I", "me", "myself", "we", "you", "our", "us" to refer to yourself or the reader.

e.g. *I* agree with Edmund's (1987) perspective that our way of dealing with stress can be unproductive. (personal pronouns)

2. To avoid Using judgemental words that indicate your feelings about a subject.

e.g. *I am convinced* by Carroll's (1996) conclusion that Australian architecture requires innovation, yet *I dislike* the way he has ignored residential design in order to reach this conclusion. (Judgem ental words)

3. To avoid Using words that are emotive.

e.g. The conditions are *appalling* and account, to a large extent, for the *terrible* morbidity and mortality statistics of this community. (Emotive words)

4. To avoid providing no evidence for the arguments being presented.

1.3.4 Explicitness

RP writing is explicit about the relationships in the text. Furthermore, it is the responsibility of the writer to make it clear to the reader how the various parts of the text are related. The effectiveness of a text is increased if the logical relationships that exist between the various parts of the text. These relationships can be made explicit by the effective control of information flow and the use of different signaling words.

Signaling Words Commonly Used in RP Writing

Time/order	at first, eventually, finally, first, firstly, in the end, in the first place, in the second place, lastly, later, next, second, secondly, to begin with
Comparison/similar ideas	in comparison, in the same way, similarly
Contrast/opposite ideas	but, despite, in spite of, even though, however, in contrast, in spite of this, nevertheless, on the contrary, on the other hand, whereas, yet
Cause and effect	accordingly, as a consequence, as a result, because, because of this, consequently, for this reason, hence, in consequence, in order to, owing to this, since, so, so that, therefore, thus

Examples	for example, for instance, such as, thus, as follows
Generalisation	as a rule, for the most part, generally, in general, normally, on the whole, in most cases, usually
Stating the obvious	after all, as one might expect, clearly, it goes without saying, naturally, obviously, of course, surely
Attitude	admittedly, certainly, fortunately, luckily, oddly enough, strangely enough, undoubtedly, unfortunately
Summary/conclusion	finally, in brief, in conclusion, in short, overall, so, then, to conclude, to sum up
Explanation/equivalence	in other words, namely, or rather, that is to say, this means, to be more precise, to put it another way
Addition	apart from this, as well as, besides, furthermore, in addition, moreover, nor, not only...but also, too, what is more
Condition	in that case, then
Support	actually, as a matter of fact, in fact, indeed
Contradiction	actually, as a matter of fact, in fact
Emphasis	chiefly, especially, in detail, in particular, mainly, notably, particularly

A logical flow of information is effective to achieving logic and coherence. It occurs across the whole text, that is to say, the movement of information between paragraphs should be logical and the movement of information with paragraphs must also be logical. Logical flow within paragraphs requires the movement from one sentence to another to be logical.

Most sentences in English have two parts a theme (or topic) and a rheme (or comment). The theme is what we are writing about — it is given information presented at the beginning of the sentence. The rheme is what you are saying about the theme—it is new information presented towards the end of the sentence.

There are three basic patterns of organizing the information flow in a text. Firstly, the new information in a sentence is presented as given information in the following sentence or sentences. This sort of sequencing creates clear and logical text. In fact, text constructed in this manner has been shown to be significantly easier to follow and learn from. Secondly, the given information is the same as the given information of the next sentence. Thirdly, a mixture of the former two is also common and possible to achieve the logic information flow in a text.

Information Pattern 1	Information Pattern 2
The complete electrical *behaviour* of any valve or transistor can be described by stating the *interrelation* of the currents and the voltages between all the electrodes. These *relationships* can conveniently be displayed graphically, and the various curves are known as the "*characteristics*" of the device. In principle, all the *characteristics* should be *available to the designer* proposing to use the device in a circuit.	*Anthropology* is the *study of humankind*, especially of Homo sapiens, the biological species to which we human beings belong. *It* is the study of *how our species evolved* from more primitive organisms; it is also the study of *how our species developed a mode of communication* known as language and a mode of social life known as culture. *It* is the study of *how culture evolved* and diversified. And finally, *it* is the study of *how* culture, people, and nature *interact* wherever human beings are found.

Information Pattern 3
A survey was conducted to find any competitive products on the Australian market that were similar to all the proposed designs. *Surveys* were conducted at hardware stores, bathroom fixture stores, and pharmacies. *These* provided information about *five competitive products*, none of which could possibly result in patent breaches. *Three of these competitive products* enable disease, or age-affected people to operate indoor house taps, hence these products do not solve the design problem. *The fourth product* does aim to solve the design problem, but it does so from a different angle. *The fifth competitive product* also aims to provide ease of operation, is similar to design C, but is intended for indoor use.

1.3.5 Hedging

It is often believed that RP writing, particularly scientific writing, is simply to convey facts and information. However it is now recognised that an important feature of RP writing is the concept of cautious language, often called "hedging" or "vague language". There are four reasons for the use of hedging.

Firstly, authors tone down their statements in order to reduce the risk of opposition by hedging. This position might associate hedges with scientific imprecision and defines them as linguistic cues of bias which avoid personal accountability for statements.

Secondly, writers want their readers to know that they do not claim to have the final word on the subject. Expressing a lack of certainty does not necessarily show confusion or vagueness. One could consider hedges as ways of being more precise in reporting results. Hedging may present the true state of the writers' understanding and may be used to negotiate an accurate representation of the state of knowledge under discussion. In fact, academic writers may well wish to reduce the strength of claims simply because stronger statements would not be justified by the data or evidence presented.

Thirdly, hedges may be understood as politeness strategies in which the writer tries to appear humble rather than arrogant or all-knowing. Hedging is a rational interpersonal strategy which supports the writer's position, builds writer-reader relationships and guarantees a certain level of acceptability in a community. Once a claim becomes widely accepted, it is then possible to present it without a hedge.

Finally, a certain degree of hedging has become conventionalized; hedging now functions to conform to an established writing style in English.

Hedging Words

Modal lexical verbs doubting and evaluating rather than merely describing	seem, tend, look like, appear, think, believe, doubt, indicate, suggest, assume, estimate, tend, argue, propose, speculate	In spite of its limitations, the study *appears* to have a number of important strengths.
Introductory phrases	to our knowledge, it is our view that, on the evidence of, according to, on the basis of, based on, for the most part, to a great extent	*It is our view* that there is no simple explanation.
Modal auxiliary verbs	will, must, would, may, might, could, can, should	Such a measure *might* be more sensitive to changes in health after specialist treatment.

Approximators of degree, quantity, frequency and time	often, sometimes, occasionally, usually, approximately, roughly, generally, somewhat, somehow	Fever is present in **approximately** a third of cases.
Modal adverbs	probably, possibly, perhaps, conceivably, practically, likely, presumably, virtually, apparently, essentially, generally, largely, usually, primarily	There is, **perhaps**, a good reason why she chose to write in the first person.
Modal adjectives	probable, possible, likely, unlikely, uncertain	It is **likely** to result in failure.
Modal nouns	assumption, possibility, probability, claim, estimate, suggestion, likelihood, evidence	This leads to the **possibility** that he will fail in the exam.
Compound hedges (double hedges, treble hedges, quadruple hedges)	It might be suggested that; it may suggest that; it seems likely that; it would indicate that; this probably indicates; it seems reasonable to assume that	it **seems reasonable to assume** that; the day-light velocity is different from the velocity at right.
"If" clauses	If anything, if necessary, if possible, if true	**If true**, our study contradicts the myth that men make better managers than women.

1.3.6 Responsibility

In RP writing we must be responsible for, and must be able to provide evidence and justification for, any claims we make. We are also responsible for demonstrating an understanding of any source texts we use, that is to say, we had better integrate the evidence we have gathered into our paper. After we look at our paper plan and decide where evidence needs to be placed in relation to the points we are making, we need to look at the particular paragraph in which a piece of evidence belongs to and decide how it can be integrated, remembering that its role will be to support or expand on a point we have already made in our own words within that paragraph. In the paragraph below, we will notice that evidence has been paraphrased or directly quoted and placed in a position that allows it to extend the point the writer is making in the topic sentence.

One phenomenon that can impact greatly on the effectiveness of groups is that as group sizes increase there is a tendency for the effort put in by the group to be less than the average effort put in by individuals engaged on the same task separately (Gabrenya, Latane & Wang 1981; Albanese & Van Fleet 1985). *The phenomenon has been described using various terms.* Writers influenced by industrial economics describe it as the "free-rider problem", where the collective nature of the "ontract" obscures the fact of one member failing to honour their part of the contract (Albanese & Van Fleet 1985). *Writers who are organisational psychologists tend to label the phenomenon as "social loafing"and typically define it as "one where everyone puts in a little less" (Gabrenya, Latane & Wang 1981, p120).* Whatever the terminology used to describe this phenomenon, it is one that is problematic for groups.	topic sentence

expansion
integration of paraphrased material

integration of paraphrased and quoted material
summarising & transition to next paragraph |

1.4　Reflections and Practice

1. Improve the following sentences by using norminalization.

(1) You can rectify this fault if you insert a slash.

(2) We can improve its performance when we use super-heated steam.

(3) It is doubtful how accurate the results are.

(4) If we add or remove heat, the state of matter may change.

2. Identify the informal expressions in the following sentences. Rewrite the following sentences, replacing the informal expressions with a more formal equivalent.

(1) You clearly can see the difference between the treated and untreated specimens.

(2) Significantly, even at this late date, Lautrec was considered a bit conservative by his peers.

(3) It focused on a subject that a lot of the bourgeois and upper-class exhibition-going public is regarded as anti-social and anti-establishment.

(4) Later Florey got together with Paul Fildes in an experimental study of the use of curare to relieve the intractable muscular spasms which occur in fully developed infection with tetanus or lockjaw.

(5) When a patient is admitted to a psychiatric inpatient unit, the clinical team should avoid the temptation to start specific treatments immediately.

(6) Therefore after six months the dieter is behaving according to all twenty-six goals and she has achieved a big reduction in sugar intake.

(7) Modern houses have so many labour-saving things that it is difficult for the person at home to have adequate exercise by doing chores, cooking, and looking after a family.

(8) Simply making the effort to reclaim this wasted stuff for fertilizer would have a positive effect on greenhouse releases.

(9) It is difficult to imagine exactly what is meant by saying that such a classification is natural as any collection of things could be classified in this way.

(10) Unfortunately, since there are so many possible explanations, the correct one is most difficult to find out.

(11) These exercises can easily be incorporated into an exercise routine, with each exercise done again a number of times.

(12) Fleming did well in isolating a streptococcus from the cerebrospinal fluid of the patient.

(13) Effective vaccines prevent such hazards, but only if a social organisation could make sure that all potential mothers are vaccinated in good time.

3. There is often a choice in English between a two word verb and a single verb—bring up/raise, set up/establish. Rewrite the following sentences, replacing the informal two-word verb with a more formal equivalent.

(1) A primary education system was set up throughout Ireland as early as 1831.

(2) This will cut down the amount of drug required and so the cost of treatment.

(3) The material amenities of life have gone up in Western society.

(4) The press reflected the living culture of the people; it could influence opinion and reinforce existing attitudes but it did not come up with new forms

of entertainment.

(5) Thus, he should have looked into how the patient coped previously.

(6) The exchange rate went up and down quite violently.

(7) In 1947 the Treasury brought up the question of excluding South Africa (and India) from the sterling area.

(8) Dieters often feel that they should totally get rid of high-fat and high-sugar foods.

(9) Thus when a Gallic bishop in 576 converted the local Jewish community to Christianity, those who turned down baptism were expelled from the city.

(10) Western scholars gradually turned out a corpus of translations from the Arabic and studies of Islam.

(11) Ms. Tucker, Lord White's 29-year-old companion, has since taken her statement back.

(12) Discussion of the outcome of experiments that have used this method will be put off until Chapter 7.

(13) They did not easily accept or put up with differences in others.

(14) My high-school friend signed up for three years with the army so he could put away enough money to go to university and study law.

(15) The solitary feeding of insectivores in forests was therefore put down to a foraging strategy involving the pursuit of cryptic and easily disturbed prey by singletons.

(16) In style, the turn toward abstraction and simplification came about earliest with Anquetin and Bernard and next with van Gogh.

(17) For Klein that cloudless day never arrived, but he never gave up his hope for a just world.

(18) Eventually the Irish party was forced to go back to Westminster.

(19) The court thinks it just and equitable to give back the property.

(20) The English liked coal fires even though they do not always give off much heat.

(21) The story told by German propaganda, however, gave away nothing of the mounting hopelessness of the 6th Army's position.

(22) These exercises can easily be incorporated into an exercise routine,

with each done again a number of times.

(23) Marx took as one of his main tasks the understanding of how this system came into being in order to find out why this system had such power.

(24) This was before he had read the guidelines on how to carry out the research.

(25) Still, the pressure to do well as an individual made most women believe that the problems they encountered were probably of their own making.

4. Read the following texts and rewrite them in a more academic style.

Text 1

Most people take drug overdoses because they find that it's difficult to sort out their problems clearly. That's why you should treat your patients in a clear way. That means you should treat your patients in a way that helps them to tell the difference between their problems and find ways to deal with them.

Text 2

I would call Wagner a subjective artist. What I mean is that his art had its source in his personality; his work was virtually independent, I always feel, of the epoch in which he lived.

On the other hand, I always consider Bach an objective artist. You can see that he worked only with the forms and ideas that his time proffered him. I do not think he felt any inner compulsion to open out new paths.

---

5. Supply proper signaling words or phrases that enhance the explicitness of the texts.

(1) _____ the difference in their ages they were close friends.

(2) If we try to analyse the conception of possession, we find two elements. _____, it involves some actual power of control over the thing possessed. _____, it involves some intention to maintain that control on the part of the possessor.

(3) Every baby's face is different from every other's. _____, every baby's pattern of development is different from every other's.

(4) In 1950 oil supplied only about 10% of our total energy consumption; _____ now it's up to about 40% and still rising.

(5) The Cold War has ended. _____ the two major world powers have

been able to reduce their arms budgets dramatically.

(6) The computer has become smaller and cheaper and _____ more available to a greater number of people.

(7) Many countries are threatened by earthquakes. _____, Mexico and Japan have large ones this century.

(8) Meetings are _____ held three or four times a year.

(9) _____, publishers are hesitant about committing large sums of money to such a risky project.

(10) He could not wait to tell Judy. _____, she had already left for work.

(11) He could not do any thing more than what he had promised _____, to look after Charlotte's estate.

(12) Sugar is bad for your teeth. It can _____ contribute to heart disease.

(13) Of course the experiment may fail and _____ we will have to start again.

(14) The winter of 1940 was extremely bad. _____ most people say it was the worst winter of their lives.

(15) This act has failed to bring women's earnings up to the same level. _____ the gulf is widening.

(16) There are many stories which describe wolves as dangerous, blood thirsty animals, but they _____ prefer to avoid human beings.

(17) They do not trust anyone, _____ people in our position.

(18) The political group will have more power, _____ because of their large numbers.

6. Improve the following sentences by using proper hedging words.

(1) The lives they chose are overly ascetic and self-denying to most women today.

(2) Weismann proved that animals become old because, if they did not, there could be no successive replacement of individuals and hence no evolution.

(3) By analogy, one can walk from one point in hilly country to another by a path which is always level or uphill, and yet a straight line between the points would cross a valley.

(4) There are cases where this would seem to have been the only possible method of transmission.

7. Study the following examples and decide whether they correctly hedged or not.

(1) On the evidence of the findings presented in Figure 1, it would appear that students in Hong Kong generally have little need to speak in English outside the classroom.

(2) The evidence proves that undergraduates rarely communicate with their parents or grandparents in English.

(3) This is undoubtedly because Hong Kong students' family members are Cantonese speakers.

(4) The students in Hong Kong University probably go on an exchange at least once in their university life.

(5) It is possible that students have relatives in English-speaking countries.

(6) There is strong evidence that academic exchanges improve the language skills of students.

(7) The students in the Hong Kong University are predominantly Cantonese speakers.

(8) It is an iron law that nothing can go faster than light.

(9) The lack of solar power stations in HK proves that HK is not suitable for solar power.

(10) Hong Kong offers the best Chinese food in the world.

8. Analyze the stylistic features of the following texts and discuss which is more academic.

Text 1
The inequity in the distribution of wealth in Australia is yet another indicator of Australia's lack of egalitarianism. In 1995, 20% of the Australian population owned 72.2% of Australia's wealth with the top 50% owning 92.1% (Raskall, 1998: 287). Such a significant skew in the distribution of wealth indicates that, at least in terms of economics, there is an established class system in Australia. McGregor (1988) argues that Australian society can be categorised into three levels: the Upper, Middle and Working classes. In addition, it has been shown that most Australians continue to remain in the class into which they were born (McGregor, 1988: 156) despite arguments about the ease of social mobility in Australian society (Fitzpatrick, 1994). The issue of class and its inherent inequity, however, is further compounded by factors such as race and gender within and across these class divisions. The relative disadvantage of women with regard to their earnings and levels of asset ownership indicates that within classes there is further economic inequity based on gender...

Text 2

Because only a few people have most of the money and power in Australia, I conclude that it is not an equal society. Society has an Upper, Middle and Lower class and I think that most people when they are born into one class,end up staying in that class for their whole lives. When all three classes are looked at more closely, other things such as the differences between the sexes and people's racial backgrounds also add to the unequal nature of Australian society.

Women earn less than men and own less than men. Why is this so?

9. In the following text, the sentences are not well written. Please rewrite the text through the effective control of logic information low.

All matter may be classified as either a solid, a liquid or a gas. The atoms or molecules of a solid are densely packed and have very little freedom of movement. Most solids require a considerable force in order to change the shape or volume of most of them. Rubber, wood, glass, iron, cotton, and sand are firm and have a definite form and so are all classified as solids.

Air, oxygen, and carbon dioxide are gases and have no fixed shape or volume of their own. Any container can be filled by these as they diffuse and spread out to fill them. The atoms or molecules of gases move very rapidly and are widely spaced. If water is put into a tyre, it will run to the bottom; if a tyre is filled with air, it fills the whole space inside it. They therefore expand or compress to fit any area.

Crystalline solids and amorphous solids are the two classes solids may be further divided into. When heated, the change to a liquid known as melting is sharp and clear for crystalline solids. Rocks, wood, paper and cotton are this type. These are made up of atoms arranged in a definite pattern. Rubber, glass and sulphur are amorphous solids. These gradually soften when heated, as the pattern of the atoms is not orderly.

A definite form does not characterize liquids. If a table has water, milk, or oil poured on it, these would flow all over the surface. So it will take the shapeof any container in which it is poured since these atoms are loosely structured and they do not keep their shape. The atoms or molecules attract each other, meaning they are able to flow.

Part II Research Process

Chapter Two   Reading Strategies

Reading furnishes the mind only with materials of knowledge; it is thinking that makes what we read ours.

—— *John Locke*

2.1   Reading Efficiently

The crucial first step in research paper writing is to select a right topic for the research paper. Usually, research papers and most examples of scholarly writing follow the following hierarchy, focusing down from a highly general subject to a highly specific thesis:

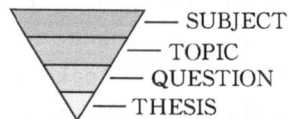

```
        —— SUBJECT
       — TOPIC
      — QUESTION
     — THESIS
```

Before the writing, the writer need to narrow his focus from a broad subject to a manageable topic, then from an intriguing research question to a strong working thesis. During this process, reading is unavoidably the path for the writer to go through, because only by reading the writer can find out the research models applied by his/her peers in their research fields and figure out the current focus of the research work in his/her fields. Efficient reading is about reading in a way that allows us to understand the writer's message without spending too much time in the process. It is also about reading with a clear purpose in mind so that we only read material that is relevant. When we are reading in preparation for a research paper or for understanding generally, remember that good reading strategies go hand-in-hand with good note-taking skills. Have we ever found that we have read a text without really understanding what the author was saying? Have we ever read mountains of books without being any wiser about what the answer to our research question might be? If we have ever had these problems, then we have been reading inefficiently.

Efficient reading starts with choosing a strategy to suit the kind of text we have to read because our purpose in reading and the nature of text to be read will determine our strategy. Our purpose in reading might be to gather information for a research paper, to learn about a particular topic, to understand a particular theory, or to prepare for an exam. In all of these cases, the nature of the text will help us decide how to read. The strategies for reading a text book, for example, are different from those used when reading journal articles.

2.1.1 Strategies for Reading Academic Texts

Academic texts are relatively formal in structure and style. They might be textbooks or just straightforward texts such as William's (1981) book "Culture". To increase the amount of information that we can extract from a single reading of a section, chapter or article in an academic text, we need to use efficient academic reading strategies. These are based on the structure of academic writing. For instance, we should begin by reading the introduction to search for the thesis point or main argument in the introduction and to verify the overview provided by the contents page, and scanning by topic sentences, ie. the sentence which makes the point of the paragraph and which is usually the first sentence of the paragraph.

The role of the introduction is to present background about the topic and to put forward the writer's thesis point (or main argument). This thesis point can often be found towards the end of the introduction. The thesis point is usually reiterated in the conclusion as well, so to gain a good idea of the argument being put forward and the main evidence being presented. We should read both the introduction and the conclusion. This will give us a framework for reading the rest of the content. In the following introduction the last sentence indicates the thesis point.

Human beings have existed on earth for about half a million years. Agriculture, the necessary basis of fixed settlements, is only about twelve thousand years old. Civilizations date back no more than some six thousand years or so. If we were to think of the entire span of human existence as a day, agriculture would have come into being at 11.57. The development of modern societies would get under way at 11.59.30. *Yet as much change has gone on in the last thirty seconds of the "human day" as in the whole of the time leading up to it.*	*Thesis point*

Once we have understood what is being argued, we need to start filling in the big picture by getting an idea of how the writer is advancing that thesis point. We can do this by looking at the way paragraphs and topic sentences are used in the text. Topic sentences play a role in advancing the argument in an organized and logical way. Remember that topic sentences indicate the point being made within a paragraph; all other sentences in the paragraph expand, explain or provide evidence for that point. They usually occur as the first sentence in the paragraph, although they often also occur as the last sentence, particularly in science writing, and they can occasionally occur in some other position. In the following paragraph the first sentence is the topic sentence.

The stress or accent pattern within a word is intimately related to the sounds in it, especially to the vowel sounds. In English, vowels are longer, louder, and often higher in pitch when they are in stressed (accented) syllables than when they are in unstressed syllables. In addition, if adding an ending to a word causes the stress to shift from one syllable to another, some of the vowels in the word may change more drastically and actually become different phonemes. These changes are often not reflected in spelling. For example, when the word *declare* is used to make the word *declaration*, the stress changes: the first syllable gains a little stress, the second syllable loses its stress while the strongest stress goes to the third syllable.	*Topic sentence*

2.1.2 Strategies for Reading Typical Textbooks

When reading a standard textbook, such as a general textbook in Nursing, information can be gathered by using a variety of strategies by noting the overall structure of the textbook in terms of the subdivision of the book into chapters, the subdivision of chapters into sections, and the subdivision of sections into subsections. It can also be extracted quickly at the level of subsections by noting the way topic sentences are used to. To show how to gather information quickly at each of these different levels, we will model this process using a textbook titled *A model for nursing based on a model for living*.

A lot of information can be gathered about this writer's message by scanning the overall book before we begin to read in depth. Some of the things to take note of are the book's title, its chapter headings, its section headings and its table of contents.

The title of the book itself is the first item that can tell us about the writer's message. The book's table of contents details the chapters/topics covered in the book. They elaborate on the message conveyed by the title.

Contents	
The Elements of Nursing: A model for nursing based on a model for living	The author wants to focus on "a model for living".
Section 1 **A model for nursing based on a model for living** Chapter 1: Nursing and health in illness Chapter 2: A model of living Chapter 3: A model for nursing	These chapter headings in Section 1 tell us that the book will first detail the concepts of nursing, health and illness and the concept of a model for living before it shows how these concepts interact to suggest a new model of nursing.
Section 2 **Nursing and the activities of living** Chapter 4: Maintaining a safe environment Chapter 5: Communicating Chapter 6: Breathing Chapter 7: Eating and drinking Chapter 8: Eliminating Chapter 9: Personal cleansing and dressing	The chapter titles in Section 2 suggest that this model's applicability to the "activities of living" will be detailed and argued throughout the rest of the book.

Chapter 10: Controlling body temperature Chapter 11: Mobilizing Chapter 12: Working and playing Chapter 13: Expressing sexuality Chapter 14: Sleeping Chapter 15: Dying	

Looking at the book in this way above-mentioned, ie. simply looking at the structure of the book, provides a good overview of the book's message and a message framework which can be validated by a closer reading of the sections within each chapter. Look at the outline of the sections and sub-sections for Chapter 1.

Chapter 1: Nursing and health in illness
What is nursing? What is health? What is illness? Why are health care systems under reform? How is nursing managing the changes and challenges?

We will see that the chapter deals with definitions of nursing, health, illness and two important questions that might indicate major issues to be detailed in later chapters: why health systems are under reform and how nursing is managing the changes and challenges? Indeed, these later sections provide the rationale for the model of nursing which is put forward later in the book. The chapter moves towards a final section which reiterates the need for a theory of nursing to underpin practice and a final paragraph which suggests that a model of nursing based on a model for living is to be presented in this book. Within its sections, it presents subtopics that detail further these major topics; for example, in the section "What is health", the question is discussed from a variety of perspectives: World Health Organisation definitions of health, health continuum, lay perceptions of health, health as coping, personal responsibilities for health, and current health targets. Skimming over this information means that we will have a "big picture" of the overall topic or issue before we begin to read in-depth. That "big picture" can make the job of reading and understanding the whole text much easier than when we begin without the "big picture". We will find that when we have an academic textbook such as this to read, making use of the structure of the textbook to "key" into the message allows us a much greater level of reading efficiency.

2.1.3 Strategies for Reading Journal Articles

Journal articles usually have a quite rigid structure that is determined by the particular journal in which they appear and by the type of research being reported; this makes extracting information from them sometimes easier than from less rigid text types. The reporting of empirical research will mostly follow the format of abstract, introduction, methods, results, discussion or conclusion. Abstract should be read first to gain a general understanding about the whole paper/research. Reading the introduction section allows us obtain a brief review of previous research, a rationale or reason for the research and an outline of exactly what it is that the research is aiming to do. As usual, we could read the Methods section for an understanding of the method used in the research, the Results section for an understanding of the results found in research, the Discussion section for an understanding of what the results mean, and the Conclusion section for an understanding of the key issues resulting from the research.

The journal article sections described above are visible in the example journal article below. The article has been annotated to highlight the structure and function of each section. We can use our knowledge of the structure and function of each section to improve the efficiency of our reading. Knowing where a certain type of information is located will reduce the time it takes to locate this information, as well as the time it takes us to read the article.

Sample Text	
Aborigines and tuberculosis: why they are at risk **Abstract** *Aborigines have higher rates of Mycobacterium tuberculosis than the rest of the community. There are insufficient contemporary data to assess how much risk tuberculosis poses to the Aboriginal community. Tuberculosis is of particular concern because of its*	*What the research is about (orientation to topic/rationale for study)*

interaction with human immuno-deficiency virus (HIV). **We aimed to ascertain the available data about tuberculosis in Australian Aborigines: to determine morbidity and mortality of tuberculosis in Australian Aborigines, to ascertain the extent of known risk factors for tuberculosis in Australian Aborigines and to consider the public health implications of our findings.** Sparse evidence suggests that Aborigines have higher rates of infection and of clinical tuberculosis than non-Aboriginal Australians, along with a high prevalence of known risk factors for tuberculosis. However, there is a paucity of data about specific risk factors and tuberculosis in Aborigines. In addition, Aborigines have a high prevalence of risk factors for HIV infection. *The existence of concurrent risk factors for tuberculosis and HIV, in a population that already has a high rate of infection with tuberculosis is cause for grave concern. Tuberculosis control is centred on correct and rapid diagnosis and appropriate treatment, as well as efficient contact tracing. These are the most important strategies for control of tuberculosis among Aborigines, and are especially important when there is concurrence of other risk factors. Appropriate preventive therapy for infected people should also be considered.*	**Research aims** Results of research *Implications /recommendations*

Introduction	
Tuberculosis was declared a global emergency by the World Health Organization in 1993. It is essentially a social disease which occurs mostly in people who live in poverty and overcrowding. There are predisposing host risk factors that increase the chance that the individual, once infected, will progress to tuberculosis disease. The infected individual carries the bacilli for variable lengths of time. Should the person's immune system become less vigilant, susceptibility to disease increases. Known risk factors for acquiring infection and progression to disease include contact with an infectious person, low body weight, alcohol abuse, diabetes mellitus, renal failure and human immunodeficiency virus (HIV) infection.	General topic about tuberculosis
There is no firm evidence of tuberculosis among Aborigines before the arrival of Europeans. High rates of tuberculosis in	*specific topic tuberculosis*

Aborigines have been documented in the post-arrival period with most reports coming from early this century. Early reports suggested that Aborigines were a group of people with no immunity to tuberculosis, who were not at great risk while they maintained relatively isolated life styles but who, on contact with outsiders, were vulnerable to tuberculosis. This vulnerability was then compounded by overcrowding and poor living conditions.	*and Aborigines*
Although comparatively little contemporary data about disease prevalence are available, it is possible to examine known risk factors for tuberculosis. This can be considered an important task while there is the possibility that one identifiable group in Australia is particularly vulnerable to tuberculosis. This study aimed to throw light on this public health concern by researching the available data on the relationship between tuberculosis and Aborigines. We aimed: **to ascertain the available data; to determine morbidity and mortality, to ascertain the extent of known risk factors and to consider the public health implications of our findings.**	**research aims**

Methodology

We began by identifying available data on tuberculosis in Australian Aborigines. We identified morbidity and mortality data available from the Northern Territory (NT), considered available data about known risk factors for tuberculosis and the occurrence of these risk factors in Aborigines. We examined the usual risk factors for tuberculosis, with the exceptions of silicosis, gastrectomy, jejunoileal bypass and miscellaneous immunosuppressive illnesses for which we could not find information specific to Aborigines.	Steps taken to gain the data which would provide answers to the research questions
We calculated the age-standardized rate ratio for hospitalization for tuberculosis for Aborigines compared with non-Aborigines in the NT for 1979 to 1988. Hospital separation diagnosis is the diagnosis when the patient leaves by discharge, death, transfer to another hospital or discharge against medical advice. Numerator data were obtained from the NT Department of Health and Community Services and denominator data from the Australian Bureau of Statistics. Indirect age-standardization was done by calculating the number of cases that would	

have been expected in Aborigines each year if Aborigines had the same rate as the same-sex non-Aborigines averaged over the years 1979 to 1988, and then taking a ratio of the observed to the expected rates.

The indirectly age-standardized rate ratio of death from tuberculosis for NT Aborigines (1979 to 1991) was compared with the total Australian rate for 1991. We examined "tuberculosis" (ICD-9 codes 010-018) and "late effects of tuberculosis" (ICD-9 code 137) separately. Indirect standardization was chosen because of the small number of deaths in the Aboriginal population, and the Australian population was chosen as the reference population because it was available (unlike the morbidity data) and because the non-Aboriginal NT population had too few deaths to use as a baseline. We grouped the years 1979 to 1991 into three-year groups with the exception of the most recent years (1988 to 1991), for which we grouped four years. Ninety-five per cent confidence intervals (CI) were calculated using the method described by Bailar and Ederer.

Lastly, we looked at data for HIV-AIDS in Aborigines and examined the potential for problems with tuberculosis control based on what was known about HIV and sexually transmissible diseases in Aborigines. We used the hypothetical and rather simple model proposed by Nunn et al. to estimate the effect HIV could have on tuberculosis rates in Aborigines.

Results

Current data

Current data were sparse. Thomson reported evidence of decreasing rates of tuberculosis in Aborigines, noting that in 1982 the rate was 26.3 per 100 000 for all forms of tuberculosis. This was still about three times the Australian rate. He quoted an annual rate of 135 per 100 000 in the NT in 1969 to 1973, declining to 30.2 in 1982. In Queensland, the rate fell from an average rate of 151.9 per 100 000 in 1950 to 1972 to 26.2 per 100 000 in 1982.

Beilby et al. noted that in 1985 there were 36 cases of tuberculosis in Aborigines in South Australia, a rate of 20.8 per 100 000, which was three times the rate in the

Incidence of tuberculosis for Aborigines and non-Aborigines across Australia

rest of South Australia without age- and sex-adjustment. Subsequent age-standardization for the years 1978 to 1988 gave an annual rate of 91.6 (Cl 56.2 to 127.0) for males and 38.6 (Cl 16.7 to 60.5) for females. Beilby et al. also undertook Mantoux test surveys in four communities and found age-standardized prevalence rates of infection of 6.2, 10.6, 21.0 and 33.5 per cent in the four communities. The authors noted that there might be problems with both denominator and numerator identification and that the rural-urban gradient was conflicting for infection and disease reports. There did not appear to be any obvious cause for this conflict, although one suggestion of the authors was nutrition-related immunosuppression affecting Mantoux-positive rates.	Incidence of tuberculosis in SA
Krause and Britton reported that the rate of tuberculosis in Aborigines in the NT was 114 per 100 000 in 1989, with seven deaths (17 per cent of Aboriginal notified cases). They reported that the rate had fallen to 60 per 100 000 in 1991, and that there was over 90 per cent compliance with treatment.	*Incidence of tuberculosis in NT*
Queensland health authorities reported that the rate of tuberculosis (per 100 000) in indigenous Australians was 25.8 in 1991, 11.1 in 1990, 20.2 in 1989, 12.1 in 1988, 20.4 in 1987, 24.5 in 1986, and 22.2 in 1985. This compares with between 3.1 and 4.5 per 100 000 for all persons in Queensland over the same period. Krause and Britton reported that the rate of tuberculosis in Aborigines in the NT was 114 per 100 000 in 1989, with seven deaths (17 per cent of Aboriginal notified cases). They reported that the rate had fallen to 60 per 100 000 in 1991, and that there was over 90 per cent compliance with treatment.	Incidence of tuberculosis in QLD
In the three years 1989 to 1991, there were 155 cases of tuberculosis notified in the NT, of which 109 (70 per cent) were in Aborigines. The NT contributes about 3 to 8 per cent of tuberculosis in Australia, and represents about 1 per cent of the total population. Aborigines represent about 24 per cent of the NT population.	
The rate ratios of hospital separation for Aborigines in the NT compared with non Aborigines are shown for tuberculosis in Figures 1 and 2. Both male and female Aborigines had an	*Pointing out a problem in data collection*

学术论文写作与发表

estimated 3 to 29 times the rate of hospital separation of non-Aboriginal Territorians. Because separations reflect events rather than the actual number of individuals, this could be a slight overestimation of cases, or, because notifications may not be as accurate as hospital separation data, it may be an underestimation. For this reason we (informally) compared the total number of notifications from the annual reports of the NT Department of Health with the total number of hospital separations. No formal evaluation could be done because the notification data were not available by unit records and data for different periods were published. However, for the years 1978 to 1988, excluding 1981, there were 325 notifications and 329 hospital separations, indicating an overall correlation between the two data sets. However, this correlation cannot be checked by year, or by individual record.

Mortality

Table 1 shows the rate ratio of death from tuberculosis and the late effects of tuberculosis for Aboriginal males and females in the NT compared with the Australian rates. The estimates of the rate ratio of death are high, although the small numbers are reflected in the wide confidence intervals.

Risk factors

Table 2 summarizes risk factors for tuberculosis and what is known about the occurrence of the risk factors in Aborigines. This table emphasises the prevalence of known risk factors for tuberculosis in Aborigines. Of particular concern is the higher risk of sexually transmissible diseases with the associated implications for the risk of HIV in Aborigines. The advent of HIV in Aborigines is likely to lead to morbidity from tuberculosis.

Little data about the occurrence of tuberculosis and risk factors are available. However, Patel et al. during a study of central Australian Aborigines from 1984 to 1986 inclusive, found nine new cases of tuberculosis, of which three were in diabetic people. Assuming that the other six were not diabetic and using the estimated Aboriginal population of the whole central Australian region, we calculated the rate of tuberculosis for both the diabetic and the non-diabetic group, estimated the crude rate ratio

and the step taken to get around the problem

Mortality data from NT

Extent of known risk factors for tuberculosis

Expands on the issue of risk factors

and calculated 95 per cent confidence intervals. The crude rate ratio of tuberculosis in diabetic Aborigines compared with non-diabetic Aborigines is 15 (CI 3 to 44). The wide confidence intervals reflect the small numbers of people with both diseases, even though the rate ratio is high. These are the only data addressing the issue of diabetes and tuberculosis in Aborigines that we could find, but they highlight the importance of diabetes in a population predisposed to tuberculosis.	
What could the future hold?	
Nunn et al. used a simple model to predict what the effect of HIV could be on a tuberculosis-infected population. Using the same argument and assuming that in the NT there are approximately 40 000 Aborigines, of whom 60 per cent are aged 15 or older, and assuming that in the adult population 25 per cent are Mantoux positive, there are 6 000 Mantoux-positive adult Aborigines in the NT. This rate of Mantoux positivity seems reasonable considering the results from Beilby et al. and the rate of tuberculosis in the NT. *Although HIV is thought to be uncommon in Aborigines at the moment, the rapid changes in HIV prevalence in Africa and Thailand, and the pre-existing risk factors for HIV in Aborigines, indicate that the prevalence could change rapidly. Assuming that 10 per cent of the adult population contracted HIV, about 600 people would have concurrent tuberculosis and HIV infection. Assuming a 10 per cent annual rate of progression of tve tuberculosis. This would be, over the total population of the NT, 60 in 40 000, or 150 per 100 000 in addition to those people contracting tuberculosis who were not HIV-infected.* This remains a frightening prospect, and one that would cause an enormous drain on health services, as well as the great personal and social costs of such an increase.	This paragraphs looks at the public health implications of tuberculosis in an Aboriginal population *The effect HIV could have on tuberculosis rates in Aborigines*

Discussion	
Aborigines already have high rates of infection and disease from tuberculosis. **They suffer from social disadvantage which in turn exposes them to the risks of poverty, underweight, homelessness, overcrowding and poor nutrition.** *As well, they have a higher than average prevalence of*	*Morbidity rates for Aborigines* **Predisposition factors** *Risk factors*

risk factors for tuberculosis, such as diabetes mellitus, renal failure, alcohol abuse and smoking. Although as yet largely untouched by HIV-AIDS, Aborigines are in considerable danger of being affected by the AIDS epidemic given their high rates of sexually transmissible diseases. *If HIV spreads to Aboriginal people, it follows that the tuberculosis-HIV interface will become a major public health problem.* **We have no knowledge about the heterogeneity of the population for either tuberculosis or risk factors for tuberculosis; it is likely that there are significant urban-rural differences at the very least. In particular, we found little evidence of tuberculosis in Aborigines in Western Australia, New South Wales or Victoria.**

Data about Aboriginal health remain of poor quality. Many routinely collected data sets fail to identify Aboriginality adequately. Census enumeration of denominator data is also imperfect. There are few data that provide more than a glimpse of the potential problem for Aborigines and tuberculosis. There is no potential to be confident about the size of the problem, nor to calculate risk versus benefits of preventive therapy. It is not possible to compare Aborigines with others with respect to the time taken for diagnosis of active disease, the effectiveness of contact tracing and the extent to which preventive therapy is used in skin-test-positive people. Completion rates of treatment have improved substantially in the NT, from a low of 34 per cent in the mid-eighties to 79 per cent in 1989, 88 per cent in 1990, 98 per cent in 1991 and 100 per cent in 1992 (unpublished data, V. Krause, 1994).

More information is necessary to develop specific public health programs. At the very least, it is essential that more information about tuberculin-skin-test positivity be obtained to consider preventive therapy for people infected with tuberculosis.

When the model proposed by Nunn et al. is applied to the Aboriginal population of the NT, **it is clear that HIV, among other things, has the potential to have an enormous impact on tuberculosis rates in the future.** The most important issues in tuberculosis control in countries such as Australia are the rapid and accurate diagnosis of disease,

and Aborigines

Public health implications of the findings **Comments on the limitations of the study and the data**

Suggested directions for future research

Implications of research Recommendations of the study

ensuring compliance with effective medication and ensuring that appropriate contact tracing measures are undertaken. These issues are more critical in high-risk groups such as Aborigines, and are compounded by insufficient information on compliance, outcomes of treatment, results of contact tracing and multi-drug resistance. Tuberculosis is a curable and potentially a preventable disease. A national tuberculosis program must recognize this at-risk group of Aboriginal people and support measures necessary to carry out effective control. With the prospect of HIV, and what it could mean for this already disadvantaged group of people, it is time to consider tuberculosis screening and, when appropriate, preventive therapy for Aboriginal people.

2.2 Critical Thinking and Reading for Academic Purposes

2.2.1 Definition of Critical Thinking and Reading

Efficient reading is not the only skill we need in the research process. We also need to read and think critically, which are the first steps towards formulating our own researches. Critical thinking and reading mean looking beneath the surface of words and images to gauge their meaning and importance. Critical thinking and reading are not necessarily negative thinking and reading. Critical comes from a Greek word meaning "to separate"; someone who thinks or reads critically separates a subject into its parts, sees how the parts work together, and judges the subject's quality and value.

Critical thinking is a means of making discoveries and organizing what we find. It is purposeful, self-regulatory judgment which results in interpretation, analysis, evaluation, and inference, as well as explanation of the evidential, conceptual, methodological, criteriological, or contextual considerations upon which that judgment is based.

To read critically, we must think critically. What does this mean? Critical thinking involves several related mental processes: analysis, interpretation, and evaluation. Each of these thinking processes helps us to question the

text in different ways. The questions put forward about the text help us make judgments about how the text is argued and identify strengths and weaknesses of the text—on a great number of levels. Critical reading is a highly reflective skill requiring us to "stand back" and gain some distance from the text we are reading. (We might have to read a text through once to get a basic grasp of content before we launch into an intensive critical reading.)

Both critical thinking and reading mean suspending judgment on a text until we have understood the message being put forward, evaluated the evidence supporting that message, and evaluated the writer's perspective. If we read or think uncritically, we may accept texts and arguments which are flawed, biased and subjectively written. Reading and writing critically will help to make sure that our study and research activities continue as soundly as possible.

Critical reading is different from common reading. The awareness of the differences between them could facilitate critical reading.

	Reading	Critical Reading
Purpose	To get a basic grasp of the text	To inform judgments about *HOW* a text works
Activity	Absorbing /Understanding	Analyzing/Interpreting/Evaluation
Focus	What a text **SAYS**?	What a text **DOES** and **MEANS**?
Questions	What is the text saying? What information can I get out of it?	How does the text work? How is it argued? What are the choices make? What kinds of reasoning and evidence are used? What are the underlying assumptions and perspectives? What does the text mean? Is the text effective? How can I use it to develop my own argument?
Direction	*WITH* the text (taking for granted it is right)	*AGAINST* the text (questioning its assumptions and argument, interpreting meaning in context)
Response	Restatement, Summary	Description, Interpretation, Evaluation

Therefore, when we are reading, highlighting, or taking notes, we should avoid extracting and compiling lists of evidence, lists of facts and examples, and avoid approaching a text by asking what information we can get out of it. We would better ask how this text works, how it is argued, how the evidence (the facts, examples, etc.) is used and interpreted, and how the text reaches its conclusions. In a word, critical reading and thinking skills are the ability to analyze, evaluate, and synthesize what one reads. They are the ability to see relationships of ideas and use them as an aid in reading.

2.2.2 Cognitive Skills for Critical Thinking and Reading

As mentioned above, critical thinking and reading are related by several mental processes: analysis, interpretation, and evaluation. These mental processes formulate the cognitive skills which are at the very core of critical thinking and reading.

Analysis is to identify the intended and actual inferential relationships among statements, questions, concepts, descriptions, or other forms of representation intended to express belief, judgment, experiences, reasons, information, or opinions, that's to say, analysis means looking at the parts of something to detect patterns. If we were a detective, this is when we would gather all our clues to see how they might relate to each other. In reading a scholarly journal, for example, we look at three main parts of the text:

● Choice of Content: What ideas and examples have been selected?

● Choice of Language: What words and sentence structures have been selected?

● Choice of Structure: What arrangement has been selected to present the ideas in?

Patterns will emerge when we look at these choices, patterns that reveal the purpose, strategies and perspective employed by the author. In looking at these patterns, our critical thinking skills will be engaged in analyzing the argument that the author is making. There are some questions that could be asked to help us conduct an analysis of articles or books.

Questions Asked through Analysis

1. What is the thesis or main idea?

2. What are the supporting points that create the argument? How do they relate to each other? How do they relate to the thesis?

3. What are the examples used as evidence for the supporting points? How do they relate to the points they support? To each other? To the thesis?

4. What techniques of persuasion are used (appeals to emotion, reason, authority, etc.)?

5. What rhetorical strategies (definition, explanation, description, narration, elaboration, argumentation, evaluation) and modes (illustration, comparison/contrast, cause and effect, process analysis, classification/ division, definition) are used?

6. In what order are the points presented (chronological, spatial, from general to specific, from similarity to difference, from cause to effect, from reason to conclusion)?

7. What sources are used? What other theorists or researchers are referred to? What schools of thought are relied upon? Analysis enables us to understand how the text works so that we can then interpret its deeper meanings and evaluate its meanings and effectiveness.

8. Have I understood the text correctly?

With regard to critical reading and thinking, there are four kinds of analysis: static abstract analysis, dynamic functional analysis, contextual analysis, and meta-analysis. The following figure define them and provide examples for us to have a better understanding of them.

Typology of Analysis			
Static abstract analysis Breaking the subject down into its component parts: 2. dimensional descriptions 3. dimensional descriptions What do these parts tell us about the meanings or values associated with subject?	**Dynamic functional analysis** Determining the function and internal relationship of those parts over time: What do those functions & relationships tell us about the meanings or values associated with the subject? How does our subject change if we change those functions or relationships? What do past or potential future changes tell us about the meanings or values associated with our subject?	**Contextual analysis** Determining the relationship of the subject to other phenomena: What does it influence? What influences it? What other relationships or contexts of significance shape it? What do these relationships and contexts tell us about the meanings or values associated with the subject?	**Meta-analysis** Evaluating the subject in light of multiple perspectives or contexts of significance: What phenomena, conditions or assumptions enable the existence of the subject or our perspective on it? What phenomena, conditions or assumptions must be absent or suppressed to enable the existence of the subject or our perspective on it? What do we learn when we shift our perspective, viewing our subject in more than one context of significance simultaneously?

Interpretation is reading ideas as well as sentences. It is when we look at the patterns in a text and make inferences about its underlying meanings. It helps us understand what the patterns of the argument mean. It can be compared to being a detective interpreting the patterns of clues in order to theorize about

whom the possible suspects are and why the crime might have been committed. At this point, context plays a greater role as a text's fuller meaning is in relationship to its context — its cultural and historical context, the context of its author, the context of dialogues within the discipline, etc. Here, we are questioning the text within its context. Thus, the more knowledge we have of the context of our discipline, the stronger our powers of interpretation, and thus evaluation.

Questions Asked through Interpretation

1. What kinds or reasoning (historical, psychological, political, philosophical, scientific, etc.) are employed?

2. What methodology or theoretical approach is used?

3. What are the implicit assumptions?

4. What is the point of view, or perspective, like?

5. What alternative perspectives remain unconsidered?

6. How might my reading of the text be biased?

Evaluation is to assess the credibility of statements or other representations which are ccounts or descriptions of a person's perception, experience, situation, judgment, belief, or opinion; and to assess the logical strength of the actual or intended inferential relationships among statements, descriptions, questions or other forms of representation.

Questions Asked through Evaluation

1. Is the thesis strong?

2. Are the points argued well?

3. Are the examples valid?

4. Are the sources reliable?

5. Is the argument logically consistent? Convincing?

6. Does the argument contribute to the discipline?

7. How can I use the text in creating my own argument?

Analysis/Interpretation/ Evaluation	Example 1	Example 2
Breaking our subject down into its **constituent parts**.	Scientific knowledge is built of slowly, "brick by brick", as each carefully designed experiment adds its one further bit of data.	The U.S. government is composed of three branches—executive, legislative and judicial —whose functions, powers and limitations are set out in the Constitution.
Approaching our subject not as a static thing, but as a changing, **dynamic, functional system of relationships,** which may change over time.	Each of those bits of data, however, does not have an equal effect on scientific theory. Some reinforce the existing paradigms; others challenge them. At irregular intervals, scientific revolutions occur in which the paradigms that had been serving as the foundations of science are crushed under the weight of new data, and new paradigms emerge to explain this data.	The precise nature and powers of the judicial branch were at first uncertain, but have largely been clarified through its evolving relationship to the legislative branch.
Stepping back from the subject to understand it not merely on its own terms, but within various larger **contexts of significance,** and appreciating how its meaning changes within those various contexts and relationships.	Therefore, science as practiced is less systematic, less regular—and quite a bit messier than our image of science.	Depending upon our point of view, we may read this ongoing story either as tragedy— a story of judicial encroachment on the legislative function— or as comedy—a story of increasing clarity and confidence about how justice is defined and delivered in the United States.
Balancing these various contexts and perspectives in order to determine **why I should care** about this subject, **what's at stake or at issue** in how we think about it—keeping in mind how our own perspective affects what we see.	But while the regular, progressive image of science is to a great extent false, it is also a very useful way of looking at science, for it enables a social climate which values the patience, objectivity and attention to detail necessary to good scientific work.	How you read this story probably has a lot to do with how you understand the concept of "interpretation".

2.2.3 Critical Reading Checklist

To read critically, we might use the following critical reading checklist to help us ask the right sort of questions of the material we have to read. The checklist consists of three levels which are designed as a guide to the process of reading academic texts critically and analytically.

Critical Reading Checklist

First level: We can critically evaluate aspects intrinsic to the text itself.

1. Is the data/information drawn on comprehensive enough for the case the author wants to make?
2. Is the data adequately and systematically analysed and otherwise dealt with?
3. Are the arguments well developed?
4. Are the arguments consistent? Can we spot inconsistencies?
5. Is the methodology used appropriate? Could the study be approached in other ways?
6. Are claims that are made sufficiently supported by the evidence?
7. Are the ideas presented relevant to the issue under discussion?
8. Are the ideas presented clearly?
9. Are there practical uses for the ideas, or are they too theoretical?
10. Is the complexity of the issues under discussion adequately dealt with, or has the writer over-simplified them?
11. Are the conclusions drawn clearly and based on the findings/discussion?

Second level: The wider context that gives rise to the text.

1. What is the writer's purpose? (Does it prejudice his/her collection and interpretation of data in obvious ways? Should we be extra cautious of his/her use of evidence, conclusions drawn and so on?)
2. How do the issues raised fit into wider debates in the discipline? Why has the author focused on these issues? Does the author have a political agenda of some sort?
3. Is the methodology the author adopts a universally accepted one in studies dealing with these issues? Could an alternative approach be used? Why? What difference might a different methodology make? Why is this important to note?
4. How do his/her conclusions compare with other related texts/studies? What grounds can we use for evaluating them?
5. What values underlie the approach or motivate the objectives of the study? Are there moral, socio-cultural or political reasons for questioning those values?

6. What social, political, moral, educational or other purposes are these findings/arguments likely to support?

Third level: Our own perspective that we bring from our wider world of experience (cultural values and beliefs, political and ideological outlook, and so on).

1. Are the ideas in the text relevant to our task/concerns?
2. Do the claims made contradict our own experience, understanding or sense of values? If so, can we justify challenging this study, or do we need to change our views?
3. Do the ideas and arguments in the study justify or implicitly support certain social relationships? Are they desirable? (Do they justify certain forms of teacher/student, gender, racial, social relationships [e.g. egalitarian/hierarchical; inferior/superior and so on]?)
4. Are the issues dealt with important in our view?
5. To what social, cultural or political purposes could the findings and conclusions of this study be put? Would we support these findings being used for such purposes? Why/why not?

Using the above-mentioned checklist, we could critically and analytically read the following excerpts from different academic journals.

Text 1	
Teams are not magic. They must have tasks that are achievable within a specified time frame. The team charged with "management" has an impossible brief and will surely fail unless effort is spent spelling out what the management task involves and what constitutes success.	What evidence does the author provide to support his or her argument?
Neither are teams a cheap option. They inevitably consume resources and time. Teams rarely resolve conflict. More often, they pressure-cook it.	*Is there evidence provided supporting this?* Would we accept this as fact? Why?
If an individual has the skills to do the job with the requisite creativity, then the individual, not the team, should do the job.	*Is this the author's opinion or fact?*

Text 2	
A third illusion is that leaders are not necessary in good teams. *Leadership is back in fashion.* But people in teams often argue that good teamwork makes	*Who says leadership is back in fashion?*

leadership redundant. Explicit or strong leadership behaviour is seen as contrary to the notional equality of teams. This illusion and the lack of leadership it produces is one of the worst things that can happen to a team. It ensures an obsession with internal power relations and a team without a champion. *A leader is the team's link with the wider organisation and the vital conduit for resources, support and credibility.* Teams need help to understand how their leadership requirements change and how to make the most of the leadership resources distributed among members.	*Is this assumed knowledge within the discipline of Management?* *This point is stated as fact. What theory is it based on? Do you agree with it?*

2.3 Reflections and Practice

1. All writers have a purpose when they write, and usually, a writer will choose or emphasize facts and details which support his or her purpose, and ignore facts which do not. In this exercise, you will read a number of quotations from different "interest groups" or "lobbies". A lobby or interest group is a group of people who have a common interest and who work together to publicize and promote their point of view. Your task in this exercise is to identify which group each quotation comes from.

Five Lobbies

- **The forestry industry:** The forestry industry makes money from cutting down trees. Therefore, they want to be able to continue to cut trees, and they want to discourage any alternative ways of producing pulp and paper.

- **The environmentalists:** The environmental lobby wants to protect the forests against logging companies, so they would like to show how destructive logging is, and how valuable the forests are.

- **The hemp farming lobby:** The hemp farmers would like fibre hemp plant to be legal so that they can grow it. They want to show how useful it is for making paper and other products, and they would like people to understand the difference between the marijuana plant and the fibre hemp plant.

● **The marijuana legalization lobby:** These people would like marijuana to be legal. They are interested in linking the fibre hemp plant with marijuana because they think it may be possible to legalize BOTH kinds of plant. They want to show how useful industrial hemp is, and at the same time, they want to convince people that marijuana is harmless.

● **The Canadian government:** The Canadian government has just legalized industrial hemp, but they want to keep marijuana illegal, so they want to show that it is dangerous. They also get lots of taxes from the forestry industry, so they do not want to restrict logging too much.

(1) "The rainforests are quite simply the richest, oldest, most productive and most complex ecosystems on Earth."

    A. the forestry industry   B. the environmentalists

    C. the hemp farming lobby   D. the marijuana legalization lobby

(2) "Some have calculated that if Canada converted the entire pulp and paper production in Canada to hemp, it would be necessary to plant hemp over 18% of the country."

    A. the forestry industry   B. the marijuana lobby

    C. the environmentalists   D. the hemp farming lobby

(3) "Farmers... can grow hemp without pesticide or herbicide application because it grows quickly and is not likely to fall to disease."

    A. the Canadian government   B. the hemp farming lobby

    C. the forestry industry   D. the marijuana legalization lobby

(4) "Each year, forest fires destroy more forests than are used for making pulp and paper."

    A. the environmentalists   B. the Canadian government

    C. the hemp farming lobby   D. the forestry industry

(5) "Decriminalizing cannabis could well result in a greater use of the drug by Canadians, thereby increasing the health and safety hazards associated with it."

    A. the marijuana legalization lobby   B. the hemp farming lobby

    C. the Canadian government   D. the environmentalists

(6) "The government added marijuana in 1923 to *The Opium Act* of 1908 without any health concerns inherent in the law whatsoever. *The Opium Act* was

introduced as a purely racist measure to deport and jail Chinese-Canadians."

    A. the hemp farming lobby   B. the Canadian government

    C. the forestry industry   D. the marijuana legalization lobby

(7) "67% of the fiber used to make Canadian pulp and paper comes from sawmill residue and recovered paper that used to be disposed of in landfills."

    A. the environmentalists   B. the hemp farming lobby

    C. the forestry industry   D. the marijuana legalization lobby

(8) "Hemp is about business and the environment. Marijuana is a moral question about the government's control of what drugs people consume. These two questions have nothing in common but the shape of the leaf, and we have to separate the issues."

    A. the hemp farming lobby   B. the marijuana legalization lobby

    C. the forestry industry   D. the Canadian government

(9)"In the Vancouver Grasstown Riot, of 1971, police attacked and injured hundreds of peaceful marijuana smokers in one day."

    A. the marijuana legalization lobby   B. the forestry industry

    C. the Canadian government   D. the hemp farming lobby

(10) "Logging is still the biggest employer and the single biggest contributor to tax revenue in BC."

    A. the hemp farming lobby   B. the forestry industry

    C. the Canadian government   D. the hemp farming lobby

2. Read each of the following paragraphs carefully. Look up any unfamiliar words if necessary. Then choose the title that best describes the main idea of each.

Text A

Universities are a microcosm of society. But they are more than a reflection or mirror; they are a leading indicator. In universities, an environment where students live, eat, and study together, racial and cultural differences come together in the closest possible way. Of all American institutions, perhaps only the military brings people of such different backgrounds into more intimate contact. With coeducation now a reality in colleges, and with the confident emergence of homosexual groups, the American campus is now sexually democratized as well. University leaders see it as a useful laboratory experiment in training young people for a multicultural habitat. Michael Sovern, president of Columbia, observes, "I like to think that we are leading society by grappling earnestly and creatively with the challenges posed by diversity."

—— Dinesh D'Souza, *Illiberal Education*

Text B

Marriage was not designed as a mechanism for providing friendship, erotic experience, romantic love, personal fulfillment, continuous lay psychotherapy, or recreation. The Western European family was not designed to carry a lifelong load of highly emotional romantic freight. Given its present structure, it simply has to fail when asked to do so. The very idea of an irrevocable contract obligating the parties concerned to a lifetime of romantic effort is utterly absurd.

—— Mervyn Cadwallader, "Marriage as a Wretched Institution", *Atlantic Monthly*

Text C

The baby mastering the skills that lead to establishment of the upright posture behaves in the same way as the novice skier. He feels compelled to repeat the activity hundreds of times until he has mastered the skill and mastered his anxiety. He often reveals that he is having difficulty in "unwinding" when we put him to bed for his nap or for the night, and if you peek into his room while he is settling down for sleep (or unsettling down for sleep), you may see him, groggy and cross-eyed with fatigue, still climbing and pulling himself upright, collapsing momentarily with weariness, then exerting himself for another climb. He repeats this over and over until finally he cannot lift himself even once more and succumbs to sleep. One set of parents discovered their eight-month-old daughter climbing in her sleep on several occasions during this mastery period. At eleven or twelve at night they could hear soft sounds in the baby's room and upon entering would find the baby standing in her crib, dazed and dimly conscious, too sleepy to protest when she was put down in her bed again. When the art of standing was perfected, the baby gave up practicing in her sleep.

—— Selma H. Fraiberg, *The Magic Years*

Text D

Considerable dispute exists about what a pidgin language is, for the simple reason that so many mistaken notions have been held for so long. Pidgin is not the corrupted form of a standard language—like the "broken" English spoken by an Italian tourist guide or that classic example of pseudo-pidgin, Me Tarzan, you Jane. Nor is it a kind of baby talk spoken by a plantation owner to his slaves, a master to his servants, or a merchant to his customers. And, finally, it is not a language that patronizingly makes concessions to the limited intelligence of "natives". A pidgin can best be described as a language which has been stripped of certain grammatical features. It is a new language that is not the mother tongue of any of its users, and it usually survives only so long as members of diverse speech communities are in contact.

—— Peter Farb, *Word Play: What Happens When People Talk*

学术论文写作与发表

(1) The best title for Text A is _____.

A. "The University Environment"B. "Sexual Democratization on American College Campuses"

C. "The University vs. the Military"

D. "The University as a Microcosm of Society"

(2) The best title for Text B is_____.

A. "Unrealistic Expectations in Western Marriages"

B. "The Failure of Romance"

C. "Why Marriages are Doomed to Failure"

D. "Marriage and Romance"

(3) The best title for Text C is_____.

A. "Babies' Nighttime Activities"

B. "How a Baby Masters the Skill of Standing"

C. "The Sleep Habits of Babies"

D. "Practice Makes Perfect"

(4) The best title for Text D is_____.

A. "A Linguistic Dispute"

B. "Pidgin Languages around the World"

C. "Lack of Grammatical Features in Pidgin Languages"

D. "What a Pidgin Language is, and is Not"

3. Read the following paragraphs and answer the questions that follow.

Paragraph 1
During the 1950s, Germany and Japan prospered once again, because American aid helped them recover from the losses they suffered in World War II.

(1) Germany and Japan had not been economically prosperous before World War II.

A. This statement is probably accurate.

B. This statement is probably inaccurate.

(2) To America, rebuilding Germany and Japan was important.

A. This statement is probably accurate.

B. This statement is probably inaccurate.

(3) Without American aid, Germany and Japan might not have returned to prosperity so quickly.

A. This statement is probably accurate.

B. This statement is probably inaccurate.

Paragraph 2

It is apparently very necessary to distinguish between parenthood and parentage. Parenthood is an art; parentage is the consequence of a mere biological act. The biological ability to produce conception and to give birth to a child has nothing whatever to do with the ability to care for that child as it requires to be cared for. That ability, like every other, must be learned. It is highly desirable that parentage be not undertaken until the art of parenthood has been learned. Is this a counsel of perfection? As things stand now, perhaps it is, but it need not always be so. Parentage is often irresponsible. Parenthood is responsible. Parentage at best is responsible for the birth of a child. Parenthood is responsible for the development of a human being—not simply a child, but a human being. I do not think it is an overstatement to say that parenthood is the most important occupation in the world. There is no occupation for which the individual should be better prepared than this, for what can be more important to the individual, his family, his community, his society, his nation, and the world of humanity than the making of a good human being? And the making of a good human being is largely the work of good parents. And it is work—hard work—not to be irresponsibly undertaken or perfunctorily performed. Yet parenthood, perhaps like politics, is the only profession for which preparation is considered unnecessary.

—— Ashley Montagu, *The American Way of Life*

---

(1) The mode of the discourse in this paragraph is_____.

A. narration   B. description   C. exposition   D. persuasion

(2) The primary method of development is _____.

A. illustration   B. steps in a process   C. comparison D. contrast

(3) Which of these is an accurate inference based on the paragraph?

A. Single parents should receive assistance from the government if they are to be good parents.

B. People contemplating becoming parents would be wise to take parenting classes or otherwise prepare themselves for the challenges ahead.

C. The number of unmarried mothers is alarming and needs an immediate solution.

D. Parenthood is not a profession in the same way that law or medicine is.

Paragraph 3

(1) In many years of hiking in the East, I've happened across bears twice. Once, in Maine, I rounded a corner on a trail, and there, three feet away, as lost in thought as I had been, sat a black bear. One look at me and she dived for the bushes—total contact time, perhaps four seconds. A few years later, walking near my house with my wife, I heard a noise in a treetop, and suddenly a black bear, roughly the size and shape of a large sofa, dropped to the ground a few yards away. She glowered in our direction and then lit out the opposite way. Time of engagement: maybe seven seconds. Those were grand encounters, and they've spiced every other day I've spent in the woods—on the way up Blackberry, for instance, I sang as I waded through the berry bushes, aware that this was where any bear with an appetite would be, especially after I found fresh berry-filled scat. But if I counted as dramatic only those days when I actually saw a big fierce animal, I would think the forest a boring place indeed.

(2) Even if you did go to the woods and saw a rare animal, and somehow managed to creep up real close, chances are it wouldn't be doing anything all that amazing. Chances are it would be lying in the sun, or perhaps grooming itself, or maybe, like the duck on the pond, swimming back and forth. A lot of animals are remarkably good at sitting still (especially when they suspect they're under surveillance), and this is something TV never captures. The nature documentaries are as absurdly action-packed as the soap operas, where a life's worth of divorce, adultery, and sudden death is crammed into a week's worth of watching. Trying to understand"nature" from watching "Wild Kingdom" is as tough as trying to understand "life" from watching "Dynasty".

—— Bill McKibben, "Reflections: Television", *The New Yorker*

(1) The main idea of the first paragraph is implied that _____.

A. nature is essentially boring

B. dramatic encounters with wild animals in nature are unusual

C. the author's two encounters with bears were the high points of his life

D. bears are afraid of people

(2) The female bear "glowered" at the author and his wife, suggesting that she was_____.

A. terrified   B. shy   C. angry   D. bewildered

(3) The main idea of the second paragraph is that _____.

A. animals stay still when they know they are under surveillance

B. animals in nature do not do very much

C. nature is quiet and not filled with constant action as portrayed in TV documentaries

D. one can learn a great deal about nature by watching TV documentaries

(4) What is the connection between paragraphs 1 and 2?

A. Paragraph 1 provides the evidence for the point made in paragraph 2.

B. Paragraph 1 is specific while paragraph 2 is general.

C. Paragraph 2 contradicts the main point of paragraph 1.

D. Both paragraph describe steps in a process.

(5) The examples at the beginning of paragraph 2 strongly suggest that

_____.

A. the author is a keen observer of nature

B. a lot of animals seldom do anything very amazing

C. wild animals will not allow people to get close to them

D. animals do little so that they can conserve energy, especially when food is scarce

(6) At the end of paragraph 2, what does the author imply about nature shows and soap operas?

A. Nature shows are modeled on soap operas.

B. The pace of action on both shows is unrealistically fast.

C. Both shows are a good way to learn about life.

D. Both shows should be made more realistic.

(7) The primary method of development in the passage is _____.

A. steps in a process   B. comparison

C. contrast   D. examples and illustration.

(8) The tone, or emotional attitude, of the last two sentences can best be described as _____.

A. hostile   B. objective   C. laudatory   D. Critical

Chapter Three   Note—taking

"When you notice yourself not feeling challenges, not feeling energized, and watching the clock, start taking note."

——Andrea Kay

3.1   Note-taking Strategies

Effective note-taking from readings is an essential skill for academic research. Good note-taking allows a permanent record for revision and a register of relevant points that we can integrate with our own writing. Good note-taking reduces the risk of plagiarism. It also helps us distinguish where our ideas came from and how we think about those ideas. If we take notes efficiently, we can read with more understanding and also save time and frustration when we come to write our paper.

Notes are not just collections of information. Note-taking, an important study skill that helps us do better in our work, involves making a permanent written record of main points and supporting details to which one may refer later. We need it to call up important information, to review information, and to store that information so we can use it later. An effective note-taking should fulfill the following standard:

Standard for Effective Note-taking

- Recognising the main ideas
- Identifying what information is relevant to our task
- Having a system of note taking that works for us
- Reducing the information to note and diagram format
- Where possible, putting the information in our own words
- Recording the source of the information

According to the standard, the following three strategies are designed to improve our ability to take more accurate, more complete, and more organized notes.

3.1.1 Being Selective and Systematic

Our research paper must be an expression of our own thinking, not a patchwork of borrowed ideas. Plan therefore to invest our research time in understanding our sources and integrating them into our own thinking. Our note cards or note sheets will record only ideas that are relevant to our focus on the topic; and they will mostly summarize rather than quote. As we take notes from a written source, keep in mind that not all of a text may be relevant to our needs. Think about our purpose for reading: whether we are reading for a general understanding of a topic or concept or for some specific information that may relate to the topic of an assignment.

Before we start to take notes, skim the text. Then highlight or mark the main points and any relevant information we may need to take notes from. Finally—keeping in mind our purpose for reading—read the relevant sections of the text carefully and take separate notes as we read.

When we take notes, we'd better not copy out exact words unless the ideas are memorably phrased or surprisingly expressed and want to use them as actual quotations in our paper. It's wise to compress ideas in our own words. However, paraphrasing word by word is a waste of time. We should choose the most important ideas, write them down as labels or headings, and then fill in with a few subpoints that explain or exemplify. We cannot depend on underlining and highlighting. It is the best way to find our own words for notes in the margin (or on "sticky" notes).

3.1.2 Sorting Out Relevant Ideas

Focus our approach to the topic before we start detailed research. Then we will read with a purpose in mind, and will be able to sort out what kind of ideas we need

to record. The following steps could help us sort out relevant ideas in note taking.

First, we could review the commonly known facts about our topic, and also become aware of the range of thinking and opinions on it. Second, we try to make a preliminary list of the subtopics we would expect to find in our reading. These will guide our attention and may come in handy as labels for notes. Third, we may choose a component or angle that interests us, perhaps one on which there is already some controversy. Now formulate our research question. It should allow for reasoning as well as gathering of information—not just what the proto-Iroquoians ate, for instance, but how valid the evidence is for early introduction of corn. We may even want to jot down a tentative thesis statement as a preliminary answer to our question. Then we will know what to look for in our research reading: facts and theories that help answer our question, and other people's opinions about whether specific answers are good ones.

Now arises an important problem: whether we need to make notes on a whole text or just part of it. This problem could be solved by identifying the main purpose and function of a text. Identifying the main purpose and function of a text is invaluable for clarifying our note-taking purposes and saving time. We could identify the main purpose and function of a text by reading the title and the abstract or preface (if there is one), reading the introduction or first paragraph, skimming the text to read topic headings and notice how the text is organized, and reading graphic material and predicting its purpose in the text.

To sum up, our aim is to identify potentially useful information by getting an initial overview of the text (chapter, article, pages...) that we have selected to read. We'd better ask ourselves: will this text give me the information I require and where might it be located in the text?

3.1.3 Identifying the Organization Pattern and Labelling Notes Intelligently

Most texts use a range of organising principles to develop ideas. While most good writing will have a logical order, not all writers will use an organising principle. Organising principles tend to sequence information into a logical hierarchy, some of which are:

- Past ideas to present ideas
- The steps or stages of a process or event
- Most important point to least important point
- Well known ideas to least known ideas
- Simple ideas to complex ideas
- General ideas to specific ideas
- The largest parts to the smallest parts of something
- Problems and solutions
- Causes and results

When we are taking notes, identify the organizing pattern of the reading materials and try to organize our notes in a way that allows for later use. To save bother later, we could developing the habit of recording bibliographic information in a master list when we begin looking at each source (don't forget to note book and journal information on photocopies). Then we can quickly identify each note by the author's name and page number; when we refer to sources in the research paper we can fill in details of publication easily from our master list. Keep a format guide handy. We should try as far as possible to put notes on separate cards or sheets. This will let us label the topic of each note. Not only will that keep our notetaking focused, but it will also allow for grouping and synthesizing of ideas later. It is especially satisfying to shuffle notes and see how the conjunctions create new ideas—ours. In addition, it is a good choice to leave lots of space in our notes for comments of our own—questions and reactions as we read, second thoughts and cross-references when we look back at what we've written. These comments can become a virtual first draft of our paper.

3.2 Useful Note-taking Skills

3.2.1 Paraphrasing

Paraphrasing is the use of another's ideas to enhance our own work. In a paraphrase, we rewrite in our own words the ideas taken from the source. Paraphrases

avoid excessive reliance on quotations and demonstrate that we understand the source author's argument. A paraphrase always has a different sentence structure and word choice. When done well, it is much more concise than the original.

Good writers signal paraphrases through clauses such as "Werner Sollors, in *Beyond Ethnicity*, argues that..." These phrases indicate the source of the paraphrase and help integrate the borrowed ideas into our own work. Because a paraphrase is our restatement of a borrowed idea, it is not set within quotation marks. Though the ideas may be borrowed, our writing must be original; simply changing a few words or rearranging words or sentences is not paraphrasing. In fact, it's plagiarism, a severe academic offense that can result in expulsion from the university and loss of reputation.

The following stages may be useful to the creation of an acceptable paraphrase.

How to Paraphrase

1. Read and understand the text.
2. Make a list of the main ideas.
   a. Find the important ideas—the important words/phrases. In some way mark them—write them down, underline or highlight them.
   b. Find alternative words/synonyms for these words/phrases—do not change specialised vocabulary and common words.
3. Change the structure of the text.
   a. Identify the meaning relationships between the words/ideas—e.g. cause/effect, generalisation, contrast.
   b. Express these relationships in a different way.
   c. Change the grammar of the text: change nouns to verbs, adjectives to adverbs, active voice to passive voice etc., break up long sentences, combine short sentences.
4. Rewrite the main ideas in complete sentences. Combine our notes into a piece of continuous writing.

5. Check our work.

    a. Make sure the meaning is the same.

    b. Make sure the length is the same.

    c. Make sure the style is our own.

    d. Remember to acknowledge other people's work.

Example 1: Wrong Paraphrase

[Original Passage] They desire, for example, virtue and the absence of vice, no less really than pleasure and the absence of pain.

Source: Mill, John Stuart. "Utilitarianism". *On Liberty and Other Essays.* New York: Oxford University Press, 1998. Quote is from page 169.

[Paraphrase] People want morality just as much as they want happiness.

[Annalysis] It is an accurate summary of the above passage, but is incorrectly paraphrased because there is no signal phrase, quotation marks, or an in-text citation to the original source. It thus appears to the reader as if the author of the paper is also the original author of the quote. Citations are a crucial link in scholarly research so that readers may find and evaluate the original source. Paraphrases, just like direct quotations, must be cited. While the words may be our own, the ideas are still borrowed, and we must acknowledge our source.

Example 2: Wrong Paraphrase

[Original Passage] If the existence of a signing ape was unsettling for linguists, it was also startling news for animal behaviorists (Davis, 26).

[Paraphrase: Version A] The existence of a signing ape unsettled linguists and startled animal behaviorists (Davis, 26).

[Paraphrase: Version B] If the presence of a sign-language-using chimp was disturbing for scientists studying language, it was also surprising to scientists studying animal behavior (Davis, 26).

[Annalysis] Version A is plagiarism. Even though the writer has cited the source, the writer has not used quotation marks around the direct quotation,

Chapter Three

学术论文写作与发表

65

"the existence of a signing ape". In addition, the phrase, "unsettled linguists and startled animal behaviorists", closely resembles the wording of the source. Version B is still plagiarism. Even though the writer has substituted synonyms and cited the source, the writer is plagiarizing because the source's sentence structure is unchanged.

Example 3: Effective Paraphrase

[**Original passage**] In the act of composing, our search for words is mostly for those that can accurately represent the elements of our message and communicate them reliably to the reader.

Source: From Peters, P. (1985). *Strategies for student writers: A guide to writing essays, tutorial papers, exam papers and reports.* Queensland: John Wiley & Sons. p.85.

[**Paraphrase**] Peters (1985, p85) explains that writers are constantly trying to find the most appropriate vocabulary which will successfully transmit their ideas to their audience.

[**Analysis**] It includes the source of the information and is about the same length as the original. Synonymous words and phrases are used to retain the original meaning (e.g. "in the act of composing, our search" = "writers are constantly trying to find" and "communicate them reliably" = "successfully transmit").

3.2.2 Summarizing

To summarize is to put in our own words a shortened version of written or spoken material, stating the main points and leaving out everything that is not essential. Summarizing is more than retelling; it involves analyzing information, distinguishing important from unimportant elements and translating large chunks of information into a few short cohesive sentences.

Paraphrasing and summarizing are very similar. Both involve taking ideas, words or phrases from a source and crafting them into new sentences within our writing. In addition, summarizing includes condensing the source material into just a few lines because a good summary shows that we have understood the text. Remember whether paraphrasing or summarizing, we should always give credit to the cited author.

The following stages may be useful to the creation of an acceptable summary.

How to Summarize

1. Read and understand the text carefully.
2. Think about the purpose of the text.
   a. Ask what the author's purpose is in writing the text?
   b. What is our purpose in writing our summary?
   c. Are you summarising to support our poins?
   d. Or are we summarising so we can criticise the work before we introduce our main points?
3. Select the relevant information. This depends on our purpose.
4. Find the main ideas—what is important.
   a. They may be found in topic sentences.
   b. Distinguish between main and subsidiary information.
   c. Delete most details and examples, unimportant information, anecdotes, examples, illustrations, data etc.
   d. Find alternative words/synonyms for these words/phrases—do not change specialised vocabulary and common words.
5. Change the structure of the text.
   a. Identify the meaning relationships between the words/ideas , e.g. cause/effect, generalisation, contrast. Express these relationships in a different way.
   b. Change the grammar of the text: rearrange words and sentences. Change nouns to verbs, adjectives to adverbs, etc., break up long sentences, combine short sentences.
   c. Simplify the text. Reduce complex sentences to simple sentences, simple sentences to phrases, phrases to single words.

6. Rewrite the main ideas in complete sentences. Combine our notes into a piece of continuous writing. Use conjunctions and adverbs such as "therefore", "however", "although", "since", to show the connections between the ideas.

7. Check our work.

a. Make sure our purpose is clear.

b. Make sure the meaning is the same.

c. Make sure the style is our own.

d. Remember to acknowledge other people's work.

Example 1

[Original text] The evaluative connotations of words are of considerable importance as you develop an argument or put forth an interpretation of some facts. Just a few are enough to signal your perspective in an otherwise neutral presentation of data. By introducing someone's proposition with the work "claim" or "assert", you imply a real possibility of challenging it and invite the reader to reserve judgement about it, if not to view it sceptically (such words are unfortunate if you really mean to endorse the proposition). But appropriately used they prepare the reader for your counter arguments long before you get to them. By describing a set of predictions in passing as either "optimistic" or "gloomy", you can very simply indicate both your criticism of them and the direction in which you think they err. The connotations of words can provide an interim commentary in a discussion before you communicate the ultimate evaluation or argument.

Source: From Peters, P. (1985). *Strategies for student writers: A guide to writing essays, tutorial papers, exam papers and reports.* Queensland: John Wiley & Sons. p.88.

[Summary] According to Peters (1985, p.88) words not only carry meaning but they also carry a positive or negative tone. She also explains how this aspect can be exploited by the writer to signal a judgement or opinion about the data or source material. It can also assist in laying the ground work for the up coming arguments by acting as a preliminary discussion.

[Analysis] This is an effective summary. In the first sentence the source and main idea of the original text has been restated. The second sentence simplifies the original second and third sentence by omitting the examples and detailed explanations. While the last three sentences of the original text have been condensed by leaving out examples and simplifying detailed explanations, an important point is retained in the final sentence. The writer has used a variety of synonymous words and phrases to keep the original meaning (evaluative connotation = a positive or negative tone) and to accurately reflect the relationships between ideas (not only... but also, also...).

Example 2

[Original text] In order to communicate effectively with other people, one must have a reasonably accurate idea of what they do and do not know that is pertinent to the communication. Treating people as though they have knowledge that they do not have can result in miscommunication and perhaps embarrassment. On the other hand, a fundamental rule of conversation, at least according to a Gricean view, is that one generally does not convey to others information that one can assume they already have.

Source: From Raymond S. Nickerson's "How We Know—and Sometimes Misjudge—What Others Know: Imputing One's Own Knowledge to Others". Psychological Bulletin 125.6 (1999): p.737.

[Plagiarism]

For effective communication, it is necessary to have a fairly accurate idea of what our listeners know or do not know that is pertinent to the communication. If we assume that people know something they do not, then miscommunication and perhaps embarrassment may result (Nickerson, 1999).

[Analysis] The writer in this example has used too many of Nickerson's original words and phrases such as "effective communication", "accurate idea","know or do not know", "pertinent", "miscommunication", and "embarrassment".

Also note that the passage doesn't have an opening tag to indicate where use of the Nickerson's material begins. A citation at the end of a paragraph is not sufficient to indicate what is being credited to Nickerson.

[Acceptable summary]

Nickerson (1999) argues that clear communication hinges upon what an audience does and does not know. It is crucial to assume the audience has neither too much nor too little knowledge of the subject, or the communication may be inhibited by either confusion or offense (p.737).

[Analysis] Notice that the writer both paraphrases Nickerson's ideas about effective communication and compresses them into two sentences. Like paraphrasing, summarizing passages is a tricky endeavor and takes lots of practice.

[Acceptable paraphrase]

Nickerson (1999) suggests that effective communication depends on a generally accurate knowledge of what the audience knows. If a speaker assumes too much knowledge about the subject, the audience will either misunderstand or be bewildered; however, assuming too little knowledge among those in the audience may cause them to feel patronized (p.737).

[Annalysis] Here the writer re-words Nickerson's idea about what determines effective communication. The writer re-phrases "generally accurate knowledge" into "reasonably accurate idea". In the second sentence, the writer re-words Nickerson's ideas about miscommunication and embarrassment using instead the words "misunderstand", "bewildered", and "patronized". Nickerson is given credit from the beginning as the originator of the ideas. This is an example of a successful paraphrase because the writer understands the ideas espoused by Nickerson, and is able to put them into her own words while being careful to give him credit.

3.3 The Cornell Note-taking Method

The Cornell note-taking method is a widely-used note taking method devised in the 1950s by Walter Pauk, an education professor at Cornell

University. Pauk advocated its use in his best-selling *How to Study in College,* but its use has spread most rapidly in the past decade.

The Cornell method provides a systematic format for condensing and organizing notes. It is a simple three-step process. First, we need to divide the paper into two columns: the note-taking column (usually on the right) is twice the size of the questions/key word column (on the left). We should leave five to seven lines, or about two inches (5 cm), at the bottom of the page. Notes from reading a text are written in the note-taking column: main ideas, supporting details, examples, etc. Long ideas are paraphrased. Long sentences are avoided, and symbols or abbreviations are used instead. Secondly, to assist with future reviews, we identify and pull out the keywords, key ideas, etc., that are written in the key word column. Finally, we should write a brief summary in the bottom, five to seven lines of the page. This helps to increase understanding of the topic.

Cornell Note-taking Method	
Keywords **Key Ideas** **etc.**	**Notes** *(Main Ideas, Supporting Details, etc.)*
Summary and Reflections	

Notes do not have to be perfect; they belong to us. We get better with more and more practice. The Cornell method is only one way of note-taking; there are many. We may already have our own style of taking notes, or may have not really settled on a method. For example, based on the Cornell note-taking method, we could classify the information we need to write down into three columns. The first column on the left is for the text reference. If it is a journal article, remember to include the page numbers. The second column is for our notes, either direct or indirect quotations, statistics, etc. Be sure to always include the page number after each piece of information. The third column is for our comments, cross-references, questions, reminders, and interpretations. This is our thinking. In addition, we could divide our note-taking page into three columns: the first column is for the thematic categorization of the notes; the second column is for the notes themselves; the third is for our own interpretations, comments and cross-referencing. Remember that some bibliographic details must be listed in the first line, such as author, title, publisher, place, and date. The following is an alternative template for the layout of Cornell method of note-taking.

Bibliographic Details: Author, Title, Publisher, Place, Date		
Headings or Themes	**Notes or Content**	**Interpretation/ Comments/Cross-references/ Ideas/Confusions/ Questions**
Use this column to indicate which theme the notes relate to.	This column is for our notes; direct or indirect quotation Always include page numbers at the end of all quotations to avoid mistakes in referencing.	This column is where you can begin the note-making process by critically evaluating the information, asking questions and cross-referencing with what you have already noted in other readings

The following examples illustrate the alternative ways of note-taking.

Theme : Tunnel Vision		
Reference	**Notes**	**Comments**
Fulop, L., Frith, F. and Hayward, H. *Management for Australian Business: A Critical Text,* Macmillan, 1992	"Tunnel vision describes a distorted or preferred way of thinking and acting...it creates or reinforces certain beliefs and attitudes among managers, and these become so entrenched that new ideas, practices and attitudes cannot flourish in an organization". p.13 "one symptom is selective focusing" p.13	This basically means that managers can get so "caught up" in their own belief systems that they are unable to see alternative perspectives. This is obvious in the case study where the manager cannot see the issue from the women's perspective. Selective focusing is a good term to use.
next reference	notes...	comments ... Does it relate to the information above?

Bibliographic Details:		
Raskall, P.N. (1997) The Psychology of Imagination. Sydney: Harper & Row.		
Themes	**Notes**	**Comments/ Cross-references**
Definition of	"Imagination is defined as that	What does this mean?
imagination	mental faculty which enables to link sensory impressions and thought" p.23	Perhaps that without imagination the world would appear to be a chaotic jumble?
Anti- imagination	"Recourse to 'imagination' in explanations of creative thought betray a type of nostalgia for a bygone romantic age which in fact never existed. There is no function of human understanding which, theoretically, cannot be adequately, and non-mysteriously, accounted for in terms of information processing and retrieval" p.39	This is rubbish! Human understanding is largely impoverished without the contributions of imagination. (see Jones & Brown, 1997, p. 115

3.4 Annotated Bibliography

3.4.1 Definition of Bibliogrphy

A bibliography is a list of sources (books, journals, websites, periodicals, etc.) that could be used for researching a topic. Bibliographies are sometimes called "references" or "works cited" depending on the style format we are using. A bibliography usually just includes the bibliographic information (i.e., the author, title, publisher, etc.). An annotation is a summary and/or evaluation. Therefore, an annotated bibliography gives an account of the research that has been done on a given topic. Like any bibliography, an annotated bibliography is an alphabetical list of research sources. In addition to bibliographic data, an annotated bibliography provides a concise summary of each source and some assessment of its value or relevance. Depending on our assignment, an annotated bibliography may be one stage in a larger research project, or it may be an independent project standing on its own.

Abstracts are the purely descriptive summaries often found at the beginning of scholarly journal articles or in periodical indexes. Annotations are descriptive and critical; they expose the author's point of view, clarity and appropriateness of expression, and authority.

There tend to be three major audiences for annotated bibliographies: the authors of the annotations, instructors, and other researchers.

Many people find it useful to craft an annotated bibliography while researching topics. Writing brief summaries of the research we consult, whether it is newspapers, journals, book, or videos, helps us remember these sources over time. More than that, by writing critical evaluations of the research we consult, we will identify common themes and methods. We will find what research is commonly cited on a topic, what methods are employed, and what a community of scholars believes needs additional inquiry.

In college and university contexts, instructors require students to craft annotated bibliographies as a preliminary step to writing a formal research paper. Asking students to construct an annotated bibliography enables instructors to ensure that students understand the bibliography style for citing references. It helps ensure the student has consulted a variety of timely and reputable sources.

Occasionally professionals will actually publish their annotated bibliographies. This happens in research fields where a lot of information is being published. Professional researchers often begin their survey of research by finding annotated bibliographies on a topic that interests them.

Writing an annotated bibliography is excellent preparation for a research project. Just collecting sources for a bibliography is useful, but when we have to write annotations for each source, we are forced to read each source more carefully. We begin to read more critically instead of just collecting information. At the professional level, annotated bibliographies allow us to see what has been done in the literature and where our own research or scholarship can fit. To help us formulate a thesis: every good research paper is an argument. The purpose of research is to state and support a thesis. So a very important part of research is developing a thesis that is debatable, interesting, and current. Writing an annotated bibliography can help us gain a good perspective on what is being said about our topic. By reading and responding to a variety of sources on a topic, we will start to see what the issues are, what people are arguing about, and we will then be able to develop our own point of view.

Extensive and scholarly annotated bibliographies are sometimes published. They provide a comprehensive overview of everything important that has been and is being said about that topic. We may not ever get our annotated bibliography published, but as a researcher, we might want to look for one that has been published about our topic.

3.4.2 Process of Creating an Annotated Bibliography

Creating an annotated bibliography consists of two stages: selecting the sources, summarizing the argument of a source, and assessing the relevance and value of sources.

First, select the sources. The quality and usefulness of our bibliography will depend on our selection of sources. Define the scope of our research carefully so that we can make good judgments about what to include and exclude. Our research should attempt to be reasonably comprehensive within well-defined boundaries. Consider these questions to help us find appropriate limits for our research:

1. What problems are we investigating? What question(s) are we trying to pursue? If our bibliography is part of a research project, this project will probably be governed by a research question. If our bibliography is an independent project on a general topic (e.g. aboriginal women and Canadian law), try formulating our topic as a question or a series of questions in order to define our search more precisely.(e.g. How has Canadian law affecting aboriginal women changed as a result of the *Charter of Rights and Freedoms*? How have these changes affected

aboriginal women? How have aboriginal women influenced and responded to these legal developments?)

2. What kind of materials are we looking for? (Academic books or journal articles? Government reports or policy statements? Articles from the popular press? Primary historical sources? etc.)

3. Are we finding essential studies on our topic? (Read footnotes in useful articles carefully to see what sources they use and why. Keep an eye out for studies that are referred to by several of your sources.)

After selecting the sources, we could create the first part of an annotated bibliography, the bibliographic information. Generally, though, the bibliographic information of the source (the title, author, publisher, date, etc.) is written in either the Modern Language Association (MLA) and the American Psychological Association (APA) styles.

Second, summarize the argument of a source. An annotation briefly restates the main argument of a source. An annotation of an academic source, for example, typically identifies its thesis (or research question, or hypothesis), its major methods of investigation, and its main conclusions. Keep in mind that identifying the argument of a source is a different task than describing or listing its contents. Rather than listing contents, an annotation should account for why the contents are there.

Example 1: Only lists contents

McIvor, S. D. (1995). Aboriginal women's rights as "existing rights." *Canadian Woman Studies/Les Cahiers de la Femme* 2/3, 34-38.

This article discusses recent constitutional legislation as it affects the human rights of aboriginal women in Canada: the *Constitution Act* (1982), its amendment in 1983, and amendments to the *Indian Act* (1985). It also discusses the implications for aboriginal women of the Supreme Court of Canada's interpretation of the *Constitution Act* in R. v. Sparrow (1991).

Example 2: Identify the argument

McIvor, S. D. (1995). Aboriginal women's rights as "existing rights." *Canadian Woman Studies/Les Cahiers de la Femme* 2/3, 34-38.

This article seeks to define the extent of the civil and political rights returned to aboriginal women in the *Constitution Act* (1982), in its amendment in 1983, and in amendments to the *Indian Act* (1985).* This legislation reverses prior laws that denied Indian status to aboriginal women who married non-aboriginal men. On the basis of the Supreme Court of Canada's interpretation of the *Constitution Act* in R. v. Sparrow (1991), McIvor argues that the Act recognizes fundamental human rights and existing aboriginal rights, granting to aboriginal women full participation in the aboriginal right to self-government.**

Identifying the argument of our source is an essential step in creating an effective annotated bibliography. It could be actualized by the following reading strategies:

1. Identify the author's thesis (central claim or purpose) or research question. Both the introduction and the conclusion can help us with this task.

2. Look for repetition of key terms or ideas. Follow them through the text and see what the author does with them. Note especially the key terms that occur in the thesis or research question that governs the text.

3. Notice how the text is laid out and organized. What are the main divisions or sections? What is emphasized? Why? Accounting for why will help us move beyond listing contents and toward giving an account of the argument.

4. Notice whether and how a theory is used to interpret evidence or data. Identify the method used to investigate the problem(s) addressed in the text.

5. Pay attention to the opening sentence(s) of each paragraph, where authors often state concisely their main point in the paragraph.

6. Look for paragraphs that summarize the argument. A section may sometimes begin or conclude with such a paragraph.

Third, assess the relevance and value of sources. Our annotation should now go on to briefly assess the value of the source to an investigation of our research question or problem. If our bibliography is part of a research project,

Note: *research question, **method & main conclusions

briefly identify how we intend to use the source and why. If our bibliography isan independent project, try to assess the source's contribution to the research on our topic. The following questions could help us assess the relevance and value of sources.

Are you interested in the way the source frames its research question or in the way it goes about answering it (its method)? Does it make new connections or open up new ways of seeing a problem? (e.g. bringing the Sparrow decision concerning aboriginal fishing rights to bear on the scope of women's rights)

Are we interested in the way the source uses a theoretical framework or a key concept? (e.g. analysis of existing, extinguished, and other kinds of rights)

Does the source gather and analyze a particular body of evidence that we want to use? (e.g. the historical development of a body of legislation)

How do the source's conclusions bear on our own investigation?

In order to determine how we will use the source or define its contribution, we will need to assess the quality of the argument: why is it of value? what are its limitations? how well defined is its research problem? how effective is its method of investigation? how good is the evidence? would we draw the same conclusions from the evidence?

Keep the context of our project in mind. How is material assessed in our discipline? Are there any similarities or differences between this work and another we have cited?

The second and the third stages allow us to create the second part of an annotated bibliography, annotations. The annotations for each source are written in paragraph form. The lengths of the annotations can vary significantly from a couple of sentences to a couple of pages. The length will depend on the purpose. If we are just writing summaries of our sources, the annotations may not be very long. However, if we are writing an extensive analysis of each source, we will need more space. We can focus our annotations for our own needs. A few sentences of general summary followed by several sentences of how we can fit the work into our larger paper or project can serve us well when we go to draft. The following is a sample of an annotated bibliography.

Annotated Bibliography Entry for a Journal Article	
Waite, L. J., Goldschneider, F. K. & Witsberger, C. (1986). Nonfamily living and the erosion of traditional family orientations among young adults. *American Sociological Review*, 51 (4), 541-554.	Bibliography information
The authors, researchers at the Rand Corporation and Brown University, use data from the National Longitudinal Surveys of Young Women and Young Men to test their hypothesis that nonfamily living by young adults alters their attitudes, values, plans, and expectations, moving them away from their belief in traditional sex roles. *They find their hypothesis*	Research question
strongly supported in young females, while the effects were fewer in studies of young males. Increasing the time away from parents before marrying increased individualism, self-sufficiency, and changes in attitudes about families. In	Conclusion
contrast, an earlier study by Williams cited below shows no significant gender differences in sex role attitudes as a result of nonfamily living.	Comment

3.5 Reflections and Practice

1. The paragraphs below provide an example by showing a passage as it appears in the source, several paraphrases that follow the source too closely, and a legitimate paraphrase. Please point out the legitimate one and the word-by-word plagiarism ones, and explain the reason.

[Original Source] (A totalitarian) society ... can never permit either the truthful recording of facts, or the emotional sincerity, that literary creation demands. ... Totalitarianism demands ... the continuous alteration of the past, and in the long run ... a disbelief in the very existence of objective truth. (written by George Orwell)

[Version A] A totalitarian society can never permit the truthful recording of facts; it demands the continuous alteration of the past, and a disbelief in the very existence of objective truth.

[Version B] A totalitarian society can't be open-minded or allow the truthful recording of facts, but instead demands the constant changing of the past and a distrust of the very existence of objective truth.

[Version C] Orwell believed that totalitarian societies must suppress literature and free expression because they cannot survive the truth, and thus they claim it does not exist.

[Version D] In his biography of George Orwell, Gordon Bowker discusses the themes of 1984, quoting a 1946 essay by Orwell: "Totalitarianism demands ... the continuous alteration of the past, and in the long run ... a disbelief in the very existence of objective truth." (Bowker p.337, quoting Orwell, 1946)

2. The paragraphs below provide an example by showing a passage as it appears in the source, two paraphrases that follow the source too closely, and a legitimate paraphrase. Please point out the legitimate one and the word-by-word plagiarism one, and explain the reason.

Original Passage
Critical care nurses function in a hierarchy of roles. In this open heart surgery unit, the nurse manager hires and fires the nursing personnel. The nurse manager does not directly care for patients but follows the progress of unusual or long-term patients. On each shift a nurse assumes the role of resource nurse. This person oversees the hour-by-hour functioning of the unit as a whole, such as considering expected admissions and discharges of patients, ascertaining that beds are available for patients in the operating room, and covering sick calls. Resource nurses also take a patient assignment. They are the most experienced of all the staff nurses. The nurse clinician has a separate job description and provides for quality of care by orienting new staff, developing unit policies, and providing direct support where needed, such as assisting in emergency situations. The clinical nurse specialist in this unit is mostly involved with formal teaching in orienting new staff. The nurse manager, nurse clinician, and clinical nurse specialist are the designated experts. They do not take patient assignments. The resource nurse is seen as both a caregiver and a resource to other caregivers... Staff nurses have a hierarchy of seniority... Staff nurses are assigned to patients to provide all their nursing care. (Chase, 1995, p. 156)

Paraphrase 1

Critical care nurses have a hierarchy of roles. The nurse manager hires and fires nurses. She/he does not directly care for patients but does follow unusual or long-term cases. On each shift a resource nurse attends to the functioning of the unit as a whole, such as making sure beds are available in the operating room, and also has a patient assignment. The nurse clinician orients new staff, develops policies, and provides support where needed. The clinical nurse specialist also orients new staff, mostly by formal teaching. The nurse manager, nurse clinician, and clinical nurse specialist, as the designated experts, do not take patient assignments. The resource nurse is not only a caregiver but a resource to the other caregivers. Within the staff nurses there is also a hierarchy of seniority. Their job is to give assigned patients all their nursing care.

Paraphrase 2

Chase (1995) describes how nurses in a critical care unit function in a hierarchy that places designated experts at the top and the least senior staff nurses at the bottom. The experts—the nurse manager, nurse clinician, and clinical nurse specialist—are not involved directly in patient care. The staff nurses, in contrast, are assigned to patients and provide all their nursing care. Within the staff nurses is a hierarchy of seniority in which the most senior can become resource nurses: they are assigned a patient but also serve as a resource to other caregivers. The experts have administrative and teaching tasks such as selecting and orienting new staff, developing unit policies, and giving hands-on support where needed.

Paraphrase 3

In her study of the roles of nurses in a critical care unit, Chase (1995) also found a hierarchy that distinguished the roles of experts and others. Just as the educational experts described above do not directly teach students, the experts in this unit do not directly attend to patients. That is the role of the staff nurses, who, like teachers, have their own "hierarchy of seniority" (p.156). The roles of the experts include employing unit nurses and overseeing the care of special patients (nurse manager), teaching and otherwise integrating new personnel into the unit (clinical nurse specialist and nurse clinician), and policy-making (nurse clinician). In an intermediate position in the hierarchy is the resource nurse, a staff nurse with more experience than the others, who assumes direct care of patients as the other staff nurses do, but also takes on tasks to ensure the smooth operation of the entire facility.

学术论文写作与发表

3. The following paragraphs are from two books. Please create an acceptable paraphrase for each of the paragraphs.

Original Passage 1
Buddhadasa's conception of human beings as active controllers of their own material and spiritual progress is most clearly presented in his view of work as integrating both social and spiritual activity. Source: Buddhadasa: A Buddhist thinker for the modern world by Peter Jackson. Bangkok, Thailand: Siam Society, 1988. p. 200.

Original Passage 2
The Republican Convention of 1860, which adopted planks calling for a tariff, internal improvements, a Pacific railroad and a homestead law, is sometimes seen as a symbol of Whig triumph within the party. A closer look, however, indicates that the Whig's triumph within the party was of a very tentative nature. Source: Foner, Eric. Free Soil, Free Labor, Free Men: The Ideology of the Republican Party Before the Civil War. New York: Oxford University Press, 1970. Quote is from p.175.

4. The following paragraph is from Oliver Sacks' essay "An Anthropologist on Mars". Please create an acceptable summarizing of the paragraph.

The cause of autism has also been a matter of dispute. Its incidence is about one in a thousand, and it occurs throughout the world, its features remarkably consistent even in extremely different cultures. It is often not recognized in the first year of life, but tends to become obvious in the second or third year. Though Asperger regarded it as a biological defect of affective contact—innate, inborn, analogous to a physical or intellectual defect—Kanner tended to view it as a psychogenic disorder, a reflection of bad parenting, and most especially of a chillingly remote, often professional, "refrigerator mother". At this time, autism was often regarded as "defensive" in nature, or confused with childhood schizophrenia. A whole generation of parents—mothers, particularly—were made to feel guilty for the autism of their children.

5. In order to create an effective paraphrase or summary, we sometimes break up or combine sentences to change the sentence structures of original texts. Please break up or combine the following sentences according to the instructions.

(1) Given the extent to which deforestation increased markedly in the four

southern states during 1987 and 1988, it is heartening news that during the early part of the 1989 dry season the burning seemed to have been curtailed somewhat, due to a combination of policy changes, better controls on burning, and most important of all an exceptionally wet "dry" season. (Break up the sentence)

(2) In 1851 the average family size was 4.7, roughly the same as it had been in the seventeenth century, but the 1 million couples who married during the 1860s, which the historian G. M. Young described as the best decade in English history to have been brought up in, raised the figure to 6.2. (Break up the sentence)

(3) Tropical forests are defined here as evergreen or partly evergreen forests. They grow in areas receiving not less than 100 mm of precipitation in any month for two out of three years. The mean annual temperature is 24-plus degrees Celsius. The area is essentially frost-free. (Combine the sentences)

(4) The third National Government followed upon the resignation of the Liberal ministers and of the free trader, Snowden. This happened in September 1932. After this it became little more than a Conservative government. A few ex-Labor and Liberal politicians were added. They all owed their seats to an electoral pact with the Conservatives. (Combine the sentences)

6. Distinguish between main and subsidiary information. Delete most details and examples, unimportant information, anecdotes, illustrations, data etc. Simplify the text. Reduce complex sentences to simple sentences, simple sentences to phrases, phrases to single words.

(1) The climatic conditions prevailing in the British Isles show a pattern of alternating and unpredictable periods of dry and wet weather, accompanied by a similarly irregular cycle of temperature changes.

(2) It is undeniable that the large majority of non-native learners of English experience a number of problems in attempting to master the phonetic patterns of the language.

(3) Tea, whether of the China or Indian variety, is well known to be high on the list of those beverages which are most frequently drunk by the inhabitants of the British Isles.

(4) One of the most noticeable phenomena in any big city, such as London

or Paris, is the steadily increasing number of petrol-driven vehicles, some in private ownership, others belonging to the public transport system, which congest the roads and render rapid movement more difficult year by year.

(5) Man has added extraneous substances to his food since prehistoric times. Salt and spices are the oldest food additives we know of, used by prehistoric man to preserve his meat and fish, and to make the taste more interesting. Today, the substances, natural and synthetic, added to food run into thousands. Most of the foods we buy contain one or more additives.

(6) Mankind is always searching for a better life. One way of improving it is to plan work so that it corresponds to the capacities and needs of the worker. Ergonomics is concerned with fitting work to man. It does not limit its goal to the elimination of physical hazards to health, but aims at making the work more satisfying to the worker.

(7) In most developing countries, two-thirds or more of the people live in rural areas, with few, if any, of the services the city-dweller takes for granted. Water taps in houses, for example, are almost unknown. At best, there may be a village well. Often the only source of water is a lake or a stream, perhaps several kilometers away. The drudgery of water-carrying can take up the better part of every day.

7. Please write a summary for the following text.

> Organization al Development (OD) practitioners assume that it is important for people to be accepted by their work and that the climate in most groups and organizations does not encourage open expression of feelings. The necessity of hiding feelings, OD practitioners believe, has a negative effect not only on group member's willingness and ability to solve problems constructively, but also on job satisfaction and performance. Encouraging openness can be difficult and risky, but it can also lead to greater job satisfaction and more effective group performance.
>
> ——Stoner and Wankel, 1986

8. Suppose you conduct your research for your research writing project. Please select some materials in your field and compile an annotated bibliography with 3 entries. Each entry in your annotated bibliography should contain a citation, a brief summary of the cited material, and an evaluation of it.

Part III Writing Process

Chapter Four   Title, Author/Affiliation, Keywords and Acknowledgements

Titles consist of only a few words, but they are serious stuff.

——*John Swales*

4.1 Title

Title is indeed text in miniature. Unclear or boring research paper title creates a negative impression on the readers and brings absolutely no desire to read the work further. Thus, take time to make a creative and an attention-grabbing research paper title that will encourage the reader.

Title is one of the major components of research papers, which appears first in a research paper, yet it may sometimes be written last. It should be formulated so that the reader would get the idea of what he/she will be reading about.

Generally, research paper title has three functions. Firstly, it generalizes the text by summarizing the central idea of the paper concisely and correctly. Secondly, an interesting title may draw particular attention among professionals. Thirdly, it helps to facilitate the retrieval as it is the first piece of information that reader acquires and a good title can help the reader in his/her search for information to be indexed frequently.

Sometimes two different notions—research paper topic and research paper title—are often mixed up. Research paper topic is what you will be investigating. Research paper topic is either given by our professor or chosen by ourselves. Usually we spend a huge amount of time on selecting the topic that we are interested in. Research paper topic is a wider notion. It presents the area of investigation. Research paper title is the formulation of the area of your investigation. The purpose of research paper title is to attract the reader's attention. That is one of the reasons why research paper title should be laconically formulated.

Most research paper titles are incomplete sentences, which is just a label or appellation. The words or phrases used in a title are very often nouns, noun phrases and gerunds, which are key words for the paper, summing up the whole text. For example, we may easily find such titles as *Database Logic, Growth Mechanism of Whiskers and Treatment for Defect Removal, Writing and Publishing AcademicPapers,* etc.

Research paper titles should be capitalized. There is not a single set of rules for capitalizing words in a research paper title. For most of us, it is a matter of selecting one convention and sticking to it. The big decision is whether to go with sentence case or title case.

Types of Title	Writing Conventions for Capitalization of a Title	Example
Sentence Case / Down Style	Only the first word of the title and any proper nouns are capitalized. This form, recommended by the Publication Manual of the American Psychological Association, among others, is popular with many online and print publications.	Rules for capitalizing the words in a title
Title Case/ Headline Style /Up Style	Capitalize the first and last words of the title and all nouns, pronouns, adjectives, verbs, adverbs, and subordinating conjunctions (if, because, as, that, and so on).	Rules for Capitalizing the Words in a Title

A good research paper title could create a positive impression and stimulate reader interest. It should be brief and concise, specific, unified and standard. A title is generally composed of no more than twenty words. It is advisable to use a subtitle if it is not limited to 15 words, for example,

International Communication Pragmatics—A New Branch of Learning of Language.
To be brief and concise, professional papers seldom use such decorative locutions
as "study of", "analysis of", "regarding", "investigation on", "some thoughts on",
"the method of "or similar constructions that lead to redundancy. Of course, the
title must be long enough to describe the content of the paper. Too short a title,
sometimes, may bring about confusion, or can not indicate the subject and scope
of a research paper with some accuracy. In preparing a research paper title, a
general and abstract title should be avoided. For example, such a title as *Computer
Retrieval* will be regarded as too general and global, vague and empty, telling
the reader nothing specific. It would be better to change the title into *Computer
Retrieval* on *Literature of Physics*, or *Computer Retrieval on International Conference
Information*, according to the content of the paper. In addition, a unified title is
preferable in preparing a research paper title, that is to say, the parallel parts of a
tile should be grammatically symmetrical. For instance, the title *The Design and
Preparing of Si₃N⁴* should be changed into *The Design and Preparation of Si₃N.* In
general, nonstandard abbreviations and symbols, or any terms intelligible only to
the specialist could be avoided, because the use of them could be unfavorable to
efficient information retrieval.

Besides these basic writing requirements above mentioned, the following
situations might be avoided in editing a research paper title.

Writing taboo of "Title"	Annotation	Example
Avoid abbreviation	In our daily life and technical communication, we often see and use many abbreviations, such as, C. P. C, SARS, and d.c., but not all readers know their meaning, especially for some technical abbreviations. Thereby, they should be avoided in the title of a research paper.	TCT (*traffic conflict technique*), SLA (*second language acquisition*).
Avoid formulae, chemical molecular formula, and symbols	Some formulae contain long and complex writing forms which is not proper for title. If included, the simple title would become complicated.	$ZeTa$, $MNaH_2PO_4$, RSO_3Na, $MNaClO_4$

Avoid patent and brand names	Patent and brand names are fixed in law form which can not be changed. For example, there are many numbers and symbols in patent name which can not be omitted or deleted, so they are unsuitable to appear in a title.	J. Smith, U.S. Pat. 2542356, 1972
Avoid jargon and nomenclature	Although jargon and nomenclature can add some flavor for writing and can be understood by some readers, they are spoken language and informal which make them unsuitable to be used in a title.	licorice stick, windy nonsense
Avoid infrequent and outdated words	Research papers purpose to investigate practical problems and phenomena. If infrequent or outdated words are used in a title, it is probable to cause misunderstanding as well as to bore readers.	cadre (from Russian)

4.2 Author/Affiliation

Author/Affiliation mainly helps the author respond to comments and questions raised from his/her paper because the author(s) must perform the entire work of paper writing in person and be responsible for the content of the paper. The names of author(s) and institutional affiliations are usually used as author indexing, designed in the formation referencing network. Readers can correspond with the author, according to the affiliation. Publication of a research paper is regarded as a norm for valuing the professional level of the researcher and the academic institution concerned. Therefore this section should be written clearly so as to publish the paper in a given international journal.

Chinese author's name is preferably spelt in accordance with the Chinese Pinyin. Nowadays, a two-character name is quite popular among the Chinese authors, for example, Li Ying, Yu Bo, which often leads to difficulty for westerners to pronounce the name, especially the family name, because they customarily take the last name as the family name. Under such circumstances, all the letters in family name are capitalized so as to distinguish the family name (last name/surname) from the personal name (first name), for example, Keqing HE and Peng LIANG.

Author's professional title, administrative rank or academic degree such as "President", "Chief Manager", "Doctor" are preferably omitted before the name of an author. The address of author's affiliation should be written from the small unit to the larger ones, for example, "School of International Studies, Xi'an Jiaotong University 710049, P.R. China". Too small internal unit in the author's affiliation is advisable to be ignored, especially those units that are incomprehensible for foreigners, such as "Technical Innovation Group of...", "Research Office of...", etc. These units are too internal and too small to be understood by foreign readers, and are difficult for author indexing.

4.3 Keywords

Keywords of a research paper are the most frequently used words and the most important words and phrases of the paper. They are representative of the theme of the paper. As it mainly functions for easiness of retrieval, "keywords" is also called "indexing terms".

Keywords of research paper appear in the form of nouns, not verbs. For example, "investigation" is used instead of "investigate". In general, the number of keywords ranges from 2 to 8. The normal limited number of keywords is four to six in one paper. As usual, keywords are chosen from the "title" and/or "abstract", where the key terms of words and phrases are usually contained.

The section of "keywords" is also variously called "keywords index", "keywords and phrases", "indexing terms", etc. Though keywords can be either above or below the abstract of a paper, they are yet, in most cases, placed below the abstract. They are in lowercase except abbreviations. There are three methods of spacing keywords: using comma, semicolon or larger partition. Full stop could not be used to space keywords. For example, "software component,(;) UML, (;) rational database".

4.4 Acknowledgements

Acknowledgements are an integral part of most RPs that recognizes the people and institutions we are indebted to for guidance and assistance during our research. This section provides an opportunity for us to show that we are a member of a community and have benefited from that membership. Sometimes the mention of a distinguished person in our profession may suggest that our paper is of high quality. In any case, academic honesty requires that assistance be recognized.

Acknowledgements occur either at the bottom of the first page or at the end. In most cases, Acknowledgments should be written in the first person—I for a single author and We for coauthors. It is possible to find phrases like "the present authors", but they are considered too formal for this situation. In this section, financial support tends to come first, followed by thanks. Disclaimers seem optional. Mentions of other versions and sources (if used) seem to come either at the beginning or at the end. But note that, in theses or dissertations, it is customary to open with thanks to supervisors, advisors, committee members, etc.

Here are some of the common elements in Acknowledgements.

Financial support	Support for this work was provided by (sponsor). This research/study was partially supported by a grant from (sponsor). This research was funded by Contract (number) from (sponsor). This project would be impossible without funds from (sponsor). We gratefully acknowledge the financial support from (sponsor) for... My work was supported by ... (Grant No.) ...(the author) are supported by ... under Grant No...
Thanks	We would like to thank A, B, and C for his encouragement and guidance throughout this project. We are indebted/ grateful to B for ... Special thanks are extended to A for...
Disclaimers	However, the opinions expressed here do not necessarily reflect the policy of (sponsor). The interpretations in this paper remain my own. None, however, is responsible for any remaining errors. However, any mistakes that remain are my own.

Other versions	An earlier/preliminary version of this paper was presented at (conference or seminar). This article is based on the first author's doctoral dissertation. This paper is based on research completed as partial fulfillment for the Ph.D. requirements at (university name).

[Example 1]

W.M. and Z.Z. are supported by grant LM05110 from the National Library of Medicine. We thank Dr. Warren Gish for helpful conversations, Dr. Eugene Kooming for assistance with samples, and Dr. Gregory Schuler for producing several of the figures.

[Example 2]

The authors gratefully acknowledge the assistance of Steven Conley and Michele Forrestall in preparing the photomicrographs.

Here are some of the names of common scientific foundation elements in Acknowledgments.

1. 国家高技术研究发展计划资助项目（863计划）（No. ） National High Technology Research and Development Program of China (863 Program)(No.) 2. 国家自然科学基金(面上项目；重点项目；重大项目)（No. ） National Natural Science Foundation of China （General Program; Key Program; Major Program）（No. ） 3. 国家"九五"攻关项目（No. ） National Key Technologies R & D Program of China during the 9th Five-Year Plan Period（No. ） 4. 中国科学院"九五"重大项目（No. ） Major Programs of the Chinese Academy of Sciences during the 9th Five-Year Plan Period （No. ） 5. 中国科学院重点资助项目（No. ） Key Programs of the Chinese Academy of Sciences（No. ） Ministry of Education of China（No. ） 6. 国家教育部博士点基金资助项目（No. ） Ph.D. Programs Foundation of Ministry of Education of China（No. ）

7. 中国科学院百人计划经费资助

100 Talents Program of the Chinese Academy of Sciences
Supported by One Hundred Person Project of the Chinese Academy of Sciences

8. 国家重点基础研究发展规划项目(973计划) (No.)

the Major State Basic Research Development Program of China (973 Program) (No.)

9. 国家杰出青年科学基金（No. ）

National Science Fund for Distinguished Young Scholars（No. ）

10. 国家教育部优秀青年教师基金（No. ）

Science Foundation for the Excellent Youth Scholars, Ministry of Education of China

11. 中国科学院西部之光基金（No. ）

Supported by West Light Foundation of the Chinese Academy of Sciences（No. ）

12. 北京市自然科学基金（No. ）

Beijing Municipal Natural Science Foundation

4.5 Language Focus: Absolutes

Suppose in a research paper on the relationship between current and magnetic field. We begin by writing:

The current changes.

The magnetic field changes.

We want to indicate the relationship between the fact that the current changes and the fact that the magnetic field changes. At first, we try to achieve the purpose by simply joining the two sentences:

The current changes and the magnetic field changes.

We are not happy with this version either, so we try again:

The current changing, the magnetic field will change.

We may like this version best, both because it is concise and because it clearly indicates the relationship between current and magnetic field. The phrase **the current changing** is called an ABSOLUTE, a group of words that is almost but not quite a complete sentence. An absolute has a full subject but only part of a predicate, often only a participle. Absolutes are useful for adding narrative and descriptive details, creating a further explanation, and suggesting cause-effect or conditional relationship. We are encouraged to practice constructing absolutes so as to make sentence expressions more specific and concise.

How would we combine the following sentences?

Resistor is R_F removed.

The wideband gain of the amplifier is 100.

We have, as always, a number of options:

Resistor RF is removed and the wideband gain of the amplifier is 100.

OR

After resistor RF is removed, the wideband gain of the amplifier is 100.

OR

Since resistor RF is removed, the wideband gain of the amplifier is 100.

Another workable option is the absolute.

Resistor RF removed, the wideband gain of the amplifier is 100.

But notice that moving the absolute to the end of the sentence produces some confusion:

The wideband gain of the amplifier is 100, resistor RF removed.

In general, absolutes work best at the middle or end of a sentence, but absolutes that either suggests a cause-relationship or refer to an earlier event work best at its beginning.

4.6　Reflections and Practice

1. Please comment on the following titles or keywords and revise them if necessary.

(1) "A Research on the Artificial Neural Network (ANN) Applied in the Analysis of Structural Mechanics"

(2) Developing Computer Internet and Spread of Culture and Information

(3) Studies on Monoclonal Antibodies in Nuclear Medicine

(4) An Investigation of Mechanisms of Retinal Damage from Chronic Laser Radiation

(5) Toward Commercialization of the Natural Gas Vehicles

(6) Can the Rate of Wash Load Be Predicted from the Bed Load Function?

(7) Phase Equilibria between Fluorothene and Organic

(8) On Learning Foreign Languages and Cultural Background Teaching

(9) Keywords: English, Vocabulary, Tendency.

(10) Keywords: Collocation Context Connotation

2. The following title, affiliation, and abstract are abridged from a journal article written by a student. Some mistakes could be found in them. Please revise them. Meanwhile, please list the keywords for the paper based on the title and abstract.

EEG and ECG assessment of mental fatigue in a driving simulator

Ding Xiaoguang[1]   Du Zhenzi[2]

1**** University, Xi'an 710049, China, 2. ****University. Xi'an 710049, China

Abstract: Mental fatigue is a contributing factor to some serious transportation crashes. Based on Electroencephalogram (EEG) and Electrocardiograph (ECG), driving mental fatigue is measured in this study. Altogether, thirteen healthy subjects performed continuous simulated driving task for 90 minutes, and their ECG and multi-channel EEG were recorded simultaneously. Some important physiological parameters were investigated with preprocessed ECG and EEG signals. The results shows that, as possible indices for measuring simulated driving mental fatigue, the EEG alpha and beta; the relative power; the amplitude of P300; the approximated entropy of ECG; the low and up bands power of heart rate variability (HRV) are significantly different before and after finishing driving task ($p<0.05$).

Key words:

---

3. Combine each of the groups of sentences below into a sound sentence containing one absolute.

(1) Air resistance is neglected.

The acceleration of gravity continually increases as the body approaches the earth.

(2) Almost all metals are good conductors.

Silver is the best.

(3) In Group 1, we have hydrogen and the alkali metals.

All of them have low density.

(4) The are many reasons for this.

One of the reasons is that simulation allows the assessment of the potential performance before a newly designed system is operable.

(5) Lasey's creation is thought to be one of today's wonders.

Laser is nothing more than a light that differs from ordinary lights.

4. Write a suitable Acknowledgments section for one of your pieces of work. If necessary, invent some forms of assistance to expand the section.

Chapter Five　Abstract

You may know the whole sack by a handful.

———*Liu Yiqing*

5.1　Purposes of Writing Abstracts

An abstract is a condensed version of a longer piece of writing that highlights the major points covered, concisely describes the content and scope of the writing, and reviews the writing's contents in abbreviated form. Abstracts typically serve three main goals.

First, abstracts help readers decide if they should read an entire article. Readers use abstracts to see if a piece of writing interests them or relates to a topic they are working on. Rather than tracking down hundreds of articles, readers rely on abstracts to decide quickly if an article is pertinent. Equally important, readers use abstracts to help them gauge the sophistication or complexity of a piece of writing. If the abstract is too technical or too simplistic, readers know that the article will also be too technical or too simplistic.

Second, abstracts help readers understand a text by acting as a pre-reading outline of key points. Like other pre-reading strategies, reading an abstract before reading an article helps readers anticipate what is coming in the text itself. Using an abstract to get an overview of the text makes reading the text easier and more efficient.

Third, abstracts index article for quick recovery and cross-referencing. Even before computers made indexing easier, abstracts helped librarians and researchers find information more easily. With so many indexes now available electronically, abstracts with their keywords are even more important because readers can review hundreds of abstracts quickly to find the ones most useful for their research. Moreover, cross-referencing through abstracts opens up new areas of research that readers might not have known about when they started researching a topic.

5.2 Types of Abstracts and Writing Skills

Abstracts falls into three categories: descriptive, informational, and structured. A descriptive abstract, also called indicative abstract or topic abstract, outlines the topics covered in a piece of writing so that the reader can decide whether to read the entire document. In many ways, the descriptive abstract is like a table of contents in paragraph form. Unlike reading an informative abstract, reading a descriptive abstract cannot substitute for reading the document because it does not capture the content of the piece. It is mainly used as the abstract of a review paper. The key elements of a good descriptive abstract are as follows:

Key Element	Writing Skills
Topic/background/purpose	Establishing the topic. Indicating the importance of the topic (optional).
Main proposition or finding	Identifying the main point of the paper which is sometimes stated in terms of the argument or the research question.
Overview of contents	Including the methodology and/or the key themes (for example, the headings of the longer paper) which should be listed in the order in which they will appear in the presentation or paper.

An informative abstract, as its name implies, summarizes the key points in the RP. It is an overview that briefly states the purpose, methods, results and conclusions with quantitative information. It is a condensed version of the research work without discussion or interpretation. An informative abstract, instead of indication the whole content in general, should be specific and quantitative, giving only essential data. One of the strategies for writing an informative abstract is to go through the research paper with a highlighter and mark the important facts and conclusions. Another is to list the headings and write a sentence under each heading using keywords for each area. Informative abstracts are written in a paragraph or two with transition words to signify the move between elements. An informative abstract usually cover the following key elements, each of which is written in a particular tense:

Key Elements	Writing Skills
Background information (optional)	Establishing the significance or context of the research. Avoiding references in abstracts. Summarizing ideas rather than attributing them to a particular author. Avoiding definitions of key terms.
Research question or aim	Identifying the research aim which is also stated as research question or hypothesis.
Methodology	The extent of information required about the methodology differing according to whether the methodology used was standard or modified, and the extent required to make sense to a reader.
Results	Summarizing the key results.
Conclusions or implications (optional)	Summarizing the key implications or conclusions.

Sometimes, informative abstracts are divided into subheadings for each of these elements. These subheadings are written in full capitalization, bold face or italic face. These abstracts are called structured abstracts. Structured abstracts appeared in the 1980s and are, by now, widely used in the major clinical journals. Many behavioral, social, biological, and basic medical sciences journals are also following the convention of structured abstracts. Some clinical journals include structured abstracts with variations on these headings. For example, some will use headings such as: Context, Background, Aim, Findings, and Interpretation. Some additional headings include: Design, Population, Setting, Participants, Intervention (method), Main Outcome Measures and other aspects relevant to the research.

Descriptive Abstract 1	
The Postmodern Appeal of Complementary and Alternative Medicines (CAM) to Australian Consumers: A Review of the Literature	
The increasing popularity of complementary and	Topic

alternative medicines (CAM) amongst health consumers and orthodox service providers in Australia is well documented. However, understandings about the reasons for increasing consumer use of CAM in Australia and elsewhere are poorly developed and invite further research. *This paper presents the results of a systematic literature review on reasons for CAM use by the Australian population.* There are four main themes: 1) criticism of conventional medicine, 2) attraction to the holistic model of health, 3) treatment options for chronic and terminal illness, and 4) lifestyle factors which are identified and explored through social change theory, namely globalization and post-modernization.

Purpose

Main proposition and overview of contents

Descriptive Abstract 2

Mechanism of Angiogenesis and Arteriogenesis

Endothelial and smooth muscle cells interact with each other to form new blood vessels. In this review, the cellular and molecular mechanisms underlying the formation of endothelium-lined channels (angiogenesis) and their maturation via recruitment of smooth muscle cells (arteriogenesis) during physiological and pathological conditions are summarized, alongside with possible therapeutic applications.

Topic
Main proposition and overview of contents

Informative Abstract 1

Assessing the Economic Aspects of Solar Hot Water Production in Greece

The long-term performance of various systems was determined and the economic aspects of solar hot water production were investigated in this work. *The effect of the collector inclination angle, collector area and storage volume was examined for all systems, and various climatic conditions and their payback period was calculated.* It was found that the collector inclination angle does not have a significant effect on system performance. Large collector areas have a diminishing effect on the system's overall efficiency. The increase in storage volume has a detrimental effect for small

Objectives (implication of the research problem)
Methodology

Results

98

daily load volumes, but a beneficial one when there is a large daily consumption. Solar energy was found to be truly competitive when the conventional fuel being substituted is electricity, and it should not replace diesel oil on pure economic grounds. Large daily load volumes and large collector areas are in general associated with shorter payback periods. *Overall, the systems are oversized and are economically suitable for large daily hot water load volumes.*	*Conclusions*

Informative Abstract 2	
Density-function Thermochemistry: the Role of Exact Change	
Despite the remarkable thermochemical accuracy of Kohn-Sham density-functional theories with gradient corrections for exchange-correlation [see, for example A.D. Becke, J. Chem. Phy. 96, 2155(1922)], *we believe that further improvements are unlikely unless exact-exchange information is considered.* Arguments to support this view are presented, and a semiempirical exchange-correlation functional containing local-spin-density, gradient, and exact-exchange terms is tested on 56 atomization energies, 42 ionization potentials, 8 proton affinities, and 10 total atomic energies of first- and second-row systems. *This functional performs significantly better than previous functionals with gradient corrections only, and fits experimental atomization energies with an impressively small average absolute deviation of 2.4kcal/mol.*	Background *Hypothesis* Arguments and model *Evaluation of the model*

Structured Abstract 1
Risk factors and mortality in patients with nosocomial staphylococcus aureus bacteremia.
BACKGROUND: Infections due to methicillin-resistant Staphylococcus aureus have become increasingly common in hospitals worldwide. S aureus continues to be a cause of nosocomial bacteremia. **METHODS:** We analyzed the clinical significance (mortality) of MRSA and methicillin-susceptible S aureus bacteremia in a retrospective cohort study in a 2900-bed tertiary referral medical center. Survival and logistic

regression analyses were used to determine the risk factors and prognostic factors of mortality. **RESULTS:** During the 15-year period, 1148 patients were diagnosed with nosocomial S aureus bacteremia. After controlling potential risk factors for MRSA bacteremia on logistic regression analysis, service, admission days prior to bacteremia, age, mechanical ventilator, and central venous catheter (CVC) were independent risk factors for MRSA. The crude mortality rate of S aureus bacteremia was 44.1%. The difference between the mortality rates of MRSA (49.8%) and MSSA bacteremia (27.6%) was 22.2% (P < 0.001). Upon logistic regression analysis, the mortality with MRSA bacteremia was revealed to be 1.78 times higher than MSSA (P < 0.001). The other predicted prognostic factors included age, neoplasms, duration of hospital stay after bacteremia, presence of mechanical ventilator, and use of CVC. **CONCLUSIONS:** Resistance to methicillin was an important independent prognostic factor forpatients with S aureus bacteremia.

5.3 Language Focus: Sentence Variety

Sentence variety is essential to research paper writing. It is the variety in sentence, ways of opening a paper and transition devices that help to avoids monotony and primer style and enables the author to express himself more effectively. Effective writing normally uses a mixture of various sentences.

Since sentence structure can be classified as simple one, compound one and complex one, the basic structure of a sentence can therefore be varied by compounding thoughts or subordinating one thought to another. It can further be effected by using different sentence structures and by varying their length. Short sentences are clear and easy to read. But too many short sentences are monotonous. Long sentences are more interesting but can be difficult to construct and read.

Which text is more interesting?	
Britain is an example of the university funding problem. Fees were introduced in 1997. Spending per student had fallen by 25% since 1990. Demand continues to grow for places on the most popular courses.	Britain is an example of the university funding problem, since although fees were introduced in 1997 spending per student had dropped by 25% since 1990, while demand continues to grow for places on the most popular courses.

Variations of sentence openings can be achieved by beginning a sentence with an adverbial clause, a prepositional phrase, a non-finite (gerund, participles, infinitives) phrase, an expletive (a word such as "there" which has no lexical functions in the sentence), a parenthetical expression (in fact, on the other hand), an adverb, an adjective, or a coordinate conjunction.

Here are some useful language expressions that could be used to enhance the sentence variety in the abstract writing:

Describing Principal Activity or Research Purpose

This article summarizes research on...
To investigate ..., we examined...
We investigated ...
For comparison purposes we present ...
This paper presents/focuses on a detailed analysis of ...
The focus/emphasis of this paper is on ...
We emphasize the following points: ...
This paper synthesizes, using a common framework, these recent developments together with new ones, with an emphasis on...
The intention of this paper is to survey ...
The present study was performed to evaluate the progress in infant immunization.

Describing Research Method

We use N-body simulations to investigate...
We tested this hypothesis in various human T cells...
We also provides a step-by-step analytic procedure, that allows...to be calculated as a function of mass in any hierarchical model.
Our program uses a maximum likelihood approach.
We apply the network to the source separation problem.
The study analyzed the frequency of the technical terms in the three texts.
This paper examines how the molecular shapes...can be used to synthesize...
We describe a new molecular approach to analyzing ...

Presenting Results

Our results suggest/show/indicate...
The results we obtained demonstrate...
We present/show...
The study revealed that...
Solar energy was found to be competitive when the conventional fuel being substituted is electricity.

学术论文写作与发表

Writing Conclusions
The article suggests... We suggest/recommend/propose...a new framework for ... Our studies indicate... In this study, we describe a psychobiological model of the structure of personality. The results suggest that abnormalities in male sex development induced by...may be mediated. Given the different factors, we conclude that...

5.4 Reflections and Practice

1. Here is an abstract of a paper in the journal of Energy Sources. Read it through looking for the main function of each sentence.

Experimental Study of the Performance of Solar Dryers with Pebble Beds
1. Major problems of the arid region are transportation of agricultural products and losses due to spoilage of the products, especially in summer. 2. This work presents the performance of a solar drying system consisting of an air heater and a dryer chamber connected to a greenhouse. 3. The drying system is designed to dry a variety of agricultural products. 4. The effect of air mass flow rate on the drying process is studied. 5. Composite pebbles, which are constructed from cement and sand, are used to store energy for night operation. 6. The pebbles are placed at the bottom of the drying chamber and are charged during the drying process itself. 7. A separate test is done using a simulator, a packed bed storage unit, to find the thermal characteristics of the pebbles during charging and discharging modes with time. 8. Accordingly, the packed bed is analyzed using a heat transfer model with finite difference technique described before and during the charging and discharging processes. 9. Graphs are presented that depict the thermal characteristics and performance of the pebble beds and the drying patterns of different agricultural products. 10. The results show that the amount of energy stored in the pebbles depends on the air mass flow rate, the inlet air temperature, and the properties of the storage materials. 11. The composite pebbles can be used efficiently as storing media.

2. Following is the abstract of a paper in the field of education. The paper examined the science education of English learners in an elementary school district in the USA. The abstract is in note form. Write the abstract based on the notes given.

Helping English Learners Increase Achievement through Inquiry-based Science Instruction
Research activity: to summarize the results of a four-year project in science education, in a rural setting, with English learners in grades K-6 in an elementary school district, southern California. **Objective of collecting data**: to measure student achievement in science, writing, reading, and mathematics. **Research method**: data analysis—number of years that students participated in inquiry-based science instruction, use of science notebooks. **Results**: achievement of English learners corresponds to number of years they participated in the project. **Conclusion**: the longer in the program, the higher the scores in science, writing, reading, and mathematics.

3. Each of the following sentences is taken from an abstract of a paper entitled "Commonly Encountered Errors on Abstract Submissions". Indicate the probable order used by the author in writing the abstract in the space below.

(1)_____ (2)_____ (3)_____ (4)_____ (5)_____

Commonly Encountered Errors on Abstract Submissions
a. It is essential for prospective presenters to follow published recommendations to ensure that their abstracts conform to conference guidelines. b. This single-blinded study utilized a convenience sample of 20 reviewers who were selected to complete a survey about commonly encountered errors on abstract review forms while evaluating abstracts submitted to a national dental hygiene research conference. The reviewers evaluated 80 submitted abstracts prior to completing the survey. The instrument used in the study contained 30 items with closed-ended responses which was previously pilot-tested with 5 other reviewers to establish content validity. Survey information was obtained through the use of an electronic online tool, and all responses remained confidential. Descriptive statistics were used to analyze the data. IRB approval was obtained from the USC School of Dentistry. c. Prospective presenters for research meetings often submit abstracts that do not conform with published guidelines. It is important for researchers

学术论文写作与发表

to know how to correctly prepare and submit an abstract.

d. The purpose of this study was to assess the types of errors encountered by dental hygiene reviewers who evaluated submitted abstracts for a national dental hygiene research conference.

e. Failure to include all of the required elements was the most commonly reported error on submitted abstracts to a national dental hygiene research conference (35%). Other errors included typographical errors (23%), lack of information about statistical methods (20%), spacing errors (7%) and failure to include affiliation (3%).

4. The following is the abstract of a paper in the journal of International Business Review. Read the abstract and analyze each sentence for the type of information it contains. Then write out a reduced version, combining method and purpose into one or two sentences and eliminating any non-essential information.

Performance of International Joint Ventures: Evidence for West Africa
(1) Performance of International Joint Ventures (IJVs) has been an important theme of research over the past two decades. (2) In the context of West Africa, however, IJV performance has received scant attention. (3) This paper examines a number of aspects of performance of 57 IJVs in the West Africa context. (4) Multivariate analysis shows that partner capabilities, capital adequacy, congruity of motives and goals are significant determinants of performance. (5) Level of control was found to have a negative impact on performance. (6) A further significant finding is that over a number of dimensions IJVs with a private sector host partner are perceived to perform better than IJVs with the host government as a partner.

5. Rewrite the following paragraphs in fewer sentences.

Text 1
Worldwide, enrolments in higher education are increasing. In developed countries over half of all young people enter college. Similar trends are seen in China and South America. This growth has put financial strain on state university systems. Many countries are asking students and parents to contribute. This leads to a debate about whether students or society benefit from tertiary education.

<table>
<tr><td align="center">**Text 2**</td></tr>
<tr><td>It is widely recognized that a university degree benefits the individual. A graduate can expect to find a better job with a higher salary. In the USA the average graduate will earn $1 million more in a lifetime than a non-graduate. Many governments now expect students to pay a proportion of tuition costs. It is argued that this discriminates against poorer students. Some countries give grants to students whose families have low incomes. Their education is seen to be beneficial for the nation as a whole.</td></tr>
</table>

6. The following sentence is too long. Please divide it into shorter ones.

China is one developing country (but not the only one) which has imposed fees on students since 1997, but the results have been surprising: enrolments, especially in the most expensive universities, have continued to rise steeply, growing 200% overall between 1997 and 2001; it seems in this case that higher fees attract rather than discourage students, who see them as a sign of a good education, and compete more fiercely for places, leading to the result that a place at a good college can cost $8,000 per year for fees and maintenance.

7. Divide the following sentence into shorter ones so that the first and last sentence is shorter.

Developing countries are under the greatest financial pressure, and may also experience difficulties in introducing loan schemes for students, since the lack of private capital markets restricts the source of borrowing for governments, which are often unable to raise sufficient cheap funds, while a further restraint has been the high default rates by students unable to repay their loans.

Chapter Six   Introduction and Literature Review

Well begun is half done.

——English Proverb

6.1 Rhetorical Pattern of Introduction

The main purpose of the Introduction is to provide the rationale for the paper, moving from general discussion of the topic to the particular question or hypothesis being investigated. A secondary purpose is to attract readers' interest in the topic. The Introduction is a key section for both the reader and the writer. First impression does matter. The reader will be more inclined to read a paper if the Introduction is clear-cut, organized, and engaging. For the writer, the Introduction serves as a transition by moving the reader from the world outside of your paper to the world within. To some extent, a carefully crafted Introduction acts as a springboard, establishing the order and direction for the entire paper. Therefore, an effective Introduction is of vital importance to a research paper. John Swales (1994) proposed a Create-a-Research-Space (or CARS) model for an effective Introduction.

Moves in Research Paper Introduction	
Move 1	Establishing a research territory a. by making a topic generalization or showing that the general research area is important, central, interesting, problematic, or relevant in some way. (optional) b. by introducing and re viewing items of previous research in the area. (obligatory)
Move 2	Establishing a niche a.by indicating a gap in the previous research, raising a question about it, or extending previous knowledge in some way. (obligatory)
Move 3	Occupying the niche a. by outlining purposes or stating the nature of the present research. (obligatory) b. by announcing principal findings. (optional) c. by stating value or justification for carrying out the present study. (optional) d. by indicating the structure of the RP. (optional)

In Move 1, centrality claims are appeals to the discourse community whereby members are asked to accept that the research about to be reported is part of a significant and well-established research area. Some typical examples of the linguistic signals of centrality claims are given below in abbreviated form.

Claiming Centrality
Recently, there has been growing interest in... The possibility of... has generated wide interest in... The development of... is a classic problem in... The... has become a favorite topic for analysis... Knowledge of ... has a great importance for... The study of... has become an important aspect of ... A central issue in... is... The... has been extensively studied in recent years.
Many investigators have recently turned to... Many recent studies have focused on...

In many ways, Move 2 is the key move in Introductions. It is the hinge that connects Move 1 (what has been done) to Move 3 (what the present research is about). Move 2 thus establishes the motivation for the study. By the end of Move 2, the reader should have a good idea of what is going to come in Move 3. Move 2 establishes a niche mainly by indicating a gap—by showing that the research story so far is not yet complete. Move 2 then is a particular kind of critique. The common ways to indicate a gap are as follows:

Indicating a Gap	
Negative verbs	However, previous research in this field has neglected/ overlooked/ overestimated/ been restricted to/ suffered from/ underestimated/ misinterpreted/ ignored/ failed to consider/ disregarded/ concentrated on/ been limited to/misinterpreted...
Negative adjectives	Nevertheless, these attempts to establish a link between secondary smoke and lung cancer are at present controversial/ incomplete/ inconclusive/misguided/ questionable/ unconvincing/ unsatisfactory...

Negative subject	However, little information is about... No attention has been paid to... No work has been done/reported on... Few/ none of data/ studies/ investigations/ are available on... Few researches have been devoted to...
Question	A question remains whether... However, it remains unclear whether... These findings suggest that this treatment might not be so effective when applied to...
Expressed needs/ interests/ desires	The differences need to be analyzed. It would thus be of interest to learn how... It is desirable/ of interest to compare... It would seem, therefore, that further investigations are needed in order to...
Contrastive statement	The research has tended to focus on... , rather than on ... These studies have emphasized... , as opposed to... Although considerable research has been devoted to..., rather less attention has been paid to...

The third and final step in the typical RP Introduction is to make an offer to fill the gap (or answer the question) that has been created in Move 2. The first element in Move 3 is obligatory. The other three steps in Move 3 are optional. Here are the beginning parts of ten opening Move 3 sentences and some examples concerning Steps c and d.

Tense and Purpose Statements
1. The aim of the present paper is to give...
2. This paper reports on the results obtained...
3. In this paper we give preliminary results for...
4. The main purpose of the experiment reported here was to...
5. This study was designed to evaluate...
6. The present work extends the use of the last model by...
7. We now report the interaction between...
8. The primary focus of this paper is on...
9. The aim of this investigation was to test...
10. It is the purpose of the present paper to provide...

Stating Value or Justification for Carrying the Current Study

1. The model described here could serve as the basis for a study of automatic measurementsystems in an instrumentation cours.
2. Both of the factors under investigation in this study may be of importance in explaining the irregular occurrence of this disease.
3. As a move in this direction, I hope that the present small-scale study could serve as starting point to later, possibly more sophisticated, research of a comparative nature.

Describing Paper Structure

1. *The paper proceeds as follows: Initially,* we review the e-commerce literature and illustrate the knowledge gap; we then discuss the research design, the measurement of the a variables and the data collection; we present the analysis and the results; *finally, we conclude with adiscussion of the implications of the finding for theory and practice.*
2. *The plan of this paper is as follows. Section II* describes the current arrangements for regulating exchange rates within the EC. In Section III a theoretical model is constructed which is designed to capture these arrangements.Experimental parameters are then tested in Section *IV. Finally, Section V offers some suggestions for modification of the current mechanisms.*
3. *The remainder of this article is divided into two sections. Section 2 gives an overview* of the literature. *It identifies* some gaps in the literature and issues of current concern. *Section 3 suggests* the way forward. It presents a framework for exploring theory and practice in LSP.
4. *After this opening introduction unit, Section Two deals with* the abstract writing. *The next two sections deal in some detail with* the many complexities surrounding the writing of a critical literature review. *Section five then moves on to some ... The final two sections switch attention to* texts that are...

The final important point with regard to the move analysis of Introduction is the cyclicity of Move 2. A number of investigators (Cooper, 1985; Hopkings and Dudley-Evans, 1998) have pointed out that the niche-establishment does not necessarily occur only at the end of a literature review, but may follow reviews of individual items, so that cycles of Move 1/Step b and Move 2 recur. Some studies have also shown that the cycles of Move 1/Step a and Move 2 are possible to be found in RP. It is likely that the longer the Introduction the greater the probability of some recycling (Crookes, 1986). The cyclicity is more evident in the social sciences than in the

natural sciences (Swales, 1990). The following texts are adopted from a research paper which indicates the typical rhetorical pattern of Introduction.

Cyclicity of Moves in Introduction Section	
(1) Urinary incontinence in women is a common distressing, and costly health problem. *(2) Studies have shown that only about a quarter of affected women consult a doctor for their symptoms, and the treatment that they are offered is probably not optimal.* (3) The condition is thus a challenge for general practitioners, who often will be the first professionals to diagnose and treat it. *(4) Several treatment options are effective in the treatment of urinary incontinence in women and most of these treatments are suitable in general practitioners and other primary care staff. (5) In two controlled trials from general practice most of the women had improved or were cured after management; similar results were found in a study in which treatments were administered by nurses.* (6) Such studies, however, are often performed by oen dedicated doctor or specially trained staff, so the results may not reflect what is attainable in ordinary practices. *(7) We conducted an observational study of treatment of urinary incontinence in women in general practice in a community where a group of general practitioners serves the total population. (8) The study was designed not to test the efficacy of one technique or specific treatment under ideal conditions, but as a comprehensively documented, although uncontrolled, effectiveness study with 12 months follow up of general practitioners' total interventions and treatment options. (9) We used both subjective and objective outcome measures.*	Claiming centrality *Reviewing the previous research* Making topic generalization *Reviewing the previous research* Indicating a research gap *Outlining purpose*

6.2 Taxomony of Literature Review

According to Creswell (2005), a literature review "is a critical summary and assessment of journal articles, books and other documents that describes the past and current state of information in a particular field". It can be a separate article, but more often it is part of a research paper. In a research paper, it can be constructed as an independent section, or incorporated part of Introductions. Occasionally, it may be integrated throughout an article as need for comparison or evaluation.

Literature reviews provide us with a handy guide to a particular topic. If we have limited time to conduct research, literature reviews can give us an overview or act as a stepping stone. For professionals, they are useful reports that keep them up to date with what is current in the field. For scholars, the depth and breadth of the literature review emphasizes the credibility of the writer in his or her field. Literature reviews also provide a solid background for a research paper. Comprehensive knowledge of the literature in the field is essential to most research papers. The review should therefore also demonstrate to the reader why the writer's research is useful, necessary, important, and valid.

In writing a literature review, our purpose is to convey to our reader what knowledge and ideas have been established on a topic, and what their strengths and weakness are, that's to say, a literature review contains two basic elements: to thoroughly describe work done on a specific area of research and to evaluate this work. Both the descriptive and evaluative elements are important parts of the review. We can not do one or the other. If we just describe past research without evaluating it, we are merely summarizing information without digesting it. If we just discuss recent theories in an area without describing the work done to test those theories, our arguments will lack supporting empirical evidence.

Literature reviews can be classified according to five characteristics: focus, goal, perspective, coverage, organization, and audience.

Characteristics	Categories of Literature Reviews
Focus	Research outcomes, Research methods, Theories, Practices or Applications
Goal	Integration , Criticism
Coverage	Exhaustive, Exhaustive with selective citation, Representative, Central or pivotal
Organization	Historical, Conceptual

The first characteristic is the focus of the review. Cooper (1988) identifies four potential foci: research outcomes, research methods, theories, or practices or applications. Literature reviews that focus on research outcomes are perhaps the most common. In terms of developing a research rationale, an outcomes-oriented review may help identify a lack of information on a particular research outcome, thus establishing a justifiable need for an outcome study.

Methodological reviews concentrate on research methods. In methodological review, research methods in the chosen field are investigated to identify key variables, measures, and methods of analysis. The methodological review is also helpful to identify methodological strengths and weaknesses in a body of research, and examine how research practices differ across groups, times, or settings. A methodological review may lead to sound rationale that can justify proposed research, if it turns out that the previous research has been methodologically flawed.

A review of theories can help establish what theories already exist, the relationships between them, and to what degree the existing theories have been investigated. A theoretical review is appropriate if, for example, the research aims to advance a new theory. In terms of the research rationale, a theoretical review can help establish a lack of theories or reveal that the current theories are insufficient, thus helping to justify that a new theory should be put forth.

Finally, literature reviews can be focused on practices or applications. For example, a review might concentrate on how a certain intervention has been applied or how a group of people tend to carry out a certain practice. In terms of a research rationale, this fourth type of review can help establish a practical need not currently being met.

While a literature review in a RP typically has a primary focus, it may also be necessary to address all or some of the foci mentioned above. For example, a review with an outcomes-oriented focus would likely also deal with the methodological flaw that might affect an outcome. An outcome oriented review may also deal with theories related to the phenomenon being investigated and introduce the practical applications of the knowledge that will ultimately be gained from the research paper.

A literature review in a research paper often has multiple goals. Because it is used to justify a later investigation, the goal place more emphasis on critically analyzing the literature, perhaps to identify a weakness and propose to remedy that weakness with the proposed research. Either way, the author must integrate reviews to present the reader with the big picture. Without integration, the map of the research landscape would be as large as the research landscape itself.

Deciding how wide to cast the net is a critical step in conducting a review. There are four coverage scenarios. In an exhaustive review, the reviewer promises to locate and consider every piece of research on certain topic, published or unpublished. However, finding every piece of research could take more time than is available. The key to the exhaustive review is to define the population in such a way that the number of articles to review is manageable, which is called an exhaustive review with selective citation. For example, the reviewer might choose only to look at articles published in journals, but not conference papers: however, a theoretical reason to exclude conference papers is advised.

A third coverage approach is to consider a representative sample of articles and make inferences about the entire population of article from that sample. However, random sampling is far from foolproof. A perhaps more certain approach is to gather evidence that demonstrates that the representative sample is actually representative. The soundest approach may be to do both.

The fourth article selection approach is to take a purposive sample, that is to say, the reviewer examines only the central or pivotal articles in a field. The key here is to convince the reader that the selected articles are, in fact, the central or pivotal articles in a field and just as importantly that the articles not chosen are not central or pivotal.

There are many formats in which to organize a review. Three of the most common are the historical format, the conceptual format, and the methodological format. In historical format the review is chronologically organized. We will group and discuss our sources in order of their appearance (usually publication), highlighting the changes in research in the field and our specific topic over time. This format is useful for papers focusing on research methodology, historiographical papers, and other writings where time becomes an important element. It is preferred when the emphasis is on the progression of research methods or theories or on a change in practices over time. For example, a literature review on theories of mental illness might present how the understanding of mental illness has changed through the centuries, by giving a series of examples of key developments and ending with

current theories and the direction your research will take.

A second common organizational scheme is built around concepts. In thematic format, we will group and discuss our sources in terms of the themes or topics they cover. This format is often a stronger one organizationally. It can help us resist the urge to summarize our sources. By grouping themes or topics of research together, you will be able to demonstrate the types of topics that are important to our research. For example, if the topic of the literature review is changes in popular music, then there might be separate sections on research involving the production of music, research on the dissemination of music, research on the interpretation of music, and historical studies of popular music.

Organization: Chronological LR

On the time consistency of optimal policy in a monetary economy

The time-consistency issue is by no means a new one in economics. Strotz [25] appears to be the first one to have raised it in relation to an individual consumer. More recently, however, Kydland and Prescott [15] have discovered a family of models exhibiting time inconsistency where the source of the problem lies in the technology and in the assumption that people hold rational expectations. Although they briefly touch upon a monetary economy, the central results of their remarkable paper are given in a context where money plays no crucial role.

Organization: Conceptual LR

Stigma of the mentally ill and perceptions of dangerousness

Regarding the mentally ill, it appears that people respond to the mentally ill with feelings of fear and rejection. Martin, Pescosolido & Tuch (2000) examined the effects of descriptions of the targets' behavior, causal attributions about the source of the behavior, the targets' perceived dangerousness, labeling and participants' sociodemographic characteristics. Twenty percent of the participants labeled a target described with depressed symptoms as having a mental illness (as compared with 54% for those described with schizophrenic symptoms or 1% with normal troubles); 37% would be unwilling to interact with the depressed person (48% for the schizophrenic and 21% for normal troubles);

and 33% felt that the depressed person would do violence to others (61% for the schizophrenic and 17% for the normal troubles). Thus, a common respond to the mentally ill are rejection and fear of violence. While, based upon research, the common response to a mentally ill person is to fear violence, diagnosed mental patients commit violence at the same rates as non-diagnosed people (Martin, et al., 2000). Public perceptions may not match reality due to the public's lack o contact with the mentally ill. Alexander and Link (2003) examined contact with the mentally ill and the stigma of mental illness, perceptions of dangerousness and social distance in a telephone survey. They found that, as a participant's own life contact with mentally ill individuals increased, participants were both less likely to perceive a target mentally ill individual in a vignette as physically dangerous and less likely to desire social distance from the target. This relationship remained after controlling for demographic and confounded variables, such as gender, ethnicity, education, income and political conservatism. They also found that any type of contact—with a friend, a spouse, a family member, a work contact, or a contact in a public place—with mentally ill individuals reduced perceptions of dangerousness of the target in the vignette. Thus, according to Alexander and Link (2003), any contact with the mentally ill is associated with reduced fear and rejection. However, since this study was observational in nature, we cannot know if contact reduces fear or having lower fear increased contact.

6.3 Language Focus: Citing Sources

One of the most important aspects of reviewing previous research is making use of the ideas of other people. This is important as we need to show that we have understood the materials that we have studied and that we can use their ideas and findings in our own way. Any academic text we read or write will contain the voices of other writers as well as our own.

There are two ways in which we can refer to, or cite, another person's work: by reporting or by direct quotation. Reporting simply means reporting other writers' ideas in our own words. We can either paraphrase if we want to keep the length the same or summarize if we want to make the text shorter. There are two main ways of showing that we have used another writer's ideas: integral reporting and non-integral reporting, which are distinguished according to whether or not the name of the cited author occurs in the citing sentence or parenthesis.

Citing Sources		Tense
Reporting	**Integral**	Brie (2006) noted (found, reported, noted, suggested, observed, pointed out) that the water boils at 100°C. Rogers (2007) observed that reducing the amount of oxygen caused the deposition rate to drop sharply. Ross (2008) suggested (hypothesized, proposed, argued) that reducing the duration of school vacations may help children to retain more of what they learn in class. Researchers such as Brie (2006), Aleanoni (2005) and Seldin (2007) have shown that the causes of illiteracy are complex.
	Non-integral	It has been shown that a weak quadriceps muscle is associated with a higher risk for knee osteoarthrits, suggesting indirect evidence that inactivity may be harmful to the joint (Slemenda, et al. 2008). As researchers have demonstrated, the procedure is harmful (Raimes, 2001; Zamel, 2003).
Non-reporting	**Integral**	According to Peters (1983), evidence from first language acquisition indicates that lexical phrases are learnt first as unanalyzed lexical chunks. The causes of illiteracy were investigated by Johnes (1987).
	Non-integral	Lexical phrases are learnt first as unanalyzed lexical chunks (Peters, 1983). Several researchers have studied the causes of illiteracy.[3]

As the above examples illustrate, there are three tense options: present indefinite simple present, past indefinite, and present perfect. The differences among these tenses are subtle. In general, a move from past to present perfect and then to present indicates that the research reported is increasingly close to the writer in some way: close to the writer's own opinion, close to the writer's own research, or close to the current state of knowledge.

The present tense choice is sometimes called the citational present and is also used with famous or important sources. For example, Plato argues that...; Confucius says...; The Constitution states...

In order to refer to the research of others or to report on their findings, we have to use reporting verbs just as Evans (1994) suggests that...; Brown (2001) argues that... The difficulty with using reporting verbs is that there are many different verbs, and each of them has slightly different, and often subtle, meaning. Using the correct words relies on making the correct interpretation of what the writer we are studying is saying.

The main reporting verbs in English may be classified in terms of their function, and their strength. Some reporting verbs are used principally to say what the writer does and does not do. These verbs do not indicate any value judgment on the part of the writer; they are called "neutral" reporting verbs. A second group of verbs is used to show when the writer has an inclination to believe something but still wishes to be hesitant; we call these "tentative" reporting verbs. Finally, if the writer has strong arguments to put forward and is absolutely sure of his or her ground, we can use "strong" reporting verbs to refer to these ideas.

Function and Strength	Example Verbs
Neutral reporting verbs	describe, show, reveal, study, demonstrate, note, point out, indicate, report, observe, assume, examine, state, etc.
Tentative reporting verbs	suggest, speculate, intimate, hypothesize, imply, propose, recommend, posit the view that, question the view that, postulate, etc.
Strong reporting verbs	argue, claim, emphasize, contend, maintain, assert, theorize, support the view that, deny, negate, refute, reject, challenge, strongly believe that, counter the view/argument that, etc.

6.4 Reflections and Practice

1. Following is an example of an introduction from the field of behavioral science. The paper is entitled "Consumer reactions toward clicks and bricks: investigating buying behavior on-line and at stores". Please complete the following table by indicating the information elements the text contains.

(1) Technological advances in the 1990s, enabled entirely new ways of conducting business in the U.S. and throughout the world. (2) Of particular

importance was the World Wide Web, an enhancement of the Internet that allowed consumers and businesses to communicate in ways that were previously unavailable and perhaps even unthinkable. (3) From the mid-1990s to early 2000, the focus of businesses was primarily on the opportunities provided by the new Internet capabilities. (4) Following the "dot-com" crash in early 2000, however, businesses began to recognize the problems associated with doing business on the Internet. (5) From this point onward, much of investors' and the media's focus shifted to companies with both Internet and "bricks and mortar" presents. (6) Numerous researchers have investigated on-line buying behavior over the past several years (e.g. Jarvenpaa and Todd, 1997; Lohse, et al., 1997). (7) However, little research has addressed the relationships between on-line purchasing ("click") and purchases made at physical stores ("bricks"). (8) The purpose of this paper is to report the results of two exploratory studies designed to assess consumers' reactions to shopping at clicks and bricks. (9) We first review background relevant to the two shopping channels and the challenges faced by companies operating in the on-line environment. (10) We next develop a research model and research questions to guide our investigations. (11) We then report the results of a large survey aimed at uncovering several of the relationships specified in the model, as well as a study of a single retailer operating in both the clicks and bricks environments. (12) These studies provide insights into consumers' experiences with shopping on-line and at physical locations, as well as guidance to how retailers can take maximum advantage of the two shopping channels.

Establishing a Context	Reviewing previous research	Advancing to present research	Research purpose	Value/finding/ paper structure

2. Following is part of the Introduction of a journal paper entitled " Enhancing Student Perceptions of Fairness: The relationship between Instructor Credibility and Classroom Justice ". Fill in the blanks with an article or add the plural(s) to a noun where necessary. Some of the blanks do not require filling in.

When student _____ perceive that their course grades, course procedures, or instructors' communication are unfair, they report _____ greater likelihood of _____ indirect aggression against their instructors (North, 2002), engaging in _____ hostility toward their instructors (Carr, 2004), resisting their instructors' requests (Brown, 2006), and giving their instructors _____ lower teaching evaluation _____ (Lee, 2001). Most instructors want their students to perceive them as fair so as to prevent such student reactions. Unfortunately, _____ empirical research examining which teacher behavior _____ student _____ find fair or unfair is limited. _____ present study addresses this limitation by examining _____ relationship _____ between _____ college students' perception _____ of _____ instructor credibility—_____ instructor competence _____, _____ character _____, and _____ caring— and their perceptions of _____ classroom distributive, procedural, and interactional justice. These associations are considered in terms of _____ communication skill _____ and perception _____ that characterize _____ interpersonal relationship _____ between _____ teacher _____ and student _____.

3. The Introduction to a research paper in the field of psychology is given below. Fill in each blank with the appropriate tense for each verb given in the brackets. In some cases, you may have to use the passive voice or add a modal verb (e.g. may, might, can, could, must).

Fifty Centuries of Right-handedness: the Historical Record Introduction

It _____ (be) common knowledge that contemporary man _____ (prefer) to use his right hand when performing tasks requiring one hand. Basically, there _____ (be) two types of theories that _____ (attempt) to explain the development of right hand preference in man. The first _____ (maintain) that there _____ (be) physiological predispositions, possibly inherited, which _____ (lead) to the preference of one hand over the other[1]. The second type of theory _____ (suggest) that social or environmental pressures (or both) _____ (lead) to the high incidence of right hand preference in man [2]. This theory _____ (support) by human and animal studies that _____ (attempt) to alter hand preference through behavioral manipulation [3].

Unfortunately, these theories _____ (be) difficult to test since written references to the distribution of hand preferences throughout history _____ (be) rare. There _____ (be), however, other sources which _____ (use) to investigate historical trends in the distribution of hand preference. Nearly all cultures _____ (have) art forms that _____ (depict) human beings engaged in various activities. We _____ (expect) that such drawings and paintings

_____ (imitate) the distribution of hand use that the artist actually _____ (observe) in his culture.

Although this possibility _____ (already, suggest) [4], no systematic studies _____ (yet, do). The purpose of this study _____ (be) to examine the works of art from various cultures at various periods of history in order to describe the history of hand preference over a period of 5,000 years. The findings reported here _____ (help) clarify whether the physiological theory or the social pressure theory of hand preference _____ (be) valid.

4. The Introduction to the paper about teacher evaluation is presented here. Except literature review represented in outline form, other moves or steps concerning Introduction writing have been given here. Using the information in the outline, write a literature review for this Introduction. You may refer to the list of references at the end of the text for your citation information.

Teachers' and Students' Perceptions of "Student Evaluation of Faculty" as a Method for Assessing Teachers' Performance

Introduction

In the past 30 years, there has been a steady increase in the use of student evaluation of instruction. With accountability and a consumer-oriented culture in vogue, quality assurance practices are also greatly advocated in the education sector in Hong Kong. Rating gained from student evaluation of faculty (referred to as SEF hereafter) have been used to appraise teachers' performance, and they also provide the source of information for department heads to make decisions on allocation of duties, contract renewal, promotions and staff development.

(literature review)

A. A number of studies—investigate evaluation practice
   1. Braskamp, Brandenburg and Ory; Aleamoni; Seldin: developed guidelines to help conduct teaching evaluations more successfully.
   2. Aleamoni & Hexner: opinions about student evaluations vary, from reliable, valid and useful to unreliable, invalid, and useless.
   3. Norris: many of the attempts to assess curricula, program content, student performance and teacher effectiveness have been "ungainly and ill-defined".

B. One reason for difference of opinions: purposes of evaluation
   Ball: (some researchers) main purpose of educational evaluation: getting funding and exerting bureaucratic control

Although student evaluations has been carried out in tertiary education in Hong Kong for nearly 10 years now, there is little agreement about what constitutes excellent, good, or unacceptable performance. Additionally, many questions have been raised about the reliability and validity of student evaluation as a model of teacher appraisal.

The purpose of this study was to investigate how robust SEF is as a measure of teaching quality in tertiary education. Three research questions are listed as follow: (1) What, according to students and teachers, constitutes good teaching in tertiary education? (2) How good a measure, according to teachers, is student evaluation of faculty, in tertiary education? (3) Is student evaluation of faculty a viable means to gain feedback on teaching performance? A second goal was to devise some guiding principles for appraising teachers in the tertiary sector in Hong Kong. This study was identified as being of importance to the healthy development of quality assurance practice in tertiary education in Hong Kong.

References

Aleamoni, L.M. (ed.) (1987) *Techniques for Evaluating and Improving Instruction.* San Francisco: Jossey-Bass.

Aleamoni, L.M., & Hexner, P.Z. (1980) "A Review of the Research on Student Evaluation and a Report on the Effect of Different Sets of Instructions on Student Course and Instructor Evaluation". *Instructional Science,* 9, 67-84.

Ball, S.J.(1999) "Global Trends in Educational Reform and the Struggle for the Soul of the Teach". *Lecture* given at the Chinese University of Hong Kong on 27th Nov., 1999.

Braskamp, L.A., Brandenburg, & Ory, J.C. (1994) "Assessing Faculty Work: Enhancing Individual and Institutional Performance". San Francisco: Jossey-Bass Higher and Adult Education Series.

Norris, N. (1990) *Understanding Educational Evaluation.* London: Kogan Page.

Seldin, P. & Associates. (1999) *Changing Practices in Evaluating Teaching.* Bolton, Mass: Anker Publishing Co., Inc.

5. Read the following paragraphs which contain literature review parts. Indicate what order of citation is used in the review?

Text 1
Knee Injuries Account for the Sports-related Increased Risk of Knee Osteoarthritis

Osteoarthritis of the knee is a public health problem. Increased risk of osteoarthritis has been found among athletes active in different kind of sports (Kujala, et al., 1995; Spector, et al., 1996; Roos, 1998; Conaghan, 2002). Knee injury is an established risk factor for knee osteoarthritis (Buckwalter & Lane, 1997; Cooper, et al., 2000). According to Buckwalter and Lane (1997), normal physical activities like running, jumping or throwing are not likely to cause injury in normal joints but the tolerance level for chronic or repetitive joint stress is not known. It has been proposed that a high level of physical activity with chronic repetitive stress and joint overuse is the likely main mechanism of osteoarthritis in both sports and certain occupational activities (Lequesne, et al., 1997). However, most researchers report that physical activity at a moderate or recreational level is not likely to be related to an increased risk of knee osteoarthritis (Lequesne, et al., 1997; Roos, 1998; Conaghan, 2002). According to Manninen, et al. (2001), moderate recreational physical exercise is associated with a decreased risk of knee osteoarthritis.

Text 2
Enhancing Student Perceptions of Fairness: the Relationship Between Instructor Credibility and ClassroomJustice

When students perceive that their course grades, course procedures, or instructors' communication are unfair, they report a greater likelihood of indirect aggression against their instructors (Chory, 2002), engaging in hostility toward their instructors (Carr, 2004), resisting their instructors' requests (Brown & Jackson, 2006), and giving their instructors lower teaching evaluations (Lee, 2001). Most of the instructors want their students find fair or unfair is limited. The present study addresses this limitation by examining the relationships between college student's perceptions of instructor credibility—instructor competence, character, and caring—and their perceptions of classroom distributive, procedural, and interactional justice. These associations are considered in terms of the communication skills and perceptions that characterize interpersonal relationships between teachers and students.

Text 3
On the Time Cnsistency of Optimal Policy in a Monetary Economy

The time-consistency issue is by no means a new one in economics. Strotz[25] appears to be the first one to have raised it in relation to an individual consumer. More recently, however, Kydland and Prescott[15] have discovered a family of models exhibiting time inconsistency where the source of the problem lies in the technology and in the assumption that people hold rational expectation. Although they briefly touch upon a monetary economy, the central results of their remarkable paper are given in a context where money plays no crucial role.

6. With reference to your own research project, write up the Introduction section of your own research paper.

Chapter Seven Methods

The mechanic that would perfect his work must first sharpen his tools.

——*Confucius, founder of Confucianism*

7.1 Rhetorical Pattern of Methods

The Methods section of a research section is usually the easiest section to write and, in fact, it is often the section that researchers write first, because they do not interpret data or reach conclusion. It is a straightforward recounting your approach. The objective of this section is to document all specialized materials and general procedures, so that another individual may use some or all of the methods in another study or judge the scientific merit of the research work. Therefore the methods section should describe what was done to answer the research question, describe how it was done, justify the experimental design, and explain how the results were analyzed. A typical rhetorical pattern in research paper Methods includes nine elements.

Information Elements in the Methods Section	
Element 1	Overview of the research/experiment (optional): one sentence that briefly tells what was done.
Element 2	Population/sample (optional): stating the people/subjects studied, or the things tested.
Element 3	Experimental location (optional): stating where the study took place.
Element 4	Restrictions (optional): describing precautions taken to make sure the data is valid.
Element 5	Sampling techniques (optional): describing how the subjects were selected for the study.
Element 6	Procedures (obligatory): stating the steps of the experiment in chronological order.
Element 7	Materials (obligatory): describing apparatuses, mathematical model, questionnaires etc.

Element 8	Variables (optional): describing the factors affecting the experimental results.
Element 9	Statistical treatment (optional): describing how the statistics were examined.

Careful writing of this section is critically important because the cornerstone of the scientific method requires that our results must be reproducible. When our paper is subjected to peer review, a good reviewer will read the Methods section carefully. If there is serious doubt that our experiments could be repeated, the reviewer will recommend rejection of our manuscript no matter how inspiring our results are. However, careful writing does not mean include all the details involved in the experiments. The Methods section is not to be a step by step description of everything we did, nor is a Methods section a set of instructions. This section should not be too lengthy; some information may be of lesser interest and can be de-emphasized by using smaller print. Sufficient information should be provided so that an interested reader can repeat the experiments. When deciding what information to include in the Methods, bear in mind that a careful reviewer will read this section to judge whether our procedures were sufficient enough to provide a valid answer to the question raised in the Introduction.

Methods sections are very variable across the disciplines, and even the term Methods is not always used, as when authors use Study, Corpus and Procedures, Data and Methodology, Methods and Materials, Experimental Procedures, or Experimental as their section heading. In some fields, it is common to have subsections in Methods that might deal with materials, the apparatus used, definitions employed, the subjects or participants in the study, or the statistical procedures used. Methods sections also vary according to how much information and explanation they contain. At one extreme, they may be very condensed; at the other, elaborately extended. If they fall in between, they can be termed intermediate.

In many of the social sciences, the methodology is very important and often described in considerable detail. Indeed, in some cases in these areas, the main point of an RP will be to announce some development in

学术论文写作与发表

methodology. However, in the natural sciences, engineering and parts of medical research, standard practices and established methods are much more widely available. In these latter areas, then, sometimes the Methods section may be largely for granted. At other times, however, it is the procedure that is newsworthy. It is explicit about details and procedures and slow paced since it does not presume much background knowledge. It contains justifications, explanations, and (sometimes) examples. The terminology is often repeated in the Methods section.

The Method describes the steps that we followed in conducting our study and the materials we used in each step. The elements included in the Methods section and the order in which they are presented may differ from department to department. However, the above rhetorical pattern may provide us with a good model.

There are generally five types of common mistakes in a Methods section: not enough information, background/introduction material included, verbose descriptions, results reported and sources of error discussed.

Common Mistakes in a Methods Section
[Original text] We mosaiced images from the THEMIS instrument.   **[Revised text]** Using USGS Integrated Software for Imagers and Spectrometers (ISIS), we mosaicked day-time thermal inertia images from the Thermal Emission Imaging Spectrometer (THEMIS) on board Mars Odyssey. The images covered the region 7°N to 34°N and 209°E to 236°E around the Olympus Mons volcano on Mars, and had a resolution of 100 meters-per-pixel. THEMIS images from October 2002 to July 2004 data releases were used. The max/min light/dark ratios were stretched manually to match individual images.   **[Analysis]** Not enough information has been provided.
[Original text] This theory was first proposed by Newton et al. (2000).   **[Revised text]** Samples were prepared using the method described by Newton et al. (2000).   **[Analysis]** Sometimes an author will include background material or explanations of concepts in the Methods section. That material belongs in the Introduction. In this section, the author should make no references to outside work, unless referencing a method or material.

[**Original text**] During image stretching, some resolution was lost, possibly interfering with counts of craters less than 5 km in diameter.

[**Revised text**] During image stretching, some resolution was lost.

[**Analysis**] Discussion materials do not belong in the Methods section. The author should not discuss sources of error or possible causes for results— in fact, the author should not discuss results at all. The interpretation of how this might affect results should be saved for the Discussion section.

[**Original text**] The samples were soaked in linseed oil for 4 hours, turning purple and developing a distinct smell of cabbage.

[**Analysis**] Sometimes, authors get so carried away describing their experiments that they report results in this section. The information about color and smell here should not be included in the Methods section, but in the Results section.

[**Original text**] Main blue-cord A was then connected via 0.25-inch screws to the third quarter-inch mark of lead pipe B, which was taped to wooden crate C with 0.5-inch-wide gray duct tape and ...

[**Analysis**] In the case of experimental setups, a diagram is worth a thousand words. Some authors—especially in chemistry or physics papers—describe elaborate lab setups with verbose, run-on sentences. A diagram is suggested to be used instead of verbose descriptions.

Avoiding these common mistakes is one of prerequisites of a good Methods section. Besides that, different journals might use different standards to judge Methods sections, but the following criteria cover the basics:

Methods Review Standards	
Materials	Enough Detail: all relevant materials used are listed Relevant Information: the materials listed are actually relevant
Methods	Enough Details: all relevant methods used are listed Relevant Information: the methods listed are actually relevant
Controls	Appropriate positive controls were used Appropriate negative controls were used
Experimental Approach	Adequate and appropriate tests of hypothesis
Materials Section Overall	Succinct: not verbose Clear: easy to read and understand Balanced: all the major topics are covered Focused: no superfluous information is included Common mistakes in a Methods

Sample Analysis	
English for College Students in Taiwan: a Study of Perceptions of English Needs in a Medical Context	
Methods	
(1) The subjects were 341 medical students in the Department of Medicine, including 97 freshmen, 74 sophomores, 90 juniors, and 80 seniors, and 20 faculty members in the medical program at Chung Shan Medical College in Taichung, Taiwan, China.	*Sample and experimental location*
(2) Two questionnaires were developed for the survey, based on two earlier survey instruments by Taylor & Hussein (1985) and Guo (1989). (3) The questionnaires were translated into Chinese, piloted, and modified according to feedback from 10 respondents: six medical students and four faculty members from Chun Shan Medical College. (4) The questionnaire given to the medical students consisted of five sections of 23 questions, the topics of which were the importance of English in college and professional careers, perceived language skill needs and problems, the activities needed in a freshman language course, and suggestions for development of course content and materials as well as demographic information. (5) The faculty questionnaire consisted of four sections of 16 questions, which were parallel to those in the version given to the students except no demographic information was gathered (see Appendix).	*Materials*
(6) One of the authors, a faculty member at Chung Shan Medical College, selected one required class for each group of students (freshmen, sophomores, juniors, and seniors). (7) Copies of the student questionnaire for administration to the students were then sent to cooperating instructors teaching these courses; copies of the faculty questionnaire were given to 20 teachers who were willing to complete the surveys. (8) Students and faculty took about 20 minutes to complete the survey.	
(9) The data were computer-analyzed using an SPSS program. (10) Chi-square, t-tests, and ANOVA analyses were conducted in order to determine the perceptions of	*Data analysis*

English language needs of medical college students and their faculty and to compare the perceptions held by the various groups.	

7.2 Language Focus: Imperatives in Research Papers

Command-like imperatives are common in textbooks, manuals, lectures, and labs.

Analyze the results in figure 1.

Complete the following sentences.

Notice the relationship between A and B.

Prepare 5cc of distillate.

Carry this total *forward*.

In RPs, however, imperatives are less commonly used because they may be offensive. They may upset the fragile relationship between the writer and the reader, since the reader can be expected to have a status comparable to or higher than the author. However, the verb let is widely used in many RP fields. Indeed, it may account for up to 50% of all the (occasional) uses of the imperative in research writing.

Let p stand for the price-cost ratio.

Let N equal the number of consumers.

A few other imperative verbs can be found in mathematical arguments, such as *suppose, substitute, and assume.* When we want to direct our readers' attention to some particular point in our paper and let them know that we have elsewhere provided full details of our data, we may write:

See Appendix A for a list of...

7.3 Reflections and Practice

1. In RPs would you accept imperative uses of the following in your field, and, if so, can you provide an example? Could you find other imperative sentences in your field?

Notice	Imagine	Compare	Refer	Take the case of
Consider	Note	Recall	Observe	Disregard

2. Read the following example of the Methods section from the field of computer assisted language learning and teaching. The study investigated the use of the World-Wide-Web for teaching writing in a British university. Identify the information elements you find in each sentence of the selection. (NOTE: Some sentences may contain more than one element.)

Use of a Writing Web-site by Pre-masters Students on an English for Academic Purposes Course

A. J. Gillett, University of Hertfordshire

Methods

(1) Two groups of international students on a one-year Pre-Masters English for Academic Purposes course, each comprising 50 students were taught academic writing by different methods and compared. (2) In each group there were 50 students from five different academic departments—computer science, business, engineering, life sciences and law. (3) The subjects were selected from the second semester—Semester B—of the University of Hertfordshire International Bridging Program in the 2004-2005academic year. (4) This program accepts only students from a narrow English Language Proficiency band (IELTS 5.00 - 5.5). (5) Thus, omparable language level among the test subjects was ensured.

(6) The subjects were selected from the 250 students on the International Bridging Program on the basis of performance at a satisfactory level in the Semester A examination. (7) Students who had performed below the minimum level on the semester A examination were excluded. (8) This criterion was employed to ensure competent understanding of the tasks and adequate motivation.

(9) One group—Group A—studied English writing in the traditional way in a class with a teacher. (10) This class met for 2 hours each week in a classroom for 12 weeks and was supplemented with written homework assignments given by the teacher each week. (11) The second group—Group B—met together in a class with a teacher for one hour per week for 12 weeks and were assigned a homework task of spending one hour per week doing exercises from the UEFAP web-site (Gillett, 2005).

(12) The test instrument employed in this study was a revised version of the University of Hertfordshire English Language Writing Test (Roberts, 1997), which permits the assessment of academic written language performance. (13) It consists of an academic reading text and comprehension

questions, followed by a discursive essay on the subject of the reading text.

(14) Both groups A and B were given the same written examination at the end of the semester. (15) The students took the examination under standard university examination conditions as part of their end of semester examination. (16) The tests were marked using the following categories: task achievement, communicative quality, organization, ideas, content and relevance, and grammar and vocabulary, by two experienced writing examiners and moderated in the standard way to ensure reliability. (17) In this way it was possible to see the relationship between the students' main academic subjects, and the improvement in their writing ability depending on the teaching method. (18) A 3×5 analysis of variance was used to test for academic department, method of teaching and language achievement differences.

3. Find a published research article in your field of specialization, and locate the section corresponding to Methods. Answer the questions below:

(1) Is the section called "Methods"? If not, what is it called?
(2) What information elements are present in the section? In what order are they presented?
(3) What are the salient features of language in this section?

4. With reference to your own research project, write up the Methods section of your article.

Chapter Eight   Results

All's well that ends well.

—— English Proverb

8.1 Rhetorical Pattern of Results Section

In short articles of single empirical studies, the Results and the Discussion are often combined. But if we need to integrate several different kinds of results or discuss several general matters, then prepare a separate discussion section. With very few exceptions, every journal requires a Results section.

The purpose of a Results section is to present the key results of the experiment without interpreting their meaning. The trick is knowing what to include. The elements included in the Results section and the order in which they are presented may differ from discipline to discipline. However, the list in the following box is typical and provides us with a good model (Weissberg & S. Buker, 1990). We might need to repeat this several times if we have different diagrams and charts.

Three-move Format of Results Section
Move 1: Location of results: showing where the results can be found
Move 2: Findings: presenting the most important findings

Move 3: Brief comment: commenting on the results this may include:
    Step 1: Generalizing from the results
    Step 2: Explaining possible reasons for the results
    Step 3: Comparing the results with what was expected or with results from other studies

The findings in a research paper are usually presented both in diagrams and text. We should avoid writing out long lists of numbers in the Results section. All the numbers and measurements in this section should be tabulated. For example:

Regional age-dating with crater counts from ejecta blanket degradation approximated ages from regular crater counts (Table 1).

The ages for each region from both methods would then appear in Table 1.

Figures and Tables are consecutively numbered in the same sequence they are first mentioned in the text. Depending on the journal, they should be in order at the end of the paper after the References, or located appropriately within the text of our results section. A heading for each figure and table should be provided. Depending on the journal, the table titles and figure legends should be listed separately or located above the table or below the figure. Each figure and table must be sufficiently complete that it could stand on its own, separate from the text. Details appearing in figure captions and table heads are not restated in the text.

It's important in Results writing to determine whether the data are best presented in the form of text, figures, graphs, or tables. We should summarize the findings and point the reader to the relevant data in the text, figures and/or tables. The text should complement the figures or tables, not repeat the same information. The data must be accurate and consistent throughout the manuscript. They are organized in either chronological order according to the Methods or in order of most to least important. Within each paragraph, the order of most to least important results should be followed. The simple past tense is preferred in the writing of Results sections.

Selective presentation of results is also important. We should state the results of statistical analyses in this section, but should not describe every detail we obtained or observed. We assume our readers know what a null hypothesis is, a rejection rule, chi-square test, etc. Determine which results to present by deciding which are relevant to the primary question(s) or hypothesis(es) presented in the Introduction. Readers and reviewers should be able to identify which specific hypotheses were supported, which received partial support, and which were not supported. Non-significant findings should not be ignored. Results of minor variations on the principal experiment should be summarized rather than included. In a well-written paper, the results section is often the shortest.

Reviewers are very interested in understanding the nature and impact of missing data. For example, information concerning the total number of participants and the flow of participants through each stage of the study (e.g.,

in prospective studies), the frequency and/or percentages of missing data at different time points, and analytic methods used to address missing data is important to include. A summary of cases that are missing from analyses of primary and secondary outcomes for each group, the nature of missing data (e.g., missing at random or missing not at random), and, if applicable, statistical methods used to replace missing data, and/or understand the impact of missing data are useful for readers.

It is often said that the Results section of an RP should simply report the data that has been collected; that is, it should focus exclusively on the present results and all evaluation and commentary should be left until the Discussion. However, research shows that this distinction between Results and Discussion is not as sharp as commonly believed. For example, Thompson (1993) studied the Results sections from 20 published biochemistry papers and found that scientists—in this case biochemists—do not present results only in a factual expository manner; they also employ a variety of rhetorical moves to argue for the validity of scientific facts and knowledge claims.

There are generally four types of common mistakes in a Results section: raw data, redundancy, methods/materials reported, and no figures or tables.

Raw Data. Occasionally an author will for some reason include all his/her raw data. This is not just unnecessary—it's mind-numbing. The author should present only the key results, meaning those results that bear on the question or problem being addressed. Generally this means presenting means, percentages, standard deviations, etc.

Redundancy. Authors will often present their results in a table, and then re-state everything in the text. This is redundant. Text should be used to clarify figures and tables—not rehash them.

Methods/Materials Reported. Often, an author will write something like this in the Results section: "We found that sample A contained pyroxene, so we ground sample B to a powder and ran the experiment again. With sample B, we found pyroxene again." The information "so we ground sample B to a powder and ran the experiment again" is Methods material and does not belong in the Results section. The author must report only results in the Results section—no new methods or material at all.

No Figures or Tables. Every Results section should have at least one table. No matter what discipline the author is writing in, he/she should have data to present. A notable exception is some mathematics or computer science papers.

Avoiding these common mistakes is one of prerequisites of a good Results section. Besides that, different journals might use different standards to judge Results sections, but the following criteria cover the basics:

Results Section Review Standards	
Results exposition	Sufficient Detail: enough to understand the key results of the study Appropriate Detail: no superfluous information Appropriate Presentation: numbers and results are tabulated, not listed
Experimentation/ number of trials	Sufficient to test the hypothesis
Statistical tests	Performed when Appropriate
Data	Believable: probably not an artifact of poor experimental setup
Results section overall	Succinct: not verbose Clear: easy to read and understand Balanced: all the major topics are covered Focused: no superfluous information is included

Sample Analysis	
Dextroamphetamine: Cognitive anBehavioral Effectsin Normal Prepubertal Boys **Results** (1) The children left the testing center 3 hours after medication or placebo had been administered; parents were asked to keep a diary record to behavior during the afternoon and evening. (2) Behavioral and cognitive effects during the drug session are given in Figure 1 and Table 1. (3) Behavioral rating showed both immediate and delayed effects which differed from each other. (4) Amphetamine administration in comparison with placebo was associated with decreased	Sentence 1: procedure Sentence 2:location of results (simple present tense) Sentences 3-6: most important findings (simple past tense)

motor activity combined with generally improved intentional performance (faster reaction time, superior memory and improved attention) and decreased galvanic skin response. (5) After drug administration, the children appeared unusually inactive, not simply less restless. (6) There was an increase in task-related descriptive speech and a decrease in speech not task-related, such as questions (Table 1). (7) These results are entirely consistent with those reported for hyperactive children on stimulant medication in previous studies.	Sentence 7: comparison the results with results from other studies (simple present tense)

8.2 Language Focus: Definition

When we write, we have to take into account the fact that our readers may not always understand the meaning of the more specialized words and expressions. If we think this is the case, we have to supply the reader with definitions of these terms.

There are mainly two kinds of definition: sentence definition and extended definition. An extended definition is a one or more paragraphs that attempt to explain a complex term. The commonly used pattern of an extended definition is a one-sentence definition plus the extended part. The language construction of one-sentence definition is:

Thing to be Defined + Verb +General Class Word + Ddistinguishing Characteristics

1. An algorithm is a finite description of a finite number of steps required to accomplish some well-defined task.
2. Computer memory is one of three basic components of computer which stores information for future use both 2.data that will be operated on as well as the programs that direct what operations must be performed.
3. Psychology may be defined as the branch of biological science which studies the phenomena of conscious Lif and behavior.

Typically, extended definitions start with a formal sentence definition then move on to supplementary information. One-sentence definition establishes the focus for the rest of the discussion.

First described in 1970 by Alos Alzheimer, a German physician, Alzheimer's disease is an adult-onset neurological disorder of unknown etiology manifested by loss of memory, impaired thought processes, and abnormal behavior. When the illness begins before the age of 65, it is termed Alzheimer's dementia of the Alzheimer's type. Approximately 5% of the U.S. population over 65 have severe dementia; an additional 10% have a mild-to-moderate impairment in memory and cognition. Of these demented individuals, approximately 40%-50% have Alzheimer's disease, making this disorder the most common cause of dementia in middle and later life.	*Sentence definition* Other supplementary definitions

8.3 Reflections & Practice

1. **Read the following example of part of a Results section from the field of computer assisted language learning and teaching. The study investigated the use of the World-Wide-Web for teaching writing in a British university. Fill in each blank with an appropriate form of a word from the brackets. Sometimes a passive verb form or a modal verb may be required.**

Use of a Writing Web-site by Pre-masters Students on an English for Academic Purposes Course

Results

　　Two groups of Students in Higher Education—Group A and Group B—on a one-year Pre-Masters English for Academic Purposes course, each comprising 50 students _____(teach) academic writing by different methods and compared. Figure 3 _____ (display) the mean percentile scores on the five subsections of the academic writing test. Students in Group B, which _____ (use) the computer assisted facilities, _____ (perform) significantly better than their non computer-assisted peers on all five subsections of the test by more than two to one in terms of scores attained in each of the subcategories. For example, in the task achievement subcategory, Group A _____ (score) an average of 80 percent, while Group B students scored an average of 14th percent. Clearly, the findings _____ (indicate) that the time spent using the UEfAP website had a positive effect on student performance. It _____ (appear) that the use of computer assisted learning programs for at least some of the teaching time available resulted in substantial differences in performance in all five categories of

the University of Hertfordshire English Writing Test. It _____ (hope) that this improvement will transfer to the students' written performance in their main subject courses.

2. Read the following Results section of a Research paper in the car industry. It describes the performance of the two makes of car in terms of consumption and reliability. Underline the verbs in each sentence and then complete the table that follows.

Results

(1) Table 1 shows the performance of two makes of car, designated A and B in the table, in tests to determine their petrol consumption and reliability. (2) The cars were between the ages of 1 and 5 years. (3) The size of the sample is indicated in column marked N and the key explains the symbols used.

(4) The results show a clear difference in the petrol consumption and reliability of the two makes of car. (5) With two exceptions, Make A was consistently more economical and reliable than the average, whereas Make B was, with three exceptions, less reliable than average. (6) Therefore, on the evidence available Make A would seem more economical and reliable than Make B. (7) However it should be noted that the Make A sample was almost three times as large as the Make B sample, and it is therefore possible that a larger sample of Make B cars would provide very different results. (8) It is also interesting to note that in neither case was there a significant correlation between the age of the car and its performance in the tests.

	Verb(s)	Tense	Function
Sentence 1			
Sentence 2			
Sentence 3			
Sentence 4			
Sentence 5			
Sentence 6			
Sentence 7			
Sentence 8			

3. A study was carried out to examine the impact of China's entry into the WTO on business professionals and college English instruction. One of the results is areas of use of English. These results are presented in the table below. Now write a text to explain the details in the table. Try to include information that is conventionally included in a Results section.

Areas of use of English	Personal officers	Employees
A: Communication with foreign counterparts	31%	17%
B: Specialist literature reading	20%	51%
C: Surfing the net	25%	20%
D: Personal promotion	25%	9%
E: Others	10%	8%

4. In your library, locate the Results section of an experimental research paper in your field. Make a photocopy of a table or a figure. Then without looking back at the original paper, write a Results text to accompany your table or figure following the convention discussed in this chapter.

5. Choose one term that names a complex concept of feature of central importance in an activity or subject you know well. Choose a word with a well-established definition, one agreed on by everyone knowledgeable about the topic. Write an extended definition of several sentences for this important term. Write for readers your own age who will be encountering the term for the first time when they read your definition.

学术论文写作与发表

Chapter Nine Discussion

Hurried readers of RP thumb through the pages to find the final paragraph of discussion where they can usually get a comprehensive conclusion of the results.

—— *Robert Blake*

9.1 Rhetorical Pattern of Discussion

Most journals require a Discussion or Conclusions section. It is not so easy to provide useful guidelines for writing Discussion or Conclusions sections. (We will not distinguish between these two terms, since the difference is largely conventional, depending on traditions in particular fields and journals.) See what is done in our own field. Sometimes the title of Discussion section is section replaced by a specific title related to the research content. The purpose of a Discussion section is to interpret the results and relate them to previous studies that the author and other authors have done.

Overall, if Results deal with facts, then Discussions deal with points; facts are descriptive, while points are interpretive. Effective Discussion sections are similar to effective lectures, which, as Olsen and Huckin (1990) note, are based on points, rather than on facts. Further, authors of Discussions have some flexibility in deciding which of their possible points to include and then which to highlight. Discussions, then, should be more than summaries. They should go beyond the results. They should be more theoretical or more abstract or more general, more integrated with the field, more connected to the real world, and more concerned with implications or applications.

Discussion sections can be viewed as presenting a series of points. Typically, they are arranged as follows:

Discussion Moves	
Move 1	Points to consolidate your research space (obligatory) Step a: A reference to the purpose or hypothesis of the study Step b: A review of most important findings Step c: Explanations for or speculations about the findings
Move 2	Points to indicate the limitations of your study (optional but common)
Move 3	Implications of the study (optional)

Move 4	Recommendations for further research and practical applications (optional and only common in some areas)

Authors usually indicate their own position through Step c, Move 2, Move 3 and Move 4 in the Discussion section. The Discussion is the bottom of the hourglass-shaped format and thus proceeds from specific matters about our study to the broadest generalizations we wish to make. It is noteworthy that the Discussion section usually begins with a clear statement on the support or nonsupport of the hypotheses or the answers to the questions we first raised in the Introduction. But do not simply reformulate and repeat points already summarized in the Results section. Each new statement should contribute something new to the reader's understanding of the problem. What inferences can be drawn from the findings? These inferences may be at a level quite close to the data or may involve considerable abstraction, perhaps to the level of a larger theory. What are the theoretical, practical, or even the political implications of the results?

This section should synthesize the whole paper. The author should re-address the hypothesis he/she discussed in the Introduction, and re-interpret them in light of the results. To interpret the results, the author should address the following questions:

1. Did the results provide answers to the (testable) hypothesis?
2. If so, what does this mean for the hypothesis?
3. If not, do the results suggest an alternative hypothesis? What is it? Why do the results suggest it? What further results might solidify this hypothesis? Have others proposed it before?
4. Do these results agree with what others have shown? If so, do other authors suggest an alternative explanation to explain the results? If not, how does this experiment differ from others? Is there a design flaw in this experiment?
5. How do these results fit in with results from other studies? Do results from related studies affect the way these results are being interpreted?

In addition to simply interpreting the results, the author should discuss the following questions (though the order may vary):

1. What factors or sources of error might have influenced these results?
2. What anomalous data turned up and how can it be explained? Is it explained by the author's theory? Someone else's theory? Error?
3. Was this experiment the most effective way to test this hypothesis? (Obviously the author thought so at the beginning, but does he/she still think so?) How could the experiment be improved to gain further insight?
4. How have the results and conclusions of this study influenced our knowledge or understanding of the problem being examined?
5. What would be the next step in this study?
6. What experiments could be run (or data found) that would lend further support to the author's hypothesis? (Either the original hypothesis, or the new one designed to explain the results.) What experiments could be run (or data found) that would disprove the author's hypothesis?

There are generally five types of common mistakes in a Discussion section: combined with results, new results, missing information, the "inconclusive" cop-out and ambiguous data sources.

Combined with Results. It's amazing how often authors combine the Results and Discussion sections. The Results and Discussion sections cannot be combined. They have two very different purposes. The Results section is for fact. The Discussion section is for interpretation.

New Results. Sometimes an author will include a new result in the Discussion section—one he/she did not report in the Results section. All results must be reported in the Results section. They can be restated in the Discussion section, but they must appear in the Results.

Missing Information. Authors often leave out critical information from the Discussion section. For example, they might forget to re-state their hypothesis and motivation, might not tie their work into the larger field of research, might not compare their work to other's, might not discuss sources of error... In short, they might not answer all the questions outlined in the "What is a Discussion Section" above. Be sure to discuss everything.

The "Inconclusive" Cop-Out. Months of research and pages of words, all leading up to a: "The results are inconclusive." What a waste! Don't waste our readers' time with a statement of "it's inconclusive". The author needs to draw what conclusions he/she can, then suggest how the experiment should be changed to properly test the hypothesis.

Ambiguous Data Sources. Often, an author will get so wound up in his/her

Discussion, that it's hard to tell when he/she is talking about the results of *this* study and when he/she is talking about the results of *other* studies. Don't let authors get away with that kind of ambiguity—*whose* study is being discussed is vital information.

Avoiding these common mistakes is one of prerequisites of a good Discussion section. Besides that, different journals might use different standards to judge Discussion sections, but the following criteria cover the basics:

Discussion Section Review Standards	
Motivation for study	Clearly restated
Interpretation of results	Sufficient interpretation of results; Logical interpretation of results
Possible limitations and sources of error	Adequate discussion; Acceptable errors: the sources of error do not lower confidence in the results
Ramifications	Clear and adequate discussion; Realistic
Discussion section overall	Succinct: not verbose Clear: easy to read and understand Balanced: all the major topics are covered Focused: no superfluous information is included

Sample Analysis	
Informal Sector: the Credit Market Channel **Discussion** (1) At the firm level, costs of being formal *include* significant fixed expenses in terms of registration fees. (2) As for benefits, they *are* generally considered as resulting from enhanced access to public goods. (3) We *have argued* that key public goods, such as property rights protection and contract enforcement, are important not only because they improve firm's productivity directly, but because they secure access to important markets, where they make interactions more efficient. (4) The model, in which costly registration *facilitates* the access to the formal credit market,	Sentences 1-3: hypothesis of the study Sentence 4: most important

学术论文写作与发表

143

provides theoretical predictions about the effect of several variables (initial assets, efficiency of credit markets, rule of law, volatility of the environment, taxes, and labor regulation) on the incidence of informality, which are consistent with the existing stylized facts.	findings
(5) From a policy point of view, this *suggests* that one important channel through which better rule of law and judicial enforcement *may* reduce informality is by making market interactions more efficient, therefore rendering the participation in formal credit markets more attractive. (6) Moreover, by reducing the need for agents to rely on informal credit mechanisms, it *may* have important welfare consequences, since one major drawback of informal lending is the generalized lack of project screening that probably leads to a lower average social value of the projects being financed. (7) Financially, our framework also *points out* to the potential benefits of micro-credit programs that make better credit mechanisms available to small entrepreneurs, while in some sense bypassing some of the costs of formality.	Sentences 5-7: implications of the study
(8) As for potential lines of research, from an empirical viewpoint, it *would* be interesting to develop more precise measures of the relative efficiency of formal and informal credit markets in and across countries. (9) From a theoretical point of view, an open question is to examine how formal and informal lenders' incentives to acquire information on loan applicants may differ, and how they select different types of credit mechanisms. (10) Finally, in a dynamic perspective, two questions emerge. (11) The first one is to assess the impact of a dual credit market structure and of the costs of entry into formality on industries' dynamics. (12) The second is to determine how the factors considered here would shape the growth potential of an economy.	Sentences 8-12: recommendations for future research

9.2 Language Focus: Taking a Stance

In academic writing, it is often necessary to make it clear to our readers what opinion we hold or what our position is with regard to a certain issue.

This is often called our "voice", our "position" or our "claim". As a writer, it is not enough to simply describe a situation or recall the facts, we need to take a stance or position ourselves in relation to the situation or the facts. This is particularly important in assessment when we have to answer a question. Of course, we need to know and reproduce the information, but we also need to use the information to give an answer to the question. Read the following sentence:

Previous studies have indicated that the intensity of physiotherapy provision may affect some patient outcomes including reduced mortality following stroke.

In the sentence above, the words "indicate", "may" and "some" show the writers position towards the facts. Instead of "indicated", the words "shown", "proved" or "suggested" could have been used. The word "may" might have been replaced by "could", "will" or nothing. "Some" was chosen, where "many", "few" or "most" were also possible.

Here are some other words and phrases that we can use to show our position:

Introductory verbs	e.g. seem, indicate, suggest
Thinking verbs	e.g. believe, assume, suggest
Reporting verbs	e.g. claim, find, confirm, assert
Evaluative adjectives	e.g. important, misguided, wrong, misguided, inaccurate, incorrect
Evaluative adverbs	e.g. accurately, unsatisfactorily
Adverbs of frequency	e.g. often, sometimes
Modal verbs	e.g. will, may, might, could
Modal adverbs	e.g. certainly, definitely
Modal adjectives	e.g. certain, definite
Modal nouns	e.g. assumption, possibility
Signaling words	e.g. furthermore, similarly

Besides these words, nominal that-clause and disjunctive adverbial are adopted in the Discussion section to indicate the writer's attitude toward the information expressed in the paper.

(1) In line with this hypothesis, we assumed that older workers in speed jobs would have poorer performance than younger workers.

(2) It is important to note that the three interacting views of discourse are not mutually exclusive, but essentially complementary to one another.

(3) Clearly, general surgery in the United States is in the midst of momentous change.

(4) Targeting pilot efforts to take advantage of existing synergies among intensification of resource use, elastic market demand, organizational capacity, and enabling policies will be critical to success. Fortunately, these conditions already exist in many communities in Africa.

9.3　Reflections & Practice

1. Part of the Discussion section of a research paper in the field of environmental protection is reproduced here. Fill in each blank space with an appropriate form of a word in the brackets. Sometimes a passive verb form or a modal verb may be required.

Protecting and Managing Private Farmland and Public Greenways in the Urban Fringe

By comparing the responses of landowners, conservationists, and sporting club leaders, the results of this study _____ (provide) new information about attitudes toward land protection, reaction and collaboration in urban fringe areas. There _____ (be) strong support among landowners for farm preservation, but only if the land could be kept in private lands. Furthermore, the economic difficulties of farming in an urban fringe area _____ (pose) a challenge to keeping farming viable in the areas, especially as upland farming areas are developed. Landowners _____ (be) willing to collaborate in efforts for land protection with other farmers and to a lesser degree with government agencies and non-profit groups. However, to date, these partnerships _____ (be) weak or non-existent.

A survey such as this _____ (be) useful as a preliminary tool for collection information from a wide sample on a range of greenway planning topics relating to farmland protection, recreation access, and collaboration. However, it _____ (be) important to accompany this research with more detailed methods of information gathering. Furthermore, these research efforts _____ (be) replicated with an even wider range of relevant groups, including local residents, landowner, conservationists, and government officials.

2. Part of the Dscussion section from a paper in the field of management is reproduced here. The paper aims to examine the impact of Internet-specific strategies on venture company performance. The first paragraph is given, but the sentences of paragraphs 2 to 4 are not yet in order. Rearrange the sentences in the order that you think the author originally wrote then.

Internet-business or Just Business
Impact of "Internet-specific" Strategies on Venture Performance
Discussion

The main aim of this paper is to test the relationship between 21 "Internet-business strategies" (drawn mainly from business literature and managerial intuition) and the self-perceived performance of Internet-trading ventures, using a large sample.

(Paragraph 2)

_____A. Only promotion-related strategies seemed to have a higher and more consistent association in more than one test.

_____B. In short, the results showed that the majority of "Internet-specific strategies" (with the expectations of "price customization" and "price lower than in the physical world") were positively correlated with venture performance in one industry or another, but their correlations were weak and their combined impact on performance was minimal.

_____C. Therefore, the one clear message of this study, which is equally relevant to both theory and practice, is that the newly emerged "Internet-specific" performance drivers (with the possible exception of promotion-related ones) did not prove to be as important as the literature and the popular press has indicated.

(Paragraph 3)

_____D. Porter argued that instead of Internet-specific strategies, the more competitive advantage will arise from traditional strengths such as unique products, proprietary content, superior product knowledge, and strong personal service and relationships.

_____E. Internet technology may be able to fortify those advantages, by tying a company's activities together in a more distinctive system, but it is unlikely to replace them.

_____F. Interestingly, our study provided empirical support to Porter's (2001) claim that the Internet does not change the rules of the game in business.

(Paragraph 4)

_____G. This study represents just a first step in testing Internet-specific strategies as drivers of performance, and, therefore, we should treat the results with caution.

_____H. They are definitely useful, but they are probably not the ones with the highest impact on venture performance. Internet business after all is still business.

_____I. A good direction for further research would be to test the additional effect of the "Internet-specific strategies" on existing and known

drivers of venture performance using the known constructs as control variables.

_____J. Finally, our message to practitioners would be not to overvalue the newly emerging "Internet-specific" strategies that are promoted by enthusiastic thinkers in (good quality) journals.

3. Find a published research article in your field of specialization, and locate the section corresponding to the Discussion part of the article. In pairs, answer the questions below:

> (1) Is the section called "Discussion"? If not, what is it called?
> (2) Identify the rhetorical pattern of the section.
> (3) What are the sentences that indicate the author's position towards the information presented? Underline the parts of these sentences in which these positions are indicated.

4. In your library, find a research paper in your field. Read the sections of "Introduction", "Methods" and "Results". Then with the help of the model we have discussed in this chapter, write the "Discussion" section of the paper.

5. The following text is from the field of Physiotherapy. Please identify the words that show the author's position.

> Patellofemoral disorders are amongst the most common clinical conditions encountered in the sporting and general population. Patellofemoral pain is usually described as diffuse, peripatellar, anterior knee pain. Symptoms are typically aggravated by activities such as ascending or descending stairs, squatting, kneeling, running and prolonged sitting.
>
> A wide variety of disorders may fall under the umbrella term of patellofemoral pain. As a result, a thorough systematic evaluation of the patient's lower extremity alignment, patellar mobility and alignment, muscle flexibility, strength, co-ordination, soft tissue and articular pain is important in determining the possible causes of patellofemoral pain and prescribing an optimal rehabilitation programme. Management of patellofemoral pain syndrome often includes reduction of pain and inflammation through cryotherapy, heat therapy, massage therapy, muscle flexibility and strength training (especially quadriceps), patellar taping, bracing, orthotics, correction of abnormal biomechanics or other causative factors, acupuncture and surgery.

Chapter Ten　Data Presentation

Since humans prefer to look at pictures rather than words, visual presentation of information aids the reader and contributes to the message of the document.

——Follett Wilson

10.1　Functions of Tables and Figures

All instructions on how to write a research paper diligently shout about the necessity of writing a research paper in the simplest way, so that even a child can figure it out. For that purpose, the very same instructions on how to write a research paper suggest using simple grammar structures, active voice and so on. But the most effective tool for writing a comprehensive research paper is often overlooked. It turns out that the key to writing a light research paper is the use of tables and figures. The proper use of tables and figures in a research paper can illustrate complicated relationships more clearly and in less space than the written word. Moreover, data tables and figures are very important in that they can make our research paper stand out from the crowd. They are the visual ways to look at the data, see what happened and make interpretations. They are usually the best way to show the data to others. Reading lots of numbers in the text puts people to sleep and does little to convey information.

Figure usually refers to any kind of graphic representation or illustration, no matter it is in the text or in an appendix. Figures include graphs, charts, drawings, diagrams, maps, photographs, blueprints, and some kinds of computer printouts. Using figures is one of the most important ways to deliver information in research papers. An accurately and canonically designed figure which is logical and compendious cannot only clarify the content of a research paper, but also can save the space of a page, and make the paper vivid to stimulate readers' interests.

Tables present lists of numbers or text in columns, each column having a title or label. Not all statistics matter need be presented in tabular form. If there are only enough data for the table to fill two rows or columns, a table should not be used. However, large quantities of statistics or numerical data should be tabulated in the interest of both brevity and clarity. If there are long series of numbers in the body of a paper, the development of an argument can be interfered, and readers may be distracted by masses of numbers in the text. In addition, do not use a table when we wish to show a trend or a pattern of relationship between sets of values—these are better presented in a Figure. For instance, if we needed to present population sizes and sex ratios for our study organism at a series of sites, and we planned to focus on the differences among individual sites according to (say) habitat type, we would use a table. However, if we wanted to show that sex ratio was related to population size, we would use a Figure.

Tables and figures in research papers should achieve two elements, unity and clarity. A table or figure may be very useful for presenting a large quantity of data, but all these data should be organized so that they can be easily traced. We should not try to present too many kinds of data or show too many types of relationships in a single table or figure. If a table or figure is very complex, it usually should be put in appendix.

10.2 Relationship of Tables or Figures and Texts

To help our readers understand the data in a table or figure, a clear introduction should be provided. The introduction may be a description of the figure or table. In most cases, the writer does not simply add the visual to the text, but includes some sort of comment. Typically the writer will include: a few words that locate the visual, a statement that draws attention to the important features of the visual, and some sort of comment on or discussion of the visual. Furthermore, the principles governing the data or the significance of the data in the table or figure might be explained and how the data serve our thesis should definitely be presented.

A well-designed figure or table can achieve its independence to the text, which means a figure should be carefully designed so that readers can read and understand it without reference to the text. Captions should be fully descriptive. Furthermore, the text should be so complete that readers can follow the development of argument without consulting the table or figure. However, the text should involve each figure and table, and explain or analyze their content.

Each table and figure should come as close as possible after the first reference to them. If space permits, it is best to finish the paragraph of the text in which the reference occurs before inserting the table or figure. If a table or figure in the research paper cannot be accommodated in the space remaining on a given page, continue the text to make a full page and place the table at the top of the next page. Avoid using imprecise phrases such as "in the following table/figure" and "in the table/figure above"; these may make our readers confused when the table or figure is not immediately visible. If a table or figure appears within the two or three pages following the first reference to it, only the number of the table or figure need be given in the text, for example, "Table 2 shows...", "Figure 3 shows..." Otherwise, both the table or figure number and the page number should be mentioned in the text, like "Table 2 on page 16 shows...", "Figure 8 on page 36 shows..."

10.3 Anatomy of Tables and Figures

Table 4 below shows the typical layout of a table in three sections demarcated by lines. Tables are most easily constructed using the word processor's table function or a spread sheet such as Excel. Gridlines or boxes, commonly invoked by word processors, are helpful for setting cell and column alignments, but should be eliminated from the printed version. Tables formatted with cell boundaries showing are unlikely to be permitted in a journal. The following three figures are typical line and bar graphs with the various component parts labeled in red.

Table 4 Population variation in hatch success (mean percent) of unfertilized eggs for females from populations sampled in 1997. N=number of females tested. ◄--- Table legend

Population	mean(%)	Standard deviation	Range	N
Beaver Creek^T	7.31	13.95	0—53.16	15
Honey Creek^T	4.33	7.83	0—25.47	11
Rock Bridge Gans Creek^T	5.66	13.93	0—77.86	38
Cedar Creek^P	6.56	9.64	0—46.52	64
Grindstone Creek^P	8.56	14.77	0—57.32	19
Jacks Fork River^P	5.28	8.28	0—30.96	28
Meramee River^P	5.49	10.25	0—45.76	45
Little Dixic Lake^L	7.96	14.54	0—67.66	71
Little Prairie Lake^L	6.86	7.84	0—32.40	36
Rocky Forks Lake^L	3.31	4.12	0—16.14	43
Winegar Lake^L	10.73	17.58	0—41.64	5
Whetstone Lake^L	7.36	12.93	0—63.38	57

◄--- Column titles

◄--- Table body (data)

^T=temporary stream,^P=permanent streams. ^L=lakes. ◄--- Footnotes

◄--- Lines demarcating the different parts of the table

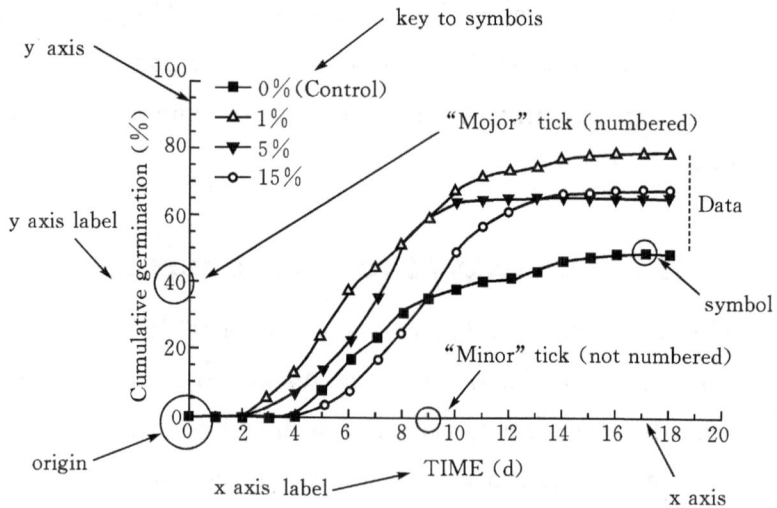

Figure1. Cumulative germination of *Chenopodium* seeds after pregermination treatment of 2 day soak in NaCl solutions. n=1 trail per treatment group (100 seeds/trial.)

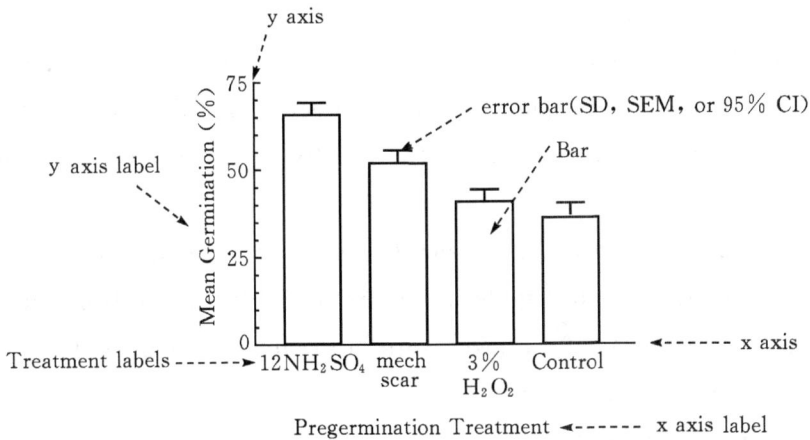

Figure 1. Mean germination（％）（＋SD）of group seeds following various pregermination treatments. N＝10 groups of 100 seeds per treatment and control. Treatments: 12 hour soak in 12 NH₂SO₄, 90 second scarification of seed coat with 80 grit sandpaper, 6 hour soak in 3％ H₂O₂. ◄------ figure legend

10.3.1 Captions of Tables and Figures

Each figure and table must have a caption, legend or title, that conveys concisely and clearly what the figure or table contains just like the title of a paper itself. The caption of a figure should be placed just below the figure while that of a table above the table. Furthermore, numbers and captions of figures and tables should appear in the table of contents.

Tables and figures, as well as other parts of a research paper, should have enough information to make them understandable on their own. The proven way to achieve the result is to place a table header that is substantial in grammar form and has no relative clauses in favor of participles. A descriptive phrase is preferred as a title of a table.

Table 3. Families Watching News Regularly, 2008

not

Table 3. Number of Families that Watch News Regularly,2008

10.3.2 Numeration of Tables and Figures

Tables and figures should be numbered consecutively, one after another.

Every table or figure in the research paper should be numbered with an Arabic numeral. A title should be given to each table or figure, even though there may be few tables or figures in the paper. The table number is placed above the table at the left margin and followed by a period. The figure number is below the figure in the center.

Tables and figures in an appendix should also be numbered continuously with those in the text. If the last table in the text is Table 18, the first one in appendix would be Table 19; if the last figure in the text is Figure 8, the first figure in appendix should be Figure 9.

Alternatively, tables and figures may be double-numbered by chapter. The numbers, separated by a period, represent the chapter number and the number of the table or figure in that chapter, respectively. For example, Table 2.3 refers to the third table in Chapter 2, and Figure 5.4 represents the forth one in Chapter 5.

Figures, as visual presentations of results, include graphs, diagrams, photos, drawings, schematics, maps, etc. If the total number of illustrations in a research paper is small, then each illustration may be labeled and numbered as a figure no matter it is a map, a graph, a diagram, or whatever. If there are more than ten illustrations of any one type in a paper (for example, more than ten graphs or more than ten diagrams), each type should be identified and a separate sequence of numbers should be given as well.

The abbreviations for figure and table are Fig. and Tbl., respectively. However, the abbreviation of table is rarely seen in text. We can also write fig. for figure. However, we should choose one convention and use it throughout the paper. We should not switch between, Figure, figure, Fig, or fig. In addition, abbreviations are not used at the beginning of sentences and a space belongs between the word/abbreviation and the number.

Figure and Table	
Incorrect	Correct
Figure.6	Figure 6, Fig. 6,
Tbl 10	Tbl. 10, Table 10

10.3.3 Body of Tables

The body of a table consists of vertical columns and horizontal rows. Columns should have appropriate descriptive headings. Each column and row in the table should have a heading label, even if the information seems obvious. The heading titles should be brief and can be abbreviated if necessary. The stub column, the first column in the table, is on the far left-hand side. This column will contain the main information of the table. Each other column contains information relating to the stub column information.

Column headings may have subheads, placed in parentheses. If two or more levels of headings are needed, then decked heads must be used. In a decked head, two or more related columns are positioned beneath a spanner head, a head spanning the width of the columns. A horizontal rule separates the spanner and column heads. In the following example of decked heads, the spanner heads are "Avg. wages in mfg." and "Avg. federal income tax", and the column heads are "Men", "Women", and "Total".

Avg. wages in mfg.			Avg. federal income tax		
Men	Women	Total	Men	Women	Total

(From Slade, C. *Form and Style: Research Papers, Reports and Theses,* 1997)

The first word of column headings should be capitalized, and end punctuation is unnecessary. Abbreviation can be used to create well-proportioned tables, but make sure they are easy to understand; otherwise they should be clarified with a note or key.

Notes can be one of three types. A general note is used for an explanation such as an abbreviation or a symbol. A specific note explains information in a particular area of the table, such as a row or column. A probability note provides some kind of statistical significance to the reader.

The body consists of the actual data the table is representing. If numbers are used, they should be consistent in measurement throughout an entire column within the table. The measurements can change by column as long as they are clearly illustrated within the table. When adding the

information to the table, consider the order in which it is placed. Many times, the results are placed in order from highest to lowest, oldest to newest or best to worst. The order in which they are placed should be carefully planned. Table entries that will be compared to each other should be situated next to each other.

A table sample: the U.S. population growth rate over the 1820-1997 period

Year	Population (in Thousands)	Annual Growth Rate
1820	9,618	2.5%
1830	12,902	2.7%
1840	17,120	2.6%
1850	23,261	2.8%
1860	31,513	2.7%
1870	39,905	2.2%
1880	50,262	2.1%
1890	63,056	2.1%
1900	76,094	1.7%
1910	92,407	2.1%
1920	106,466	1.9%
1930	123,188	1.2%
1940	131,028	0.8%
1950	151,683	1.7%
1960	180,684	1.6%
1970	204,880	1.1%
1980	227,757	1.2%
1990	253,684	1.1%
1997	272,679	0.9%

Source: Banks, A.S. Cross-National Time Series Archive.

10.4 Graphic Display Tools

10.4.1 Choice of a Graphic Display Tool

Several types of graphic display tools exist, including: (a) charts displaying frequencies (bar, pie and Pareto charts), (b) chart displaying trends (line graphs, run and control charts), (c) charts displaying distributions (histograms), and (d) charts displaying associations (scatter diagrams).

Different types of data require different kinds of graphic display tools. There are two types of data. Attribute data are countable data or data that can be put into categories: e.g., the number of people willing to pay, the number of complaints, percentage who want blue, percentage who want red, or percentage who want yellow. Variable data are measurement data, based on some continuous scale: e.g. length, time, cost. When creating graphic displays, the following table can help us identify which tool is the most suitable one to present data in our research paper.

Choosing Graphic Display Tools		
To Show	**Use**	**Data Needed**
Frequency of occurrence: Simple percentages or comparisons of magnitude	Bar chart, pie chart, pareto chart	Tallies by category (data can be attribute data or variable data divided into categories)
Trends over time	Line graph, run chart, control chart	Measurements taken in chronological order (attribute or variable data can be used)
Distribution: Variation not related to time (distributions)	Histograms	Forty or more measurements (not necessarily in chronological order, variable data)
Association: Looking for a correlation between two things	Scatter diagram	Forty or more paired measurements (measures of both things of interest, variable data)

学术论文写作与发表

10.4.2 Bar and Pie Charts

Bar and pie charts use pictures to compare the sizes, amounts, quantities, or proportions of various items or groupings of items. Pie chart is a circle graph divided into pieces, each displaying the size of some related piece of information. Pie charts are used to display the sizes of parts that make up some whole.

Bar and pie charts can be used in defining or choosing problems to work on, analyzing problems, verifying causes, or judging solutions. They make it easier to understand data because they present the data as a

picture, highlighting the results. This is particularly helpful in presenting results to team members and other interested parties. Bar and pie charts present results that compare different groups. They can also be used with variable data that have been grouped. Bar charts work best when showing comparisons among categories, while pie charts are used for showing relative proportions of various items in making up the whole (how the "pie" is divided up).

We may choose from three types of bar charts, depending on the type of data we have and what we want to stress: simple bar charts, grouped bar charts, and stacked bar charts. Simple bar charts sort data into simple categories. Grouped bar charts divide data into groups within each category and show comparisons between individual groups as well as between categories. It gives more useful information than a simple total of all the components. Stacked bar charts, which, like grouped bar charts, use grouped data within categories. They make clear both the sum of the parts and each group's contribution to that total.

How to Use a Bar Chart

Step 1 Choose the type of bar chart that stresses the results to be focused on. Grouped and stacked bar charts will require at least two classification variables. For a stacked bar chart, tally the data within each category into combined totals before drawing the chart.

Step 2 Draw the vertical axis to represent the values of the variable of comparison (e.g. number, cost, time). Establish the range for the data by subtracting the smallest value from the largest. Determine the scale for the vertical axis at approximately 1.5 times the range and label the axis with the scale and unit of measure.

Step 3 Determine the number of bars needed. The number of bars will equal the number of categories for simple or stacked bar charts. For a grouped bar chart, the number of bars will equal the number of categories multiplied by the number of groups. This number is important for determining the length of the horizontal axis.

Step 4 Draw bars of equal width for each item and label the categories and the groups. Provide a title for the graph that indicates the sample and the time period covered by the data; label each bar.

How to Use a Pie Chart

Step 1 Taking the data to be charted, calculate the percentage contribution for each category. First, total all the values. Next, divide the value of each category by the total. Then, multiply the product by 100 to create a percentage for each value.

Step 2 Draw a circle. Using the percentages, determine what portion of the circle will be represented by each category. This can be done by eye or by calculating the number of degrees and using a compass. By eye, divide the circle into four quadrants, each representing 25 percent.

Step 3 Draw in the segments by estimating how much larger or smaller each category is. Calculating the number of degrees can be done by multiplying the percent by 3.6 (a circle has 360 degrees) and then using a compass todraw the portions.

Step 4 Provide a title for the pie chart that indicates the sample and the time period covered by the data. Label each segment with its percentage or proportion (e.g. 25 percent or one quarter) and with what each segment represents (e.g. people who returned for a follow-up visit; people who did not return).

Stacked Bar Charts Sample

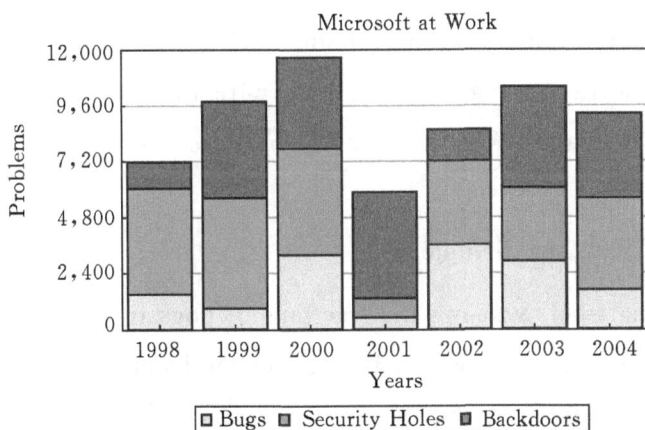

Imperfect Grouped Bar Chart Sample

A double bar graph is similar to a regular bar graph, but gives 2 pieces of information for each item on the vertical axis, rather than just 1. The bar chart below shows the weight in kilograms of some fruit sold in two different days

by a local market. This lets us compare the sales of each fruit over a 2-day period, not just the sales of one fruit compared to another. We can see that the sales of star fruit and apples stayed most nearly the same. The sales of oranges increased from day 1 to day 2 by 10 kilograms. The same amount of apples and oranges was sold on the second day.

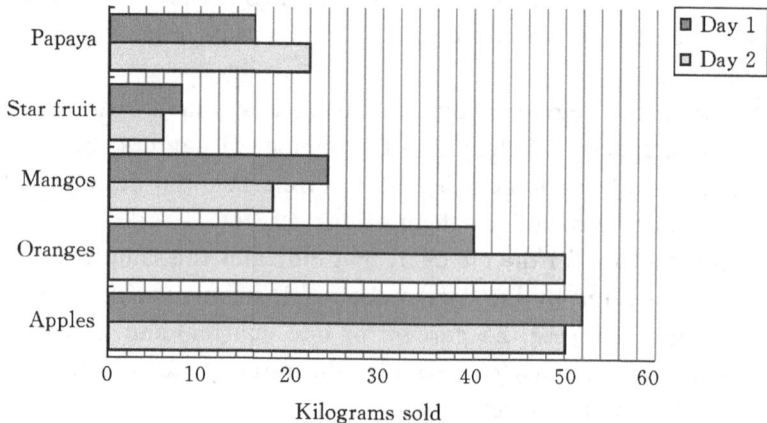

Analysis

This column chart is not well displayed because it does not show the precise numerical value of each column. Such a design could combine the virtue of the table (giving exact values) with that of the graph (quickly presenting the message). What is more, the bars are not arranged in decreasing order of size.

Imperfect Pie Chart Sample

The pie chart below shows the fractions of dogs in a dog competition in seven different groups of dog breeds. We can see from the chart that 4 times as many dogs competed in the sporting group as in the herding group. It is indicated that the two most popular groups of dogs accounted for almost half of the dogs in the competition. Suppose 1000 dogs entered the competition in all. We could figure the number of dogs in any group by multiplying the fraction of dogs in any group by 1000. In the toy group, for example, there were $0.12 \times 1000 = 120$ dogs in the competition.

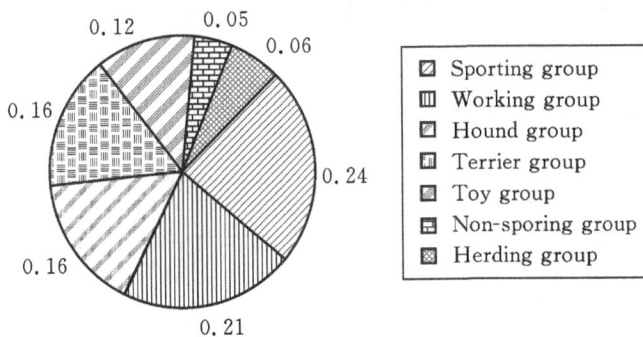

0. 12   0. 05
0. 06
0. 16
0. 24
0. 16
0. 21

☑	Sporting group
Ⅲ	Working group
☑	Hound group
☐	Terrier group
☑	Toy group
⊟	Non-sporing group
☒	Herding group

Analysis

This pie chart sample remains to improve because it does not completely follow the standard of a good pie chart. A good simple pie chart must have the following characteristics: (1) the largest segment begins nearly at 12 o'clock; (2) it continues with proportionally smaller portions in the clockwise direction; and (3) labels are placed outside the circle.

Be careful not to use too many notations on the charts. Keep them as simple as possible and include only the information necessary to interpret the chart. Do not draw conclusions not justified by the data. For example, determining whether a trend exists may require more statistical tests and probably cannot be determined by the chart alone. Differences among groups also may require more statistical testing to determine if they are significant. Whenever possible, use bar or pie charts to support data interpretation. Do not assume that results or points are so clear and obvious that a chart is not needed for clarity.

10.4.3 Line Graph

A line graph is a way to summarize how two pieces of information are related and how they vary depending on one another. The numbers along a side of the line graph are called the scale. A line graph is a rectangular which should not be too long or too flat, and the rate of its width and length normally is 5:7. It shows the relationship between two or more variables with vertical and horizontal scales. Value and unit must be placed with it. Graphs are often

学术论文写作与发表

used to show the results of studies, especially when they involve some kind of change over time.

Sample of Line Graph: 1

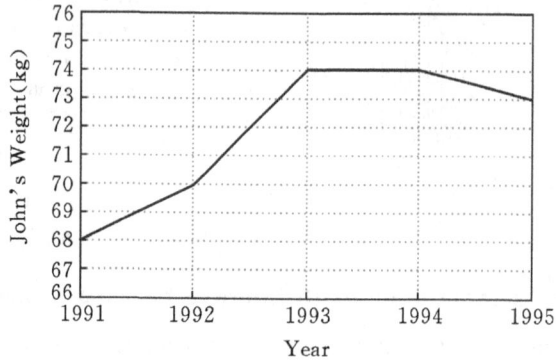

The graph above shows how John's weight varied from the beginning of 1991 to the beginning of 1995. The weight scale runs vertically, while the time scale is on the horizontal axis. Following the gridlines up from the beginning of the years, we see that John's weight was 68 kg in 1991, 70 kg in 1992, 74 kg in 1993, 74 kg in 1994, and 73kg in 1995. Examining the graph also tells us that John's weight increased during 1991 and 1995, stayed the same during 1991, and fell during 1994.

Sample of Line Graph: 2

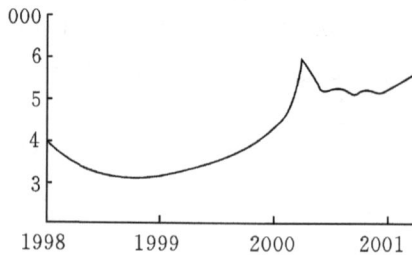

figure 1.Sales of mobile phones per month

The Figure above shows sales of mobile phones per month. As can be seen, it covers the years 1998 to 2001 and shows that the sales of mobile phones declined steadily in 1998, then remained steady from May until the end of the year. The sales rose more and more steeply, throughout 1999, with a steep increase at the end of the year, and reached a peak of 6,200 in February 2000. A sharp fall followed but sales leveled off at about 5,300 per month in April, fluctuated slightly through the year, and are now increasing again. The figures seem to indicate that we have recovered from the problems in mid-2000 and are on target to improve on our February 2000 peak by the end of 2002.

Language Expressions for Referring to a Graph, Chart etc.		
As can be seen It can be seen We can see	from/in	the chart (diagram, table, graph, figures, statistics)
can be seen is shown	from/in	the chart (diagram, table, graph, figures, statistics)
from the chart (diagram, table, graph, figures, statistics)	It can/may be	seen (concluded, shown, estimated, calculated, Inferred)
the chart (diagram, table, graph, figures, statistics)	shows	that

Describing Change		
There was a(n) (very)	barely noticeable (slight, slow, gradual, steady, marked, dramatic, steep, sharp, rapid, sudden)	rise (increase, upward tend, fluctuation, downward trend, decrease, decline, reduction, fall, drop)
...	increased (shot up, grew, rose, declined, reduced, decreased, dropped, fell)	slightly (slowly, gradually, steadily, markedly, dramatically, steeply, sharply, rapidly, suddenly)
...	reached a peak/ leveled off	
...	increased (shot up, grew, rose, declined, reduced, decreased, dropped, fell)	by
There was a(n)	rise (increase, decrease, decline, reduction, fall, drop)	of

10.4.4 Other Data Display Tools

Pareto Chart. A Pareto chart, named after Vilfredo Pareto, is a type of chart that contains both bars and a line graph, where individual values are represented in descending order by bars, and the cumulative total is represented by the line. The following is a simple example of a Pareto chart using hypothetical data showing the relative frequency of reasons for arriving late at work.

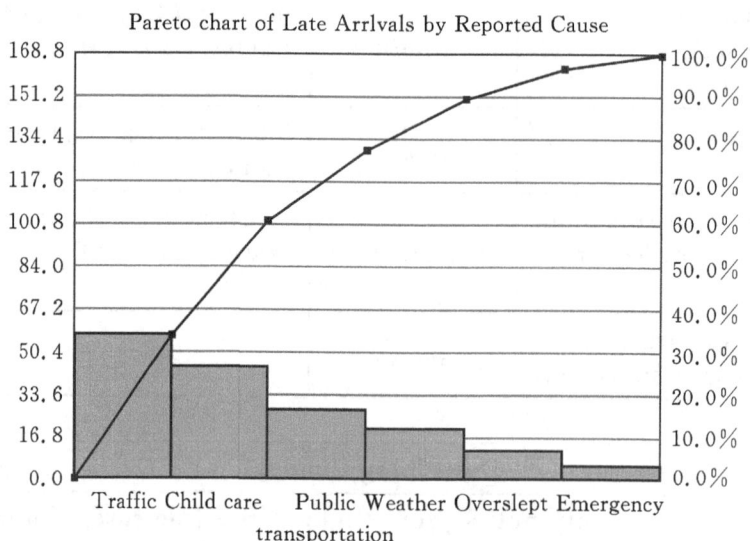

Pareto chart of Late Arrlvals by Reported Cause

168.8		100.0%
151.2		90.0%
134.4		80.0%
117.6		70.0%
100.8		60.0%
84.0		50.0%
67.2		40.0%
50.4		30.0%
33.6		20.0%
16.8		10.0%
0.0		0.0%

Traffic Child care Public Weather Overslept Emergency
transportation

The left vertical axis is the frequency of occurrence, but it can alternatively represent cost or another important unit of measure. The right vertical axis is the cumulative percentage of the total number of occurrences, total cost, or total of the particular unit of measure. Because the reasons are in decreasing order, the cumulative function is a concave function. To take the example above, in order to lower the amount of late arriving by 80%, it is sufficient to solve the first three issues. The purpose of the Pareto chart is to highlight the most important among a (typically large) set of factors. In quality control, it often represents the most common sources of defects, the highest occurring type of defect, or the most frequent reasons for customer complaints, and so on.

Run Chart. A run chart, also known as a run-sequence plot is a graph that displays observed data in a time sequence. Often, the data displayed represent some aspect of the output or performance of a manufacturing or other business process. Here is a simple run chart showing data collected over time.

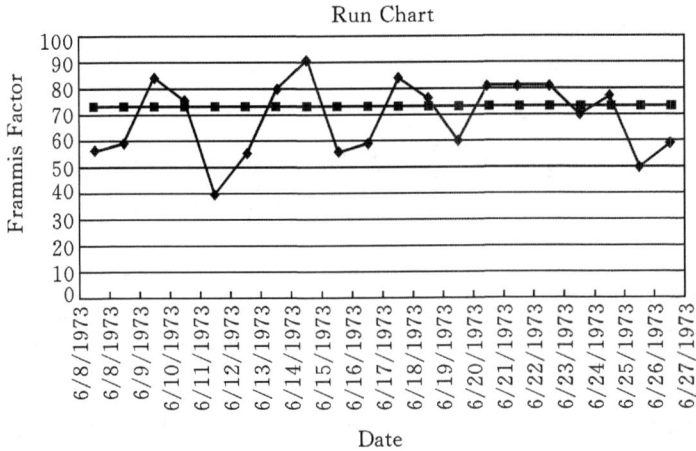

Run Chart

Control Chart. Control charts, also known as Shewhart charts or process-behavior charts, in statistical process control charts are tools used to determine whether or not a manufacturing or business process is in a state of statistical control. A control chart consists of:

1. Points representing a statistic (e.g. a mean, range, proportion) of measurements of a quality characteristic in samples taken from the process at different times (the data).

2. The mean of this statistic using all the samples is calculated (e.g. the mean of the means, mean of the ranges, mean of the proportions).

3. A center line is drawn at the value of the mean of the statistic.

4. The standard error (e.g. standard deviation/sqrt(n) for the mean) of the statistic is also calculated using all the samples.

5. Upper and lower control limits (sometimes called "natural process limits") that indicate the threshold at which the process output is considered statistically "unlikely"are drawn typically at 3 standard errors from the center line.

学术论文写作与发表

xbar chart for quality characteristic XXX

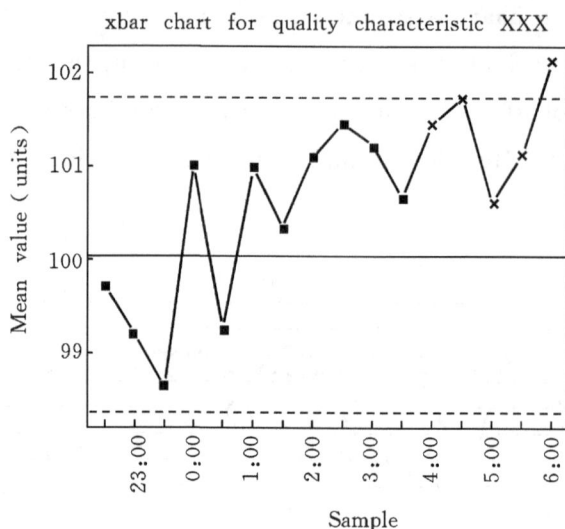

Number of groups = 16
Center = 100.0356
StdDev = 0.9725694

LCL＝98.35107   Number beyond limits＝2
UCL＝101.7202   Number violating runs＝5

Histogram. In statistics, a histogram is a graphical representation, showing a visual impression of the distribution of data. It is an estimate of the probability distribution of a continuous variable and was first introduced by Karl Pearson. A histogram consists of tabular frequencies, shown as adjacent rectangles, erected over discrete intervals (bins), with an area equal to the frequency of the observations in the interval. The height of a rectangle is also equal to the frequency density of the interval, i.e. the frequency divided by the width of the interval. The total area of the histogram is equal to the number of data. A histogram may also be normalized displaying relative frequencies. It then shows the proportion of cases that fall into each of several categories, with the total area equaling 1. The categories are usually specified as consecutive, non-overlapping intervals of a variable. The categories (intervals) must be adjacent, and often are chosen to be of the same size.

Histograms are used to plot density of data, and often for density estimation: estimating the probability density function of the underlying variable. The total area of a histogram used for probability density is always normalized to 1. If the length of the intervals on the x-axis are all 1, then a histogram is identical to a relative frequency plot.

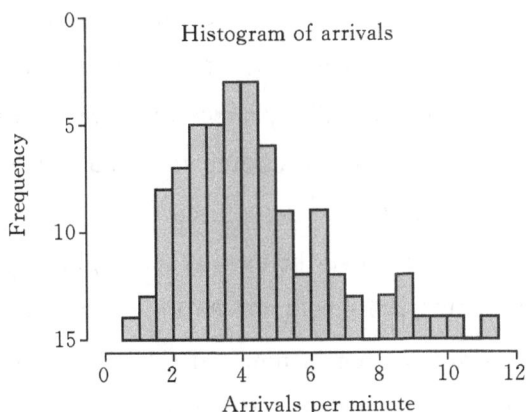

Histogram of arrivals

Scatter Diagram. A scatter plot or scatter graph is a type of mathematical diagram using Cartesian coordinates to display values for two variables for a set of data.

The data is displayed as a collection of points, each having the value of one variable determining the position on the horizontal axis and the value of the other variable determining the position on the vertical axis. This kind of plot is also called a scatter chart, scatter diagram or scatter graph.

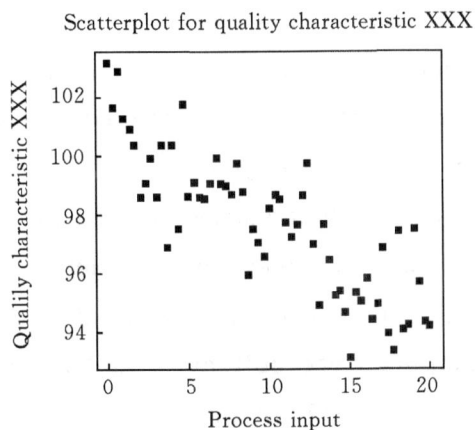

Scatterplot for quality characteristic XXX

10.5 Language Focus: Numbers and Equations

It is common occurrence that some student writers, both Chinese and western, do not seem to know when numbers should be written in numerals or need to be spelt out. Frequently some writers write Arabic numerals instead of

学术论文写作与发表

spelling out in English. For Chinese writers, this probably stems from the fact that Mandarin is a symbolic language and not alphabetic. Thus, the writer will find it easier to write a symbol that expresses the idea instead of the word. In academic English, however, there are circumstances under which numerals are undesirable and full spelling of word is required.

- Arabic numerals should never be used at the beginning of sentences.

  Twelve parameters were selected for the experiment.

- Larger numbers are written in numerals. Numbers that are less than 10 should be spelt out rather than written in numerals. But there are three exceptions: (1) when a measurement unit is involved; (2) when numbers are shown as decimal fractions or expressed as precise mathematical relations; (3) when the number is directly linked to some category that has more than one type.

  ① Distance between the two points is 6 mm.

  ② Using the equation $S = 6A0.12$, the number of species S on an island with area $A = 9m2$ would be 7.8—or about 8 species.

  ③ Only specimen no. 23 contained trace minerals.

- Arabic numerals should be used to give data in technical papers; however, they should not be used to provide general information.

  [Incorrect] The 3 author from 3 studies grouped the 4 age classes into <2 years, 2-5years, 6-10 years, and >10 year.

  [Correct] Author from three studies grouped the age classes into <2 years, 2-5years, 6-10 years, and >10 year.

- In academic English, dates should always have the month written in letters.

  Aerosol samples were collected on 15 January 2006 in Guangzhou (23°13'N, 113° 32'E).

- Equations should be introduced as much as possible, not inserted in place of words. Most journals, like the International Journal of Production Research, discourage the use of even short expressions within the text.

  [Incorrect] If the power battery SOC > SOClo and the driving torque belongs to the middle load...

[Correct] If the power battery SOC is greater than SOClo and the driving torque belongs to the middle load...

10.6　Reflections and Practice

1. Study the graph below and complete the description with phrases from the table below.

Sports centre membership 1)_____ in 1992, and then 2)_____ until 1995, reaching a peak of 4,900. It 3)_____ in 1996, but 4)_____ the next year. In 1998 there was a 5)_____, then a peak of 6,700 in 1999, followed by a 6)_____ in 2000.

Verb ↗	Adverb	Verb ↘	Adjective + noun
Grew	Slightly	Dropped	A slight drop
Rose	Gradually	Fell	A gradual fall
Increased	Steadily	Decreased	A sharp decrease
Climbed	Sharply		

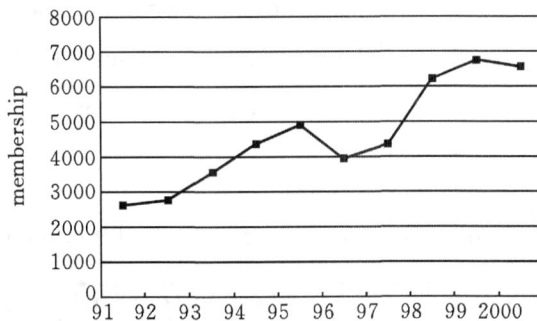

Sports centre membership 1991–2000

2. Complete the following description of the chart below.

The chart shows population 1)_____ in a variety of countries around the world. It 2)_____ the extreme contrast 3)_____ crowded nations such as South Korea (475 people per sq. km) and much 4)_____ countries such

as Canada (3 people per sq. km). Clearly, climate plays a major 5)_____ in determining population density, 6)_____ the least crowded nations 7)_____ to have extreme climates (e.g. cold in Russia or dry in Algeria).

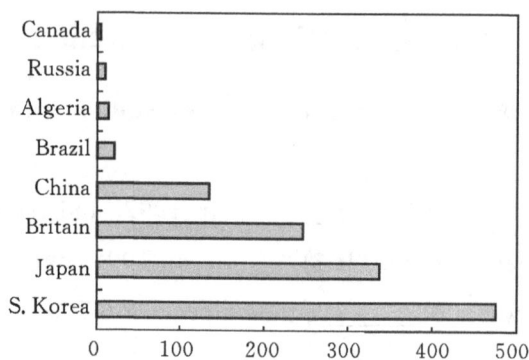

Population density (people per square kilometer)

3. Complete the following description of the table below.

The 1)_____ shows the wide variations in marriage and divorce rates in a 2)_____ of countries. The 3)_____ rate varies from 10.7 per thousand in 4)_____ to 4.0 in South Africa, while the divorce 5)_____ ranges from 4.7 in the United States to 0.5 in Turkey and 6)_____ It appears that in the United States more than 7)_____ of all marriages end in divorce, while in Turkey the 8)_____ is less than 10%. This suggests that in countries such as the United States and Britain the high marriage rate may be a 9)_____ of the high divorce rate.

Marriage and divorce rates (per 1,000 population)

Country	Marriage Rate	Divorce Rate
Britain	10.7	3.4
United States	8.6	4.7
Turkey	8.0	0.5
Iran	7.8	0.5
Japan	6.2	1.8
Russia	5.2	3.2
Spain	5.2	0.8
South Africa	4.0	0.9

4. Complete the following description of the table below.

Table 1 Gender balance in the School of Computing 1996–2000

	Men	Women
1996	109	34
1997	112	45
1998	125	41
1999	108	56
2000	118	72

Table 1 shows_____.

Part IV Research Paper Publication

Chapter Eleven Procedures of Paper Publication

Successful publication is more a matter of planning and persistence than brilliance.

—— *F. Mosteller*

11.1 Choice of Target Journals

Although most researchers would like very much to publish their work, the problem for new authors is breaking the ice by submitting their first manuscript to a journal. Some are plagued by a lack of confidence and fear of having an article rejected. These individuals spend considerable time "planning" to publish, but continually put the actual task off until a "tomorrow" that never comes. Others suffer from not knowing how to publish with regard to writing style and the selection of an appropriate journal. These individuals are willing to make a try, but often experience disappointment as a result of submitting the wrong article to the wrong journal.

To select an appropriate journal is the first important decision for the publication of our study after the completion of our research paper. Journals differ considerably in their orientations and standards for quality. No matter how well written our manuscript may be, unless it provides a good fit with the particular journal, it will probably not be accepted. In fact, the only review we may receive is the editor informing us of inappropriateness. Successful authors learn to make good selections of publication outlets, and not waste time having their articles reviewed (and rejected) by inappropriate journals.

Each journal has a set of guidelines that we will need to follow strictly before submitting our manuscript. Usually, we will find these guidelines on the Journal's homepage under the Instructions to Authors or Information for Authors section. There are many ways to choose the most appropriate journal and this is a really important decision that we should not take slightly. We are recommended to evaluate in the following order:

The scope. We will usually find information on the field of expertise of each journal on their homepage or in a specific rubric. Depending on the journal, the scope can be really vast or on the opposite really narrow. The larger the scope, the more difficult it is to publish an article usually, considering the number of submissions we would have to compete with. If we find a journal that specializes in it, we might have a better chance to publish your article.

The impact factor. This is the most widely used criterion to estimate the value of a journal and even of a scientist. The impact factor is based on the number of times a journal or article is referred to in other publications, and gives an authority index. All impact factors are indexed every year in the Thomson's Reuter's Journal Citation Reports and in the ISI Web of Knowledge. They can depend highly on the discipline but in any case a higher number means a more important contribution.

The last articles published and the guidelines. A good indication to what article could be accepted in a specific journal would be the publications of the last issues. Indeed, trying to publish an article on the genetics of a neurological disease in a journal of neurology that never published any genetic studies might not be a very smart decision. Thankfully, the editor who receives our paper is the one who decides if the article is suitable for the journal and if not, will send it back to us within a week. On another hand, if the journal we are interested in just published a study very similar to ours, we might want to try another journal. Check also the guidelines. Some journals are more stringent than others

学术论文写作与发表

and if we are having trouble formatting our article, we might want to consider another journal.

The turnaround and publication speed. It is almost impossible to predict how long it will take for us to receive an answer from the editor and the reviewers, since it is different for each paper. However, the usual turnaround time varies between 1 week and 6 months. An option is to ask colleagues who published in the same journal to have an idea of how long they waited. Concerning the publication speed, we can find it in most articles, usually on the first page, where the journal will publish an article history with the dates of reception, acceptance and final publication.

Past experience and editor. After all, who knows better than ourselves where to send the article? Think carefully about our article and estimate its level of importance. Keep in mind the other articles we read on the same subject and where they were published. Remember the other articles we published and where we had the most pleasant experience. We can also investigate the editor's identity; it is a good indication on the authority of the journal.

Importance of paper. The importance of our paper is also an important factor to consider in the choice of a target journal. We are suggested to try the highest journal we'd like and if our paper gets rejected, to send it to a lower authority journal, etc... until it is finally accepted for publication.

11. 2 Process of Paper Publication

When the target journal is selected, the next step is to submit the paper for publication. Particularly when the paper is submitted to a major journal it can be a very exhausting and sometimes dead-end way to the paper finally appearing in a printed or online issue of the journal. Essentially there are two obstacles: the editors and the reviewers, who ensure the scientific quality of journal papers.

The most important function of an editor (can also be a group of persons) is to make the final decision whether to accept or to reject a submitted paper.

Indeed, the comments of the referees just serve as suggestions. Nevertheless, as the editor alone would not be able to review and comment on all submissions in detail, he usually relies on the advice of his editorial board, where he/she can choose from a pool of experts in diverse fields of the journal's main topics. If there is consensus on acceptance or rejection, the editor's life is fairly easy. It becomes difficult only when there is significant disagreement in the reviewer's suggestions. In such a case the editor may make a final decision based on his/her own opinion or after consulting additional referees.

Important activities in the publishing process of journal papers are depicted in Figure 11.1. The vertical swim lanes separate the areas of responsibility of the main actors in the process. An article from submission to its final publication has to go through a series of process including manuscript submission, manuscript referral and final decision.

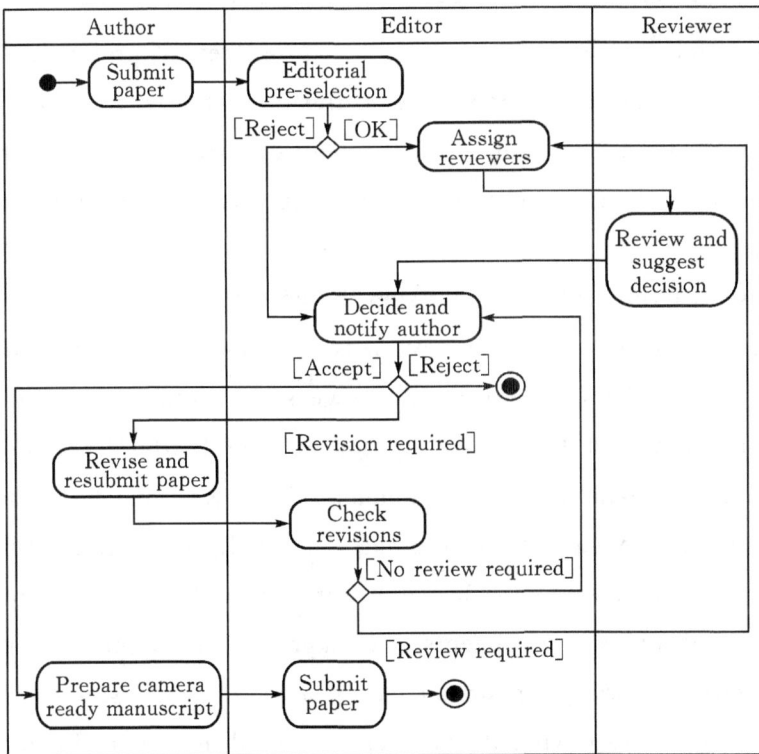

Fig.11.1 The process of publishing a paper in a journal

Manuscript submission. After choosing an appropriate journal for submission, the author has to submit the paper according to the instructions issued by the journal editor. Most journals today offer the opportunity to submit the paper via the journal's web site. At this stage, it is very important that the author follows the instructions at the utmost accuracy, because papers submitted not compliant with (parts of) the instructions will most likely be rejected without taking into account the paper's actual content. Here are some common authors' mistakes at the stage of paper submission:

Common Authors' Mistakes at the Stage of Paper Submission

(1) Not adhering to the journal's paper formatting and layout guidelines (e.g. using the wrong font size, line spacing, page numbering, referencing style, figure and table placement and visual guidelines, etc.).

(2) Exceeding maximum paper length (word count, page count).

(3) The paper's thematic focus is not within the scope of the journal's subject areas.

If any of the above is evident when the editor does the preliminary review, the paper will be directly rejected regardless of its scientific contribution and quality. On the other hand, if these conditions are met, the paper will be considered for publication. The submitting author is notified of either one of these decisions.

Manuscript referral. The next step the editor takes is to select referees for peer reviewing the paper. Peer review is often used to determine academic papers suitability for publication. Reviewers are usually a community of experts in a given (and often narrowly defined) field, who are qualified and able to perform impartial review. The number of referees involved in the review process may vary from journal to journal, but usually the editor forwards the paper to at least three referees who are experts in the topic that is covered by the paper. Besides making comments and suggestions for improvements to the authors, referees generally support the editor in making a decision by providing information on the following general issues, which may vary in importance among different journals. Here are some general issues usually answered by referees in manuscript referral:

General Issues Answered by Referees in Manuscript Referral

(1) Thematic relevance to the journal's scope of subjects.
(2) Significance of contribution. (Does the paper contribute new findings to the body of knowledge in the field?)
(3) Originality of the work. (Is similar research already published elsewhere?)
(4) Coverage of relevant literature. (Did the authors report related work?)
(5) Writing style of the paper. (The following aspects influence reviewers' recommended decision.)
  - Clarity of writing: readability, organization, conciseness, and technical quality of the paper.
  - Appropriate title and abstract.
  - Appropriate use of well-designed figures and tables.
  - Sound conclusion and discussion.
  - Length of the paper relative to its usefulness.

Final Decision. When the assigned referees have finished reviewing and commenting the paper, the editor collects their recommendations and makes a decision which is sent to the corresponding author of the paper (usually the first author). Generally, the notification by the editor will carry one of the following messages:

"**Accept as is**". The editor accepts the paper without modifications. The paper will be published in one of the journal's forthcoming issues. This outcome is very unlikely upon initial submission. Only in very rare cases the paper will be accepted right away. It is more likely that the paper has to be revised.

"**Accept conditionally**". The editor requests revision of certain parts of the paper. The author has to modify the paper according to the suggestions and comments of the reviewers and the editor (i.e. conditions for acceptance) in order to be further considered for publication. After revising the paper accordingly, the author may resubmit the paper to the journal. Resubmission typically requires authors to enclose a letter to the editor where they must present and discuss in detail how they addressed the reviewer and editorial comments in their revised version. After receiving the revised version the editor typically forwards the paper to the same referees who conditionally accepted the

initial submission.

"Reject". The editor does not see any chance for the paper to be published in the journal. Unfortunately, this is by far the most frequent outcome of the review process of a journal. The editor usually encloses detailed reasons for rejection provided by the referees, which should be read carefully by the author. Most likely, one or more referees found the paper out of the journal's scope, fundamental flaws in the paper's argument, data, etc. or no improvement with regard to previous submissions of the same paper.

If modification is required and the author feels unable to comply with the editors recommendations, the author may either politely tell the editor about the disagreement, or alternatively the paper may be sent to another appropriate journal in the field. The same applies to rejected papers.

11.3　Correspondence between Author and Editor

During the paper submission and publication process, the author needs to communicate with the editor(s), which are usually through letters or, now mostly, emails. There are two main types of letters within this process: query letter, cover letter and other contacts.

11.3.1　Query Letter

11.3.1.1 The Value of a Query

A query letter is a formal letter sent to magazine editors. Writers write query letters to propose writing ideas, and to probe the possibility or permission to send in manuscript. A well-structured query letter benefits both editors and writers.

As editors become increasingly swamped with inappropriate manuscripts, more and more publications are closing their doors to unsolicited submissions. Editors much prefer to review a one-page letter than a 10-page manuscript, so queries could help them spend less time in the slush pile. They also enable an editor to determine, quickly, whether we:

- Can write effectively.

- Have a coherent, well-thought-out idea that fits the publication's content.

- Have a basic grasp of grammar and spelling.

- Have read the publication.

- Have the credentials or expertise to write the article.

- Are professional in your approach to writing.

Queries save us time by insuring that we do not invest time and energy into writing an article that will not be accepted. Keep in mind that articles are often rejected for reasons that have nothing to do with quality. An editor may already have a similar piece on file, or assigned, or have covered something similar in a recent issue. It is much easier to find this out through a query, than to tailor an article for a publication and then have to rewrite it and send it somewhere else.

By querying first, we also give the editor a chance to provide feedback on our idea. The editor may want to suggest a particular length, or approach, or recommend experts to interview. S/he may want us to cover other aspects of your subject in sidebars. By finding out what the editor wants before we start writing, we will avoid having to revise the piece later.

A well-written query can also result in assignments we did not expect. If the editor is impressed by our style and credentials, s/he may offer us some other assignment, even if our original idea is not usable. This can often be the beginning of a long, rewarding relationship!

All in all, a query, a letter of introduction, is our first and only opportunity to get our foot through that particular door. If we make a good impression, we're likely to be invited back (even if our original pitch is rejected). If we make a bad impression, we may find that door forever closed.

11.3.1.2 Paper Query Letter Components

But how do we "sell" an editor our article when we have no more than a page to explain our concept and display our writing skill? The answer is: by including everything the editor needs to know about our article—and about us. A successful query letter generally includes these five basic components: the hook, the pitch, the body, the credentials and the close.

The Hook. Our very first line should grab an editor's attention. It must demonstrate that we can write effectively. Certain hooks scream "amateur" and are guaranteed to speed a query to the rejection pile, including:

The personal introduction. Never start with a line like "Hi, my name is John, and I'd like to send you an article about..." Do not offer irrelevant information, such as "I'm a housewife and mother of three lovely children. Recently I decided to pursue my lifelong dream of writing..."

The "suck-up" hook. Editors want to know that we have read their publication, but they also want us to prove it by offering an appropriate query—not by saying, "I've been a subscriber for 20 years and just love your magazine..." (This is even less effective if our query goes on to prove that we have never actually read the magazine!)

The "bid for sympathy". Do not tell an editor that we have never been published before, or that we need to publish an article or we will not be promoted.

The "I'm perfect for you" hook. Never sing our own praises: "I am a highly experienced professional and will be an asset to your magazine." Do not inform the editor that our article is "perfect" for his readers. Never declare that our article is "wonderful" or "fascinating". We need to prove it with a good query.

The "I'm an amateur" hook. Never announce that we have never been published before, or that we have tried to sell the same article to 20 other magazines, or that our writing teacher (or mother or spouse) suggested that we send this to a magazine. Even if we have not published any paper before, we can still act like a professional.

The Pitch. Once we have an editor's attention, move on to the pitch. Usually, this is our second paragraph, and its purpose is to explain exactly what we are offering. For example, a pitch in a query goes like this:

I'd like to offer you a 1,500-word article titled "Internationalizing Your Online Market". The article would discuss how small businesses can take advantage of "localizing" agents to tailor their products and market strategies to the international marketplace.

If possible, our pitch should include a working title for your article (titles help editors "visualize" what we are proposing), a word-count (make sure we have checked the publication's guidelines!), and a brief summary of what the article will cover.

The Body. This is where we really start to "sell". The body of our query will usually presents the details of our article. Remember that an editor wants to know exactly what the article will cover, so by this time we should have a working outline of the piece in our own mind. A good way to present an overview of our topic is to break it into logical subtopics — e.g. the sections that would be likely to appear under subheads in the finished piece.

The Credentials. Editors want to know why we are the best person to write the article we have proposed. This is where your credentials come in. Don not assume, however, that these must include writing credits. While a list of previous articles on relevant topics is nice, we may also be able to prove our qualifications with credentials such as:

- Professional experience (some publications accept material only from qualified experts).
- Academic degrees or training.
- Teaching experience in the subject area.
- Personal experience (especially if the article relates to personal issues/ problems).
- Writing experience.
- Interviews with experts (a way to demonstrate that even if you do not have the credentials, you will be able to get information from those who do).

Credentials are usually listed in the last or next-to-last paragraph. Here is an example:

> As webmaster of www.musicphotographer.com, it has been my job to
> connect music writers and photographers with the markets that need
> their work. This is the only site devoted to music journalism on the Web.
> I am also writing the first guide on the topic. Reviews for my last book,
> The Van Halen Encyclopedia, are available at Amazon.com.

The Close. Use the final paragraph of our article to thank the editor for reviewing our proposal and to offer one last "nudge" to encourage the editor to respond. A time-estimate could usually be included in this paragraph—e.g. "If you are interested in this article, I can have it on your desk within xx days." Here is a typical closing paragraph:

I hope this topic interests you, and look forward to your response. If you would like to see the article, I can have it on your desk within two weeks of receiving your go-ahead. Thank you for your time!

A Typical Paper Query Letter

Dear Dr. Rebecca Talley,

As a constant reader of Physical Review Letters, I have found 4 articles on simple phenomenological model published in your journal sine July 2010. But to my knowledge, they are all written in the light of theoretical considerations. I am now preparing a paper on the same topic, however, with its emphasis on the experimental aspect, and wonder whether it is acceptable in your journal. I would be very grateful to you for an early reply, even though it could turn out to be a negative one.

Yours sincerely,
Vukani G. Nyirenda

11.3.1.3 Query Letter Format and Follow-up

The presentation of our letter can be as important as our content. A traditional paper query should include seven basic elements:

A decent letterhead. At the very least, our name and address and other contact information should be printed at the top of our letter (not at the bottom or under our signature) in an attractive font. We can have an inexpensive letterhead designed and typeset at our local printing shop, or online through iPrint.com. We can also design our own on our computer.

A business-style body. Our query letter should fit onto a single sheet of paper, no questions asked. It should be formatted as a business letter, that is, from the top of the page, all aligned to the left margin and a blank line is always included between paragraphs.

A formal salutation. Do not address the editor by first name unless we know him/her personally.

Clean, proofread copy. Do not rely on our spellchecker; review our query ourselves before mailing it out.

Quality paper. Use at least 20-lb. bond paper for queries. Some writers like to use fancier papers on the theory that a nicer paper with a professional tint will stand out amidst all the white paper on an editor's desk. We are suggested not to go to "colors", because pink paper and blue type scream for rejection.

A SASE (self-addressed stamped envelope). Do not use "insert" envelopes; fold a full-size business envelope(#10) in thirds and use that. Be sure it has adequate postage. If we are submitting a query from another country, be sure that our SASE has the correct postage for the target country.

Clips. Many editors ask for clips so that they can review a sample of our writing style. Clips are simply copies of previously published materials. Never send copies of unpublished works! Don't send clips of work we have self-published or posted on our own website. And remember, bad clips are worse than no clips at all.

It is best to send clips that are relevant to the proposal, if we have them. If we don't, send samples from our most prestigious publications. If most of our published works are electronic, print out copies from our website; don't just ask the editor to "visit" unless we are sending an e-mail query.

If we have no clips, don't despair. Most editors consider the merits of a query first and the clips second. (To be honest, many editors don't even have time to read clips, even though they request them.) If your query is strong enough, the absence of clips shouldn't be enough to trigger a rejection, unless the publication works only with published writers.

After we send editor a query, arises the net issue how long we should wait for a response. Usually, we should wait at least as long as the publication's guidelines suggest (e.g. 4 to 6 weeks) and then add another two weeks "grace period". Then, send a polite follow-up. Attach a copy of our original query, so that the editor won't have to search the files for it. If we still hear nothing after another 3-4 weeks, consider a polite phone call. (No, it won't cause our article to be rejected.) If we still can't get an answer, and we would like to withdraw the query, send a final letter informing the editor that, as we have received no response, we are officially withdrawing the query from consideration. This protects us from charges of "simultaneous submissions" if the first editor finally decides to reply after we've already sent the query on to someone else.

✖ 11.3.1.4 E-mail Query Letter Essentials

While some editors still prefer paper queries sent by surface mail, an increasing number prefer e-mail queries. E-mail queries save postage and time. Our query will reach the editor in seconds rather than days. We may also receive a response within days (or even hours). While e-mail queries contain many of the same elements as traditional "paper" queries, they also contain elements that need special attention. These include the header, the text, and the credentials.

The header. With e-mail, we can't impress an editor with nice paper or a snappy letterhead. Instead, we must rely on our header to provide vital information about ourselves and our query. Be sure to address our query to the right person at the right address. Try to locate the exact e-mail address of the editor we wish to contact. Be sure to set up a professional "personality" in our e-mail program that includes our real name and a professional-sounding e-mail address. The word "Query" may be included in your subject line, along with a brief (two to three words) description of our proposal—e.g. "Query: (article title/subject) or Article submission: Title." Never leave this line blank. Avoid cuteness or excessive informality; a subject line like "May I have a moment of your time?" looks too much like "spam" and could cause our query to be deleted.

The text. The easiest way to handle the text of an e-mail query is to treat it just like a traditional paper query. However, many editors find that they actually prefer shorter queries by e-mail. The less the editor has to "scroll" to read our query, the better. Thus, more writers are turning to brief, one-to three-paragraph e-mail queries. The hook is often eliminated entirely, allowing the writer to get straight to the pitch, followed by a single paragraph of description, and closing with the writer's credentials. When crafting an e-mail query, therefore, give serious thought to ways that we can "condense" our information into a compact summary that the editor can view on a single screen. Just be sure that our summary actually covers all the salient points that we wish to make!

The credentials. It is perfectly acceptable to list our credentials in an e-mail query just as we would in a traditional query. Many writers also use this opportunity to provide a link to a Web site where editors can learn more about the writer's qualifications, or perhaps view writing samples. Here is an example:

> I have been chosen as a Poet of the Year 2000 for the poetry that I submitted to Poetry.com and have been invited to Reno Nevada to receive a trophy and a medallion for my poetry from the actor and poet, Ed Asner. My poetry can be seen at http://www.poetry.com.

Some editors will check the sites we list; some won't. It is wise, therefore, to state our credentials explicitly, and offer Web sites only as a backup. Never send "clips" in an attachment.

The address block. In a traditional query, our name, address and other contact information would go at the top of the page (or be incorporated into our letterhead). In an e-mail query, it should go at the bottom, below our typed signature:

Athena Smith

1042 Gloriana Lane

Whippet, IL 60606

(555)123-4567

(555) 123-4568 (fax)

athenasmith@126.com

The signature block. We may wish to use a standard "signature block" to include our Web site and any special credentials we'd like to list. We can also include our surface-mail address and contact information in a signature block, but be sure we only use this block for queries and professional correspondence; we don't want to broadcast that information on the Web. Avoid overly cute signature blocks, or blocks that involve graphic elements.

Editors will be even happier with our electronic submissions if we follow these guidelines:

Guidelines for Electronic Submission

Do use a large, readable font. Make sure your font size is set to "normal" — or to a minimum of 12 points. If we're not sure how "large" our type looks (it may look fine on our own screen), ask someone else how our e-mails look.

Do keep e-mail queries as short as possible. Try to present our query succinctly enough to minimize (or eliminate) the need to scroll through our message.

Don't use HTML formatting in our e-mail. Not every editor has their e-mail program set up to accept HTML. Turn off any commands that automatically convert our e-mail to an HTML document.

Don't use colors. Just as we wouldn't type a query in yellow ink, don't send an e-mail query in any font color other than black.

Don't use emoticons. These are more appropriate for personal correspondence.

Don't send "clips" as attachments. It's always difficult to send clips with electronic queries. One option is to state the availability of clips, to be sent by e-mail or surface mail on request; another is to provide links to online clips

Don't expect an editor to respond to an e-mail submission "instantly". Although some editors do respond more quickly to e-mail submissions than to surface mail. Nothing irritates an editor like a writer who asks after a submission only days after sending it in.

Do keep a copy of all correspondence with editors. This will make it much easier for us to send a copy of our original query if we need to follow up.

11.3.2 Cover Letter

When we submit a scientific article for publication, we are usually required to upload a cover letter. This letter, also called covering letter, is the first document the editor of the journal will read upon submission. It should thus contain key information that will trigger the interest of the editor and encourage her/him to evaluate the manuscript. Based on the cover letter and the abstract of the article, the editor will then choose to send our application to anonymous reviewers and referees for a deeper analysis. A cover letter serves at least three functions: (1) establish the author's credibility, (2) help ensure that the manuscript is seriously considered for publication, and (3) initiate a positive rapport with the editor and editorial staff of the journal. What points are important when writing the letter and what information should be included to achieve these functions?

First of all, the cover letter must be rich in arguments to incite the editor to read our paper. It is really important to present our work in a way that incites the editor to know more about the work we performed. One way to do so is to briefly summarize the aim of the study and the main results obtained. In this case, try to be precise without entering too much into details, especially if the experimental part is complex. The idea is not to overwhelm the editor with information but to fuel her curiosity.

We can also clearly state which are the key attributes of our work, such as the innovative technology used, the incredible amount of samples analyzed, the great impact it has on the research field, the potential clinical interest for affected patients, etc. Define very well the main points and instead of explaining everything, focus on the three that we think are the most relevant for the editor of the specific journal where we will send the article. For example, it could also be that our paper confirms the results already published in the same journal by another research group, or on the contrary fails to replicate results that were considered revolutionary in our field.

Additionally, the cover letter could contain information about us and our research team. Present for example the main investigator, the research interests of our lab or the overall study where this particular paper is involved. In this paragraph, we can also add relevant information such as the reason for choosing this particular journal (and why not another) or the reason for choosing to study this particular protein in this particular disease, etc. If the study is the result of collaboration with other groups we could also mention it here.

If we decide to summarize our main results or findings, be sure to explain what we did and how we did it and emphasize the interest that our study should have on the readers of the journal. Mention what is known in the field and which new information we are bringing with this manuscript.

It is also interesting for editors to have a quick overview of possible applications of your work. This includes the direct applications, for example in further research studies that can develop based on these findings, in clinical practice if the results can be applied to treat patient or to develop preventive means, but also indirect applications in other fields, for example if our main interest is myocardial infarction, maybe our results are promising for other vascular diseases such as stroke?

Of course, our letter must be free of grammatical and orthographical errors. Do not hesitate to ask our university for a professional translator or editor service if necessary, who could help us proofread the letter as well as the manuscript, in particular if English is not our native language. Make an effort also to present a beautiful letter with formatting, headers from our institutions and a pleasant font. Avoid long letters, one or two pages maximum but instead

be concise and focus on the key elements of our study, the ones we think are especially relevant. Finally avoid copying and pasting the abstract.

Be creative and positive, but most of all defend our work as if it was the best paper ever published and you will convince the editor to review it!

Here are a few examples of cover letters we can use as templates to prepare our own letter.

Cover Letter Sample 1

Dear editorial board of *European Journal of Human Genetics*,

Please find enclosed the manuscript: "The oestrogen receptor alpha gene is not a risk factor for breast cancer", by Sandy Olsson et al., to be submitted as an original article *to European Journal of Human Genetics* for consideration of publication. All co-authors have seen and agreed with the contents of the manuscript and there is no financial interest to report. We certify that the submission is original work and is not under review at any other publication.

In this manuscript, we report the results of the first study on the genetic and functional roles of the oestrogen receptor alpha gene on the risk of suffering a breast cancer in a Caucasian population. Indeed, we genotyped the rs352498 polymorphism in 1000 breast cancer cases and 1000 healthy controls, and then performed functional studies by measuring serum oestrogen receptor alpha protein level and activity in healthy controls and breast cancer patients. The results from our study did not reveal any association of the oestrogen receptor alpha variant with breast cancer, which did not affect oestrogen receptor alpha protein level, and breast cancer patients showed similar oestrogen receptor alpha level than controls.

We believe that our findings could be of interest to the readers of *European Journal of Human Genetics* because they bring new and strong evidence that the oestrogen receptor alpha gene is not a risk factor for breast cancer.

We hope that the editorial board will agree on the interest of this study. Sincerely yours,

Danny Zuko on behalf of the authors.

Corresponding author: Danny Zuko at Breast Cancer Research Laboratory and Oncology Unit, Research Institute Rydell High, Madison Avenue 119-129, 10098 New York, USA, solsson@grease.com, phone number: 212-878-1011, fax number: 212-878-1010

Cover Letter Sample 2

Dear editorial board of *Neurobiology of Aging*,

Please find enclosed the manuscript: ACE Variants and Risk of Alzheimer's Disease, by Sarah Hamilton et al., to be submitted as an Original Research Article to *Neurobiology of Aging*. All co-authors have seen and agree with the contents of the manuscript and there is no financial interest to report. We certify that the submission is not under review at any other publication.

In this manuscript, we report the results of a genetic and functional study in a white population of sporadic Alzheimer's Disease patients on the risk of suffering cognitive impairments.

We believe that our findings could be of interest to the readers of *Neurobiology of Aging*, because they could have a great impact on the diagnostic, prognostic and treatment of patients with Alzheimer's Disease. Indeed, the ApoE gene is the only well recognized risk factor for Alzheimer's Disease at the moment (Goder et al. 1998), and we report here evidence that the ACE gene could also be involved in this disease. Moreover, we show that the variant studied modulates ACE levels and increase the predictive value of the ApoE gene.

This study could thus have a great pharmacogenetic interest and bring new and important light in the field of Alzheimer's Disease management and we hope that the editorial board and the reviewers will agree on the interest of this study.

Sincerely yours,

Sarah Hamilton on behalf of the authors.

Corresponding author: Sarah Hamilton at Cardiovascular Research Laboratory, Marie Curie Research Institute, 75000, Paris, France, shamilton@mariecurie. fr, phone number: +33582246789, fax number: +33582246789

11.3.3 Some Other Letters

There are other kinds of correspondence between author and editor, mainly involving manuscript improvement, suggested modification, further alterations, counter-proposals to the suggested revisions, and manuscript withdrawal. These types of letters have the similar patterns with the previous two types, but are more concentrated to serve their specific purposes.

Manuscript Improvement

Dear Editor,

In the light of the paper presentation and helpful discussions during the 3rd International Symposium on Atomic Collision her of held in my institute last month, I have made a number of improvements on my research project, and the experiment result turned out proves much better than that recorded in the previous draft submitted to you on March 30. For the sake of the journal, the reader, as well as the author, I would therefore beg to withdraw my manuscript (register No.11-4-8) and would like to resubmit it to you after the experimental result and the conclusion are updated. Could it be possible? Please let me know. Thank you.

Suggested Modification

Dear Dr. Enzo Montanero,

I have received your letter dated May 6, 2011, giving me your suggestions and advice for further modifications on my paper. I think they are very helpful and constructive, and revisions have been made accordingly. We hope that all these changes fulfill the requirements to make the manuscript acceptable for publication in Atherosclerosis.
Enclosed please find the improved manuscript together with the original version.

Thank you for your continued attention.

Manuscript Withdrawal

Dear Professor John Lee,

Thank you for letter dated July 8, in which I have noticed that my article is accepted for publication but has to wait its turn due to the backlog of the accepted articles and you would like to know my preference about its publication. Since the journal of Scientific Instruments is approaching me about a solicited Review and I think my article submitted to you may be more suitable to the journal, so could it possible for you to return the article if there is not too much trouble?

I thank you again for your constant attention to my manuscript, and apologize to you for the trouble because of the withdrawal.

Further Alterations

Dear Professor William Cart,

Thank you very much for your standard notice of receipt of April 2, 2011, acknowledging the acceptance of my paper. But if the manuscript has not yet been sent go the press, I would like to alter in the abstract the statement "And its cross-section is measured" into the expression "And its cross-section is $(6.25 \pm 0.02) \times 10^{-28}$ m^2", so as to let the reader get the information more concretely and quantitatively.

I hope the above alteration will not cause you too much trouble.

Counter-proposals to the Suggested Revisions

Dear Editor,

I appreciate very much your valuable suggestions and advice on my submitted manuscript. You will notice that the modifications have been made and the figures and plates redrawn according to your instructions.
But here I would like to add some explanations as follows.

Concerning the title, I did not change "A dynamical nuclear magnetic resonance" to "Nuclear magnetic resonance in a chemical conversion system" because I thought the implications of the two seemed to be similar or equivalent, and the former appeared simpler and also in common use internationally. However, I also agree to the change if you think the latter is much better.

In respect to your proposal of supplementing the effect of the radioactive field, the detailed program of the computation and examples of the speed conversion, etc., I think the suggestions are very good indeed, and therefore I am planning to prepare another article about them.

11.4　Reflections and Practice

1. Distinguish the types of the following two letters according to their functions and purposes.

Letter 1
Dear Sir, Madame, or Other,
We would like to submit the manuscript entitled "***", which we wish to be

considered for publication in ***.

We certify that we have participated sufficiently in the work to take public responsibility for the appropriateness of the study design and method, and the collection, analysis, and interpretation of the data.

We have reviewed the final version of the manuscript and approve it for publication. To the best of our knowledge and belief, this manuscript has not been published in whole or in part nor is it being considered for publication elsewhere.

Best Regards.

Yours Sincerely,

Authors : ***,***,***
(Submitting author: ***, ***University. EMAIL: ***;
Corresponding author: ***,*** University. EMAIL: ***)

Letter 2

Mr. Editor,

In November 2006, Rudolfo Maestro, the son of Mexican immigrant parents, and a teacher within the urban school district of SampleCity, Minnesota, was one of just 50 teachers nationwide to receive the prestigious Sample Educators Award. As I'm sure you may know, the Sample Awards have been called "the Academy Awards of Teaching", and come with a purse of $100,000 —no strings attached.

With the mass exodus of many Caucasian, middle class students from urban districts like SampleCity, MN, the honor is quite an achievement for this young, 9-year veteran teacher. Add to that the fact that Mr. Maestro was raised and educated in the very same district where he now teaches, and the human-interest appeal is even greater.

I propose a 2,000 word interview with nationally recognized educator Rudolfo Maestro, focusing on the teacher's role within school districts that are slowly becoming re-segregated. How does this teacher, himself a minority, promote racial harmony and social justice within the "microcosm"of his classroom? What challenges has he faced in his short teaching tenure? What can other educators and social activists learn from his work?

Since his award, Mr. Maestro had been interviewed for various publications, including Sample Newspaper, Sample Magazine, and Sample Trade Publication, but he has agreed to grant me an exclusive interview on this particular angle in relation to his award.

The personality of this educator is of great magnitude. As an interviewer, I've found him to be gregarious, talkative and very forthcoming. I am positive I can convey this personality into an article, and that other teachers, both minority and otherwise, will be able to take a little piece of his practice from this article.

I could have a rough draft to you within three weeks of acceptance. I anticipate a question and answer format, but am flexible based on your magazine's needs.

I also ask that you take a look at my resume attached. I am an experienced editor, writer and proofreader, with cognate education in Teacher Preparation, making me knowledgeable in this subject field. I am currently working for Sample City's Sample Magazine.

Thank you for this opportunity.

Yours in writing,

Author's name

2. Write the letters called for in the following imaginary cases, making up headings, address, dates, signature, and other additional details, if necessary.

(1) Suppose that you are going to submit your paper for publication in a famous journal in your area. Prepare a cover letter.

(2) Assume that you have received a letter from the editor, saying your paper has been accepted, but need some revisions. Write a reply to the editor.

(3) Write a letter to your editor, assuming you want to revise your manuscript that has been accepted by the journal.

3. Following is a submission letter in the field of chemistry. Read and comment on it in terms of the correctness and appropriateness of the language used. In pairs, revise or rewrite the letter.

Dear Editors,

The attached files include the revised manuscript A and the revised manuscript B in which our revised points were described by using blue letters according to the referees' comments. In addition, we did some additional experiments to see that if the substrate and product remaining in the ionic liquid solvent could improve the reaction yield during the recycled runs. The experimental results revealed that 2%-3% N-acyl-a-amino acid remaining in the ionic liquid solvent did improve the recycling yields about 2%-3%. Meanwhile the isolation yield was slightly higher than extraction yield by 3%.

The details of corrections and modifications in our manuscript were presented in P.S.

Yours sincerely,
Dawei Li
Professor of Chemistry
Department of Chemistry
XZY University 31000
P.R.China

Part V Writing Accuracy

Chapter Twelve   Common Errors in Research Papers

To err is human.

——English proverb

Since the intended goal of research paper writing is the transmittal of scientific information, even the most well-written research paper is ineffective if the facts, theories, and observations presented are in error. The content must be as scientifically accurate as is humanly possible. Accurate content is important to RP writing. However, it is quite difficult to produce accurate content without the help of accurate language expressions. Accuracy is one important aspect of the total fabric of good writing. One minor mistake with a preposition or plural in a sentence might not be concerned. But if a writer is making mistakes in every other word, there is likely to be serious confusion about meaning. The most common error types are highlighted in this chapter: lexical, sentential, and textual.

12.1   Errors at the Lexical Level

12.1.1   Confusion of Words / Phrases

Some English words/phrases are by very easily confused for their similar meanings, which has become a big problem for authors in English writing.

Below are some of these words or Phrases.

"**In this paper**" **and** "**in this study**". These two phrases are often confused by many authors. Two errors occur when these phrases are used. The first is overuse. In some papers written by learner writers, these phrases can occur as much as twice per page. In papers written by expert writers, these phrases are reserved for primarily two uses:

1. In the Introduction and Conclusion to emphasize the content of the paper.
2. In the body of the paper, after referring to the work not done by the author.

Therefore, if either phrase occurs more than three times in a paper, its use is questionable. Actually, the reader is aware that the work presented is by the author (unless the author states otherwise), so there is no reason to repeat these phrases. The second error is more subtle. The two phrases are wrongly interchanged.

[Awkward] In the paper, a SZG4031 towing tractor is used as the sample vehicle, it components equivalent physical parameters are obtained by UG design and testing.

[Correct] In this study, a SZG4031 towing tractor is used as the sample vehicle, it components equivalent physical parameters are obtained by UG design and testing.

The "study" is the work the author/s did. The paper is the mode to present this work and is what the reader is holding/ reading. Keep it in mind that the writer can also use other phrases such as "in this research", and "this paper present".

"**Respectively**". "Respectively" refers back to two or more persons or things only in the order they were previously designated or mentioned. If two lists are given, "respectively" pairs the list entries according to the order in which they are given. In this case the use of "respectively" is to allow the writer to give a lot of information without confusing the reader or writing several short sentences. For example, *Bobby, Nicole and Daren wore red, green and blue coats, respectively.* This sentence means that Bobby wore a red coat; Nicole wore a green coat; Daren wore a blue coat.

"Respectively" is usually at the end of the sentence. The word is used to mention the order that must be important to the meaning of the sentence; otherwise it is not used. With regard to the usage of this word, three kinds of errors often occur as the following examples indicate.

1. "Respectively" is misplaced in the sentence; it is put before the nouns to which it refers.

[Incorrect] Equations 2~6 can be respectively linearized as:...

(equations given) ...

[Correct] Equations 2~6 can be linearized as...(equations given)...,

respectively.

[Incorrect] The weights of the two experts are respectively 0.600 and 0.400.

[Correct] The weights of the two experts are 0.600 and 0.400,

respectively.

2. "Respectively"s inserted to show that there is a certain order in which something is done. However, the order is already implied elsewhere in the sentence or does not need to be expressed because it does not add value to the meaning of the sentence.

[Incorrect] If both the core technology score and core quality score of a bottleneck process are, respectively, below certain scores, then we refer to strategy 1, otherwise, if either is, respectively, above a certain score, then we refer to strategy 2. Similarly, if the core technology and core quality are, respectively, above a certain score, then we refer to strategy 3, otherwise, if either is, respectively, below a certain score, then we refer to strategy 4.

[Incorrect] If both the core technology score and core quality score of a bottleneck process are below certain scores, then we refer to strategy 1, otherwise, if either is above a certain score, then we refer to strategy 2. Similarly, if the core technology and core quality are above a certain score, then we refer to strategy 3, otherwise, if either is below a

certain score, then we refer to strategy 4.

[Incorrect] Then, the rows of vortex due to both of the long and short blades are transformed into two singularities on the ζ-plane and integrate the induced velocity along the blades respectively.

[Correct] Then, the rows of vortex due to both of the long and short blades are transformed into two singularities on the ζ-plane and integrate the induced velocity along the blades.

3. It is unclear to what "respectively"refers.

[Incorrect] The dynamic characteristics of a rotor with asymmetric stiffness or with initial warp have been studied before respectively [1-4].

[Correct] The dynamic characteristics of a rotor with asymmetric stiffness or with initial warp have been studied before [1-4].

[Incorrect] The inlet and outlet temperature of the air cooler were measured using two thermocouples respectively.

[Correct] The inlet and outlet temperature of the air cooler were measured by using two thermocouples.

"**such as**" **and** "**etc.**". "Such as" and "etc." are commonly misused by Chinese English writers. "Such as"means "for example" and implies that an incomplete list will follow; etc. means "and so on" and is used at the end of a list to show it is not complete. Therefore, using "such as" and "etc." together is redundant.

[Incorrect] Studies of methodology and process of implementing remanufacturing mainly focus on durable products such as automobile motors, printers, and etc.

[Correct] Studies of methodology and process of implementing remanufacturing mainly focus on durable products such as automobile motors, and printers.

[Incorrect] Compared to traditional industry, Micro-electronic fabrication has three characteristics such as high complexity, high precision and high automation.

[Correct] Compared to traditional industry, Micro-electronic fabrication
has three characteristics: high complexity, high precision and
high automation.

Scientists or researchers. Invoking scientists or researchers often makes their text sound like a creature of a 1950's press release. Usually, these words are used to indicate the importance of an idea:

Many scientists have studied PHB, mostly because of its potential use
as a biodegradable plastic.

Such a statement can be interpreted in two ways, depending on the reader's opinion of scientists:

Scientists are always right, therefore, PHB is important.

Scientists are full of baloney, therefore, PHB is unimportant.

The sophisticated reader wants to know which scientists; at a bare minimum, cite all the many scientists involved. Better yet, get rid of the pesky scientists because they are not important to the story of PHB.

The potential use of PHB as a biodegradable plastic has prompted
numerous studies of its physical properties and its production and
purification. [1,2,3,4]

The scientists have disappeared. The people who produced the studies can be tracked down through the references if necessary.

Misuse of " a, an, the " . The single most common mistake is the omission of articles "a, an, the". This occurs because Mandarin has no direct equivalent of articles and the rules for using them are somewhat complicated for a non-native speaker.

Articles signal that a noun will follow and that any modifiers between the article and the noun refer to that noun (a big blue bicycle / the first award). "a , an" are indefinite articles; "the" is a definite article. Every time a singular non-count noun, a common noun that names one countable item, is used, the noun requires some kind of determiner. These articles are usually wrongly used as the following examples indicate.

1. The articles are omitted where they are required.

[Incorrect] Figure 2 shows the distribution of relative velocity on

学术论文写作与发表

surface of main and splitter blades.

[Correct] Figure 2 shows the distribution of relative velocity on the
surface of the main and splitter blades.

[Incorrect] Watt is unit of electrical power.

[Correct] A watt is the unit of electrical power.

2. The articles are used where they are not needed or contribute to wordiness.

[Incorrect] The voltage induced in the primary winding is proportional
to the primary inductance according to the Faraday's law.

[Correct] The voltage induced in the primary winding is proportional to
the primary inductance according to Faraday's law.

3. An article is put in the wrong place of a sentence.

[Incorrect] Aluminum is not as a good conductor as copper.

[Correct] Aluminum is not as good a conductor as copper.

4. The definite article and the indefinite article are wrongly interchanged.

[Incorrect] The software PowerSHAPE is chosen to be a 3D modeling
tool; it is good at dealing with free surfaces and curves.

[Correct] The software PowerSHAPE is chosen to be the 3D modeling
tool; it is good at dealing with free surfaces and curves.

12.1.2 False Collocation

Novice authors often feel at a loss when choosing an appropriate word for certain context. Some collocation problems are related to incorrect parts of speech, which are relatively more obvious to find out; some involve the mismatching of words and contexts, which is more difficult to detect and demands the writer's much proficiency of English. Of the various collocation problems, the matching of words and prepositions is the most frequent one.

[Incorrect] The academy is in charge of developing satellite technology
and making space research.

[Correct] The academy is in charge of developing satellite technology
and conducting space research.

[Incorrect] It is worthwhile to point out that heating may bring about certain change in the structure of any material.

[Correct] It is worthwhile pointing out that heating may bring about certain change in the structure of any material.

[Incorrect] Since these reasons, it has become desirable for a computer to separate the text from images.

[Correct] For these reasons, it has become desirable for a computer to separate the text from images.

12. 2　Errors at the Sentential Level

A sentence is the basic unit of communication in all forms of English. One of the most important skills a writer can have is the ability to compose clear, complete sentences. A sentence is a group of words with a subject and a verb that expresses a complete thought. The most egregious errors that novice writers, especially Chinese writers, can make include run-on sentences, sentence fragments, faulty parallelism, excessive use of passive voice, dangling modifiers, too long sentences, and punctuation errors.

12.2.1　Run-on Sentences

A run-on sentence is two or more independent clauses that are not jointed properly, including combining two complete sentences using a comma.

Rubidium has no major uses, however, it is more common in the earth than zinc, copper, or nickel.

This is a run-on sentence. The writer does not recognize that "however" is an adverb, and therefore cannot join two independent clauses. Such run-on sentences occur frequently in writing, but they can be easily corrected once identified. The alternative revisions of the sentence above are as follows:

1. By ending the first sentence with a period and starting a new sentence with the new thought.

Rubidium has no major uses. This metal, however, is more common in the earth than zinc, copper, or nickel.

2. By placing a semicolon between the two sentences.

Rubidium has no major uses; however, it is more common in the earth than zinc, copper, or nickel.

3. By placing a comma and conjunction after the first sentence.

Rubidium has no major uses, but it is more common in the earth than zinc, copper, or nickel.

4. By making one of the sentences dependent on the other.

Rubidium, which has no major uses, is more common in the earth than zinc, copper, or nickel.

While using any of the methods is acceptable and grammatically correct for revising a run-on sentence, sometimes it makes more sense to use one method over another. Concerning the example sentence above, the third revision is better than the others.

When the run-on sentence contains two short and related sentences, like the example sentence above, it makes more sense to connect the two using a semicolon. Likewise, if the sentences are lengthy and/or unrelated, it makes more sense to write two separate sentences.

12.2.2 Sentence Fragments

Fragments are incomplete sentences. Usually, fragments are pieces of sentences that have become disconnected from the main clause. One of the easiest ways to correct them is to remove the period between the fragment and the main clause. Other kinds of punctuation may be needed for the newly combined sentence.

Below are some examples with the fragments. Notice that the fragment is frequently a dependent clause or long phrase that follows the main clause.

[Incorrect] Purdue offers many majors in engineering. Such as electrical, chemical, and industrial engineering.

[Correct] Purdue offers many majors in engineering, such as electrical, chemical, and industrial engineering.

[Incorrect] The current city policy on housing is incomplete as it stands. Which is why we believe the proposed amendments should be passed.

[Correct] Because the current city policy on housing is incomplete as it
stands, we believe the proposed amendments should be passed.

Some fragments are clearly not pieces of sentences that have been left
unattached to the main clause; they are written as main clauses but lack a
subject or main verb.

[Incorrect] A story with deep thoughts and emotions.

[Possible Revision A] She told a story with deep thoughts and emotions.

[Possible Revision B] Gilman's "The Yellow Wallpaper", a story with
deep thoughts and emotions, has impressed
critics for decades.

[Incorrect] With the ultimate effect of all advertising is to sell the product.

[Possible Revision] The ultimate effect of all advertising is to sell the product.

[Incorrect] By paying too much attention to polls can make a political
leader unwilling to propose innovative policies.

[Possible Revision] Paying too much attention to polls can make a political
leader unwilling to propose innovative policies.

These last two examples of fragments with no subjects are also known as mixed
constructions, that is, sentences constructed out of mixed parts. They start one way
(often with a long prepositional phrase) but end with a regular predicate. Usually the
object of the preposition (often a gerund, as in the last example) is intended as the
subject of the sentence, so removing the preposition at the beginning is usually the
easiest way to edit such errors.

12.2.3 Faulty Parallelism

Look out for faulty parallelism whenever you use one of the following
constructions:

> *a* **and** *b*
>
> *a*, *b*, **and** *c*
>
> *a* **or** *b*
>
> *a*, *b*, **or** *c*

The clauses or phrases joined by the conjunctions should have similar grammatical structures to ensure that our readers can follow the logic of our sentences, and to avoid awkwardness. Consider the following sentence,

> My first-year philosophy professor was informative, lively, and a source
> of inspiration.

Notice that the first two phrases in the *a, b,* **and** *c* construction are adjectives, while the third is a noun phrase. This sentence suffers from faulty parallelism.

To repair the faulty parallelism here, we will have to change the elements *a* and *b* into noun phrases or the element *c* into an adjective. Always choose the simplest option. In this case it is easiest to change the final element, *c*, into an adjective:

> My first-year philosophy professor was informative, lively, and inspiring.

Often faulty parallelism can be repaired by paying close attention to where we place our verbs. Look at the following sentence:

> My philosophy professor *not only* demonstrated how to reason
> persuasively *but also* how to avoid logical fallacies.

Note that element *a* begins with a verb but element *b* doesn't. To repair the faulty parallelism, you can add a verb to the start of element *b*. However, since the same verb will work for both parts of the construction, the more elegant solution is to drag the verb demonstrated to the front of the whole construction:

> My philosophy professor demonstrated *not only* how to reason
> persuasively *but also* how to avoid logical fallacies.

Problems with parallelism often arise from the careless use of clauses beginning with the subordinating conjunction *that*:

> He warned me to revise my essay and that I should pay close attention
> to parallel structures.

To repair the problem, choose either an infinitive *(to + verb)* or a that clause on both sides of the *a* and *b* construction. In this example, the infinitive provides the more elegant solution:

> He warned me to revise my essay and to pay close attention to parallel
> structures.

Another major error that forms a typical core typicalmistake is the excessive use of passive sentences in the paper. In English, all sentences are in either "active" or "passive" voice:

[Active] Werner Heisenberg formulated the uncertainty principle in 1927.

[Passive] The uncertainty principle was formulated by Werner Heisenberg in 1927.

In some sentences, passive voice can be perfectly acceptable. We might use it in the following cases: 1) the actor is unknown; 2) the actor is irrelevan; 3) we want to be vague about who is responsible; 4) we want to emphasize the person or thing acted on.

We are writing in a scientific genre that traditionally relies on passive voice. Passive voice is often preferred in lab reports and scientific research papers, most notably in the Materials and Methods section:

The sodium hydroxide was dissolved in water. This solution was then titrated with hydrochloric acid.

In these sentences we can count on our readers to know that we are the one who did the dissolving and the titrating. The passive voice places the emphasis on our experiment rather than on us.

Historically science has encouraged the use of passive voice, because passive voice helps emphasize the objectivity of the sciences. However, too many passive sentences in a paper often make our writing more awkward, less direct, and less clear. In the past several years there has been a movement in science away from the passive voice. Scientists often now prefer active voice in most parts of their published reports, even occasionally using the subject "we" in the Materials and Methods section. One reason for this is a philosophical shift in our thinking about science: we are more ready to acknowledge the role of the observer or investigator in the shaping of knowledge. In fact, many journal editors have responded to a growing demand for greater transparency in science by requiring that published scientific papers clearly identify the role

and the source of funding of each contributor. Active voice does a much better job of emphasizing agency—the idea that every action has an actor. Another good reason behind this growing preference for active voice is stylistic: the active sentence is easily understood.

Learn some simple sentence patterns that will help our writing benefit fully from the directness of active voice. For example, refer to figures, tables, equations, "results" , "studies" and "evidence" at the beginning of the sentence rather than at the end.

Figure 1 illustrates the quadratic relationship between distance and velocity.

Experimental evidence shows that the typical dose-response curve has an inverted J-shape.

If we are referring to a technique or procedure, we can also achieve greater directness by making it the subject of our sentence:

PCR analysis produced clones of the toxin B DNA originally isolated in cultures of C. difficile from hospital patients.

12.2.5 Dangling Modifiers

The term dangling modifier refers to a word or phrase that modifies a word not clearly stated in the sentence. Dangling modifiers surface from time to time in academic writing. Even experienced editors sometimes miss them. But once you know how to spot dangling modifiers, they are reasonably easy to fix.

Having finished the instructions above, the tube was put into a refrigerator.

"Having finished" is a participle expressing action, but the doer is not the tube (the subject of the main clause): the tube don't finish assignments. Since the doer of the action expressed in the participle has not been clearly stated, the participial phrase is said to be a dangling modifier.

Observe that the opening modifier implicitly raises the question of who has finished the instructions above. To fix the problem here, we can choose a noun or a phrase that does answer the question of who, that's to say, we could name the appropriate or logical doer of the action as the subject of the main clause:

Having finished the instructions above, the student put the tube into a refrigerator.

Another solution would be to change the phrase that dangles into a complete introductory clause by naming the doer of the action in that clause. Then the opening no longer raises a question that needs an immediate answer:

The student having finished the instructions above, the tube was put into a refrigerator.

Sometimes we could combine the dangling modifier and the main clause into one:

[Incorrect] To improve his results, the experiment was done again.

[Correct] He improved his results by doing the experiment again.

Dangling modifiers are often followed by the expletive it. (Expletives are words that play a role in a sentence without contributing anything to the meaning.)

To institute a carbon tax, *it* is essential first to address the increasing influence of corporate lobbies.

Some uses of the expletive it are unavoidable ("it is raining outside"), but many just make sentences wordy and vague. Fixing this kind of dangling modifier can therefore solve more than one problem at once. But the solution requires that we think carefully about exactly to whom or what the modifier is trying to connect. The answer is not always that obvious. Though occasionally the collective "we" may work, always be as precise as we can:

To institute a carbon tax, reforming politicians must first address the increasing influence of corporate lobbies.

Dangling modifiers coupled with the expletive phrase *it* is show up especially frequently in science papers, largely because some scientific contexts prefer the passive voice. However, the passive voice can sometimes lead to awkward, not to mention ungrammatical, constructions:

Before adding the compound, it was determined that the solution's PH was 6.4.

It, of course, cannot add compounds to solutions, so the question of who

did so remains. Often—though not always—we can rewrite the modifier and preserve the passive voice:

Before the addition of the compound, it was determined that the solution's PH was 6.4.

But if our discipline provides any leeway (many science writers overuse the passive voice out of mere habit), the active construction will provide a much clearer solution:

Before adding the compound, I determined that the solution's pH was 6.4.

12.2.6 Too Long Sentences

Too long sentences are especially common in our writing. One can usually recognize a too long sentence by its length—sixty words or more. However, sentences of smaller lengths can also be too long because so many of us are so used to padding our writing that it's hard even to imagine how to cut the fat. Writing to required page lengths is one of the reasons many writers are inclined to write wordy sentences. Here's a typical example from a technical paper. The passage specifies the protocol for tracking changes in an accounting system:

To ensure that the new system being developed, or the existing system being modified, will provide users with the timely, accurate, and complete information they require to properly perform their functions and responsibilities, it is necessary to assure that the new or modified system will cover all necessary aspects of the present automated or manual systems being replaced. To gain this assurance, it is essential that documentation be made of the entities of the present systems which will be modified or eliminated.

Revising this isn't easy. For one thing, what information can be dispensed with, and what should be preserved? Is it important, for instance, to note that information should be "timely, accurate, and complete"? Or is this obvious from the context? There's no absolute right answer. It depends on what our own voice is, and what our readers expect. Here's one possible revision that maintains a fairly formal tone:

> To ensure that users have all the information needed to do their jobs, the new system must preserve the present system's critical functions. Therefore, all modifications to the present system must be documented.

The revision reads much better than the bloated original. Remember that concision is a constant battle. The keys are to build around strong verbs, prefer the active voice to the passive voice, be suspicious of adverbs, and toss out empty words and phrases.

Besides wordiness, more than one idea contained in a sentence might result in too long sentences. It is acceptable to put several supporting ideas in one Chinese sentence to show their relationship, but the main idea and each supporting idea are typically written in separate English sentences.

> The rate gyroscope itself consists of a very rapidly spinning wheel and electronic components which sense changes in the axis of rotation of the wheel, and which modify and output a digital signal accordingly.

The sentence is awkward, confusing and obscure because it violates the rhetorical principle—one idea per sentence. Such too long sentences can be avoided by giving each idea a sentence of its own and connecting the sentences. Semicolons might be used where we really want to emphasize the relationship between ideas.

> The rate gyroscope itself consists of a very rapidly spinning wheel. Changes in the wheel's axis of rotation are sensed by electronic components, which modify and output a digital signal proportional to the changes.

Look at another example:

[Original] Today, society is witnessing the steady progression of women towards equality with their increasing presence in the working world and in government and their gradual move outside the home.

[Revision] Today, society is witnessing women's steady progression towards equality. Moving beyond the limits of the home,

women are claiming new and increasing authority in government, business, and other historically male-dominated areas.

The basic idea of the revision is to separate one sentence into two by putting actions into verbs and actors into subjects. In the original, "women" was the logical actor, but grammatically it was the object of a preposition, "of". In the revision, "women" becomes the subject of the verb in the second sentence: women are claiming. The revision then builds its argument around that core subject-verb clause. True, the revision is longer, but in and of itself that's not very important. It reads more easily, has some rhythm, and lets the reader pause: a much easier-to-read opening. The first sentence of the revision is simple and general, and the second starts developing the detailed argument. That's a pattern that good writers use a lot.

12.2.7 Punctuation Errors

Punctuation marks are the traffic signs and signals placed along the reader's road. They tell him when to slow down and when to stop, and sometimes they warn him of the nature of the road ahead. Chinese students often punctuate wrongly in technical context as a result of partial understanding of the use of punctuation in English. Detailed examples will be provided in this section.

1. Some Chinese punctuations including "书名号、顿号、着重号和分隔号", don't appear in English.

[Incorrect] 《Science and Nature》

[Correct] *Science and Nature*

2. When a sentence ends with an abbreviation, the period should be saved as there is already a dot behind the abbreviation.

[Incorrect] The diameter of this rope is 2 in.

[Correct] The diameter of this rope is 2 in.

3. No colon between the predicate and its object.

Some important vitamins found in vegetables are vitamin A, thiamine, niacin, and vitamin C.

4. No colon after words such as "says", "tells", "shows", etc. while quoting.

"If you could go down to the corner hardware and say you want wire," says a physicist at the University of California at Berkeley, "and they would say, what kind, normal or superconducting? That would certainly change the world."

5. No colon after "such as", "including", or "for example".

The trees on our campus include many fine Japanese specimens such as black pines, gink goes, weeping cherries, and cut leaf maples.

6. Semicolon should be used to separate a series of items in a list which contains internal commas.

Discharges of these hazardous substances occurred through the following: spills when loading vehicles; spills and over-spills when filling the tanks; leaks from supply pipes; and corroded welds, rust holes, and cracks in the seams of the tanks themselves.

7. No comma after coordinating words like "and", "but", "or", "nor", "for", "yet", "so".

Occasionally soap operas are taped, but more often they are being performed as they are telecast.

8. No comma after "such as".

Many shade-loving plants, such as begonias, impatiens, and coleus, can add color to a shady garden.

9. Missing comma after abbreviations "i.e.", and "e.g."

The amount of solute you obtain in this way depends not only upon the volume of solution but also upon the concentration of solute, i.e., the amount of solute in a given amount of solution.

10. Commas separate introductory phrases and clauses.

After cooling, the exhaust gases continue to expand.

12.3 Errors at the Textual Level

12.3.1 Lack of Unity

Unity is a very important characteristic of good writing. Unity, which is also named singleness of purpose, means that one paragraph is about ONLY ONE main topic. In other words, all the sentences in a paragraph are telling the reader about ONE main topic. Unity contributes to an effective paper which is coherent and easy to follow.

If a paragraph contains a sentence or some sentences that are NOT related to the main topic, then we say that the paragraph "lacks unity", or that the sentence is "off-topic". With regard to science writing, this "off-topic" error is easy to be found. Another error easily committed is the poorly written topic sentence, which also contributes to the lack of unity.

The topic sentence is the single idea concentrated on by all the sentences in a paragraph. A good topic sentence usually declares a single point. Such a single point is the controlling idea of the paragraph. Sometime we want to declare several points in a topic sentence, but we fail to indicate the relationship between these points according to the supporting sentences. Although all the information we want to express has been included in the paragraph, the paragraph still lacks unity. Here is a typical example :

It has only been since the early 1960s that isokinetic devices i.e. devices that allow for movements to be performed at controlled velocities, have been available on the commercial market. These devices, such as the Cybex II Isokinetic Dynamometer (Lummex Inc.), measure the torque produced throughout the range of voluntary limb movements held at constant pre-set velocities. They provide an ideal means of measuring an individual's torque generating capacities, and thereby greater information on the expression of strength in maximal voluntary limb movements. This is what traditional methods could not do.

In the paragraph above the author has put two points in the topic sentence, without indication, through punctuation. This could be easily improved by putting one point, not two, in the topic sentence. In most cases, we prefer to keep the two points in the topic sentence, using two commas to show which is more important. We could revise the example above in two ways:

Either

It has only been since the early 1960s that isokinetic devices, which allow for movements to be performed at controlled velocities, have been available on the commercial market.

Or

Isokinetic devices, which have only been available on the commercial market since the early 1960s, allow for movements to be performed at controlled velocities.

The words in bold mark the main point; the point between the commas is secondary. The first option means that the main point of the paragraph is the commercial availability of the devices; the second option means that the main point is what these devices do. According to the developing sentences in this paragraph, it can be seen that the second is a better choice.

12.3.2 Lack of Coherence

Imagine that we have gotten this far: we have the thesis, the topic sentence, and truckloads of evidence to support the whole lot. But even though we have followed our outline and everything is "there", the paper just doesn't seem to hold together. The writer has a problem with coherence. A lack of coherence is easy to commit and diagnose, but not so easy to cure. An incoherent essay doesn't seem to flow. Its arguments are hard to follow. The reader has to double back again and again in order to follow the gist of the argument. Here is typical example:

According to Maxwell, the correlation between equality and gender characterized the first regime of the women's movement that began in the late nineteenth century. Indeed, the crafters of the constitution never intended women to be included in the governing of the United States, but at no point did they ever envision that women might be able to vote. The significance of the "all men are created equal"

clause of the constitution becomes clear, as Maxwell states, when one acknowledges that women were not considered to be men, as they are now. At this point, Maxwell highlights a key component in the success of women's suffrage: women needed first to convince society that they were indeed people.

This paragraph has so many different sentence subjects that the paragraph is hard to follow. When faced with a paragraph like this, readers often ask the writer to think about which of the five grammatical subjects, if any, is actually the subject of the paragraph. When this happens, it's a good idea to make sure that the grammatical subjects are consistent. Besides keeping the subjects consistent, repetition and transitions could be used to create a sense of unity. However, overuse of them certainly results in redundancy. Look at the following paragraph:

> The ancient Egyptians were masters of preserving dead people's bodies by making mummies of them. Mummies several thousand years old have been discovered nearly intact. The skin, hair, teeth, fingernails and toenails, and facial features of the mummies were evident. It is possible to diagnose the disease they suffered in life, such as smallpox, arthritis, and nutritional deficiencies. The process was remarkably effective. Sometimes apparent were the fatal afflictions of the dead people: a middle-aged king died from a blow on the head, and polio killed a child king. Mummification consisted of removing the internal organs, applying natural preservatives inside and out, and then wrapping the body in layers of bandages.

Though weak, this paragraph is not a total washout. It starts with a topic sentence, and the sentences that follow are clearly related to the topic sentence. In the language of writing, the paragraph is unified (i.e. it contains no irrelevant details). However, the paragraph is not coherent. The sentences are disconnected from each other, making it difficult for readers to follow the writer's train of thought.

Below is the same paragraph revised for coherence. Italics indicates pronouns and repeated/restated key words, boldface indicates transitional tag-words, and underlining parts indicate parallel structures.

The ancient Egyptians were masters of preserving dead people's bodies by *making mummies* of them. **In short**, mummification consisted of removing the internal organs, applying natural preservatives inside and out, and then wrapping the body in layers of bandages. **And** *the process* was remarkably effective. **Indeed**, *mummies* several thousand years old have been discovered nearly intact. *Their skin*, hair, teeth, fingernails and toenails, and facial features <u>are still evident</u>. *Their diseases* in life, such as smallpox, arthritis, and nutritional deficiencies, <u>are still diagnosable</u>. **Even** *their* fatal afflictions <u>are still apparent</u>: a middle-aged king died from a blow on the head; a child king died from polio.

The last effective method to create a sense of unity is to follow the principle of moving from old to new. If a writer puts the old information at the beginning of the sentence and the new information at the end, he/she will accomplish two things. First, he/she ensures that his/her reader is on solid ground, moving from the familiar to the unknown. Second, he creates sentences that end emphatically. Thus each sentence can be seen to be a little bridge to what has already been presented: the sentence starts out on the familiar ground and then takes a step forward. Good writing consists of linking these many little steps into a sustained argumentative journey (of course with a few bold exceptions every so often). Anyhow a writer is usually advised to shift less important ideas to the front of the sentence, and to shift more important ideas to the end. These two paragraphs are identical except for their final sentences:

> **[Original]** True capitalists distrust governments, and don't think they make good arbiters of morality. They believe that individuals are best qualified to manage their own lives and pursue happiness in their own way. Freedom is what capitalists believe in, in other words.

> **[Revision]** True capitalists distrust governments, and don't think they make good arbiters of morality. They believe that individuals are best qualified to manage their own lives

and pursue happiness in their own way. In other words, capitalists believe in freedom.

The original throws away its energy in that last sentence because freedom comes right at the beginning of the sentence. The revision saves the new information for the sentence's natural emphasis point, its end. The principle is of fundamental importance: start sentences with familiar material, and end with new.

12.4 Ways to Steer Clear from Errors

12.4.1 Proofreading

The two words, "editing" and "proofreading", are easily confused. They should be differentiated from one another. Proofreading a research paper simply means reviewing texts, spotting errors and even marking them with proof correction symbols to make our copies clear and consistent; while editing means revising parts of sentences or paragraphs or changing the whole thing.

Proofread is a great help to get rid of punctuation and grammar mistakes in our research paper. Read the actual page proofs. It's not a good idea to proofread the draft of our research paper over the computer. What we see in our PC monitor is different from what we can read in real page proofs. In some publication companies, proofreaders are allowed to read their works at the top of their voices. Proofread our research paper backward. This may sound funny, but we can spot errors when reading the pages from right to left, instead of left to right, and from bottom to top, rather than the usual way around. Some useful suggestions about how to proofread our papers are as follows:

"**Bigger is better.**" Why not enlarge the font types and sizes of our preliminary draft? Why use black font color when we can also try pink, violet or orange? Doing this is very elementary, but that's the essence of it all: Altering the overall look of your research paper will make it less familiar to us, so we have to have a fresher set of eyes. Just don't forget to put it back to its previous appearance when we're all done.

Use helpful icons in our PC. And these include the word count, spell checker, grammar checker and Thesaurus all found in the Microsoft Word program in our computer. But don't depend on them totally as they don't get to catch every single mistake in research papers all the time.

Get a second opinion. Believe it or not, but detecting our own mistakes will be two times harder than in others', work. Might as well get a "fresh set of eyes" not only to correct our output, but to get clarifications and suggestions for improvement.

Follow our instinct. Even if the final output of our research paper has already been printed, if we are still in doubt, then check it out! Beware of repetitive mistakes such as misspelled words (*occasion* not *ocasion*, *millennium* instead of *millenium*, *tomorrow* and not *tomorow*, and so on); typing errors ("form" which means "from"); and how to use *which* and *that*, *can* and *could*, *will* and *would*, *shall* and *should*, *may* and *might*, etc.

As mentioned earlier, errors in research papers are just normal. But what isn't normal is when we keep on doing these boo-boos all over again. Brush up our proofreading skills: It's like giving importance to the minutest details in our research paper that brings out the difference.

12.4.2 Content Editing

Most writers understand how to proofread for grammar, punctuation, and misspelled words, but editing for content can be a bit trickier. Content editing goes beyond the usage.

At the most basic level, content editing helps us determine that our paper has been written in the same point of view throughout, and that it is in the most appropriate point of view for the context. A basic content edit will also ensure that the content is in the correct order, such as that facts are presented consecutively and the plot doesn't backtrack (unless on purpose).

There are many questions about the clarity of our writing that can be answered by a thorough content edit:

1. Are the explanations clear and unambiguous?

2. Do the explanations lead readers to the appropriate conclusions?

3. Are the facts, details, and evidence consistent throughout the text?

4. Are the case studies appropriate for the context?

5. Are images, lists, and side stories in the right places?

6. Does the information flow cleanly from one idea to the next?

7. Do page numbers or section references match?

8. Content editing will also help you decide if anything is missing.

9. Are there any gaps in the information or explanation provided?

10. Have there been any new developments that should be added to the context?

11. What could be added to the paper to make it even better?

A content editor can offer the service to us. If we don't have access to a content editor, we may be able to find a freelance editor who is willing to review our manuscript for content errors and suggestions. At the very least, read our writing aloud to check for the flow of ideas and pass it on to someone we trust. Another person is most often able to find all those nagging details that a reader unfamiliar with the content of the paper is most likely to trip up on.

12.5　Reflections and Practice

1. Please improve the following wrongly translated English sentences.

(1)［汉语原句］这种新方法具有效率高、容易调整的优点。

［英语错句］This kind of new method have the advantage of high efficiency, easy adjustment.

(2)［汉语原句］本文首先讨论了这种信号的特点，然后讨论了它的产生。

［英语错句］This paper first discusses the features of this signal, and then its generation is described.

(3)［汉语原句］这太设备的特点是操作简便、价格低廉。

［英语错句］The features of this device are easy in operation and low in price.

(4)［汉语原句］强调指出了光强随圆柱体直径变化的正弦规律。

［英语错句］The sine law of the variance of the light intensity brought due to the variance of the cylinder diameter has been pointed out emphatically.

(5)[汉语原句]我们的方法与以前同一问题的文章中所述的不同。

[英语错句] Our method is different from previous articles discussed the same problem.

(6)[汉语原句]只有通过对该系统性的研究，我们才能了解它的优点。

[英语错句] Only through studied the performance of the system, its advantages can be understood.

(7)[汉语原句]若自偏电路设计不当，LC 振荡器会出现间歇振荡。

[英语错句] If the self-bias circuit does not design good, the LC oscillator will take place chopping oscillation.

(8)[汉语原句]本文对提高打印速度和印字质量提供了一种机辅设计手段。

[英语错句]This paper provided a kind of means of computer aid design for progressing the printing speed and the printing quality.

(9)[汉语原句]同时给出了三轴稳定跟踪的数学描述及全补偿条件。

[英语错句]The mathematical description and the full-compensation conditions of the 3-axes steady-tracking principle are also given.

(10)[汉语原句]文中比较了STM和ATM，表明ATM将是BISDN的基础。

[英语错句]STM and ATM are compared. It shows that ATM should be the ground of BISDN.

(11)[汉语原句]对构件的承载能力作了具体的分析。

[英语错句]The detailed analysis of the ability of bearing loads of the components is given.

(12)[汉语原句]共有M个多边形，其顶点数为N。

[英语错句]There are M polygons altogether, whose vertex number is all N.

(13)[汉语原句]这是由于在PN结上存在一个电容之故。

[英语错句]This is due to that there exists a capacitance on the PN junction.

(14)[汉语原句]这个方法需要精确的定位，这就使得它的实现具有一定的难度。

[英语错句]This method requires accurate location and this makes its realization have a little difficulty.

(15)[汉语原句]对A的识别和对B的确定是使用这一方法的先决条件。

[英语错句]The recognition of A and determining B are the

prerequisite for the use of this method.

(16)[汉语原句]最后提出了实现这种方法应注意的一些问题和解决方法。

[英语错句]At last, we provided some problems that could be noted in implementing this method and solving ways.

(17)[汉语原句]由于缺陷的存在，构件的疲劳寿命将大大降低。

[英语错句]Because of the existing of the defect, the fatigue life of the components will decrease very much.

(18)[汉语原句]导出了一个计算电荷分布的简单公式，最后举了若干例子。

[英语错句]A simple formula to calculate the charge distribution is derived and some examples are given in the end.

(19)[汉语原句]并讨论了这一方法与扫描法相比的优点。

[英语错句]As compared with the scanning methods, the advantages of this method has discussed also.

(20)[汉语原句]已知常数K，就能算出C来。

[英语错句]Giving the constant K, C can be calculated.

(21)[汉语原句]这种生成器产生的序列的周期几乎都大于任意给定的值。

[英语错句]Almost all of the periods of sequences generated by such generator are greater than arbitrary given value.

(22)[汉语原句]这个信号太小了以至于不能使晶体管Q4导通。

[英语错句]This is a too small signal that it cannot make transistor Q4 conduct.

(23)[汉语原句]锡的熔点没有铅的高。

[英语错句]Tin does not have a melting point as high as lead.

(24)[汉语原句]该电阻上的电压为零点几伏特。

[英语错句]The voltage on the resistor is zero point several volt.

(25)[汉语原句]这台新设计的仪器质量很好。

[英语错句]This new designed instrument is in good quality.

(26)[汉语原句]这台转动的机器将在一二分钟后自动停下来。

[英语错句]This running machine will stop of itself after one minute or two minute.

(27)[汉语原句]所有这一切表明采用PECVD方法制备Tisi2薄膜的工艺是完全可行的。

[英语错句] All these illustrate the technology of TiSi2 thin film by PECVD is quite workable.

(28)[汉语原句]在这种情况下，输入不会下降，输出也不会下降。

[英语错句]In this case, the input does not fall; the output does not fall, too.

(29)[汉语原句]导体的电阻不仅取决于制成导体的材料，而且也取决于导体的尺寸和温度。

[英语错句]The resistance of a conductor not only depends on the material with which the conductor is made, but also on the size and temperature of the conductor.

(30)[汉语原句]在10月8日早上又发射了一颗通信卫星。

[英语错句]Another comsat has been launched in the morning of the 8th of October.

(31)[汉语原句]这个问题有待解决。

[英语错句]This problem waits to solve.

(32)[汉语原句]在宇宙中似乎只有两种电荷。

[英语错句]There seems to be only two kinds of electric charge in the universe.

(33)[汉语原句]这个电荷与存在的其他电荷相互作用。

[英语错句]This charge interacts with other present charges.

(34)[汉语原句]现有的教科书没有提到这一点。

[英语错句]The now existed textbooks do not make mention of this point.

(35)[汉语原句]X的所有值均不能满足这一方程。

[英语错句]All values of X can't satisfy this equation.

(36)[汉语原句]这个电压几乎是测不出的。

[英语错句]This voltage almost can not be measured.

(37)[汉语原句]铜的导电率比铁高。

[英语错句]The conductivity of copper is higher than iron.

(38)[汉语原句]在这个实验室中，这台仪器比其他的灵敏。

[英语错句]In this laboratory, this instrument is more sensitive than any one.

(39)[汉语原句]这本书的序言写的很好。

[英语错句]The preface of this book was well written.

(40)[汉语原句]为了发射无线电波，必须产生高振荡。

[英语错句]Sending out radio waves, high-frequency oscillations must be generated.

(41)[汉语原句]波能绕其通道上的障碍物的边缘弯曲行进，这一特性称为绕射。

[英语错句]Waves are able to bend around the edge of an obstacle in their path, this property is called diffraction.

(42)[汉语原句]这条曲线显示了该电路中的电流随外加电压的变化情况。

[英语错句]The curve shows the situation of the current in the circuit varying with the applied voltage.

(43)[汉语原句]他们对这一论题很感兴趣。

[英语错句]They are very interesting in this topic.

(44)[汉语原句]其他类型的电动机也广泛地用在工业上。

[英语错句]Other types of the electric motor also are widely used in industry.

(45)[汉语原句]任何学生均不会解这种特殊的方程。

[英语错句]Any student cannot solve this kind of special equation.

(46)[汉语原句]直到发明了显微镜后对细菌的真正研究才成为可能。

[英语错句]Until the invention of the microscope the real study of bacteria became possible.

(47)[汉语原句]必须了解这种材料是否能经受住这么大的力。

[英语错句]It is necessary to know if this material can stand a so large force or not.

(48)[汉语原句]两小时后该机器会自动地再次启动。

[英语错句]The machine will automatically start to operate again two hours later.

(49)[汉语原句]该实验是从八点钟开始的。

[英语错句]The experiment began from eight o'clock.

(50)[汉语原句]电压是用伏特来度量的。

[英语错句]Voltage is measured with volt.

(51)[汉语原句]这两位工程师正忙于设计一种新型的软件。

[英语错句]This two engineers are busy to design type of new software.

(52)[汉语原句]铜是一种物质，而空气也是一种物质。

[英语错句]The copper is a kind of matter and so does air.

(53)[汉语原句]他们将赴北京参加一个通讯国际会议。

[英语错句]They will leave to Beijing to attend a international conference of communications.

(54)[汉语原句]这种材料很难加工。

[英语错句]This material is very difficult to be machined.

(55)[汉语原句]若把式（7）代入式（8）就得到a=b。

[英语错句]Eq.(7) is substituted in Eq.(8), we obtain a=b.

(56)[汉语原句]声音传播的速度比光慢的多。

[英语错句]Sound travels less faster than light is.

(57)[汉语原句]功等于力乘以距离。

[英语错句]Work equals to force multiplying distance.

(58)[汉语原句] 这个设备有它的一些独特的优点。

[英语错句]This equipment has a few advantage all it's own.

(59)[汉语原句]我们已定义了度量m的质量单位。

[英语错句]We have defined mass units to measure m.

(60)[汉语原句]所得结果与测量值相吻合。

[英语错句]The results obtained fit the experimental values.

(61)[汉语原句]本文讨论了三维多通道稳态流场和温度场的数值计算与实验。

[英语错句]Numerical computation and experiment for the steady-state flow and temperature fields in three dimensional multi-channels are discussed in this paper.

(62)[汉语原句]定义了一种描述图论中某些工程问题求解的算法语言（我们称之为图论算法语言）。

[英语错句]An algorithm language (we call it the Algorithm Language for the Graph Theory) to describe the solution of some engineering problems in the graph theory is defined.

(63)[汉语原句]通过观察一种新药对病人的影响，我们才能看出它的治疗效果。

[英语错句]Through observing the effect of a new kind of drug to patient, one can see its efficiency of cure.

(64)[汉语原句]铁的导电性能几乎与铝一样好。

[英语错句]The iron is almost as good conduct as the aluminum.

(65)[汉语原句]我们容易确定该物体的重量。

[英语错句]We are easy to determine the weight of the body.

(66)[汉语原句]磨檫使得输入机器的功大于由机器所做的有用功。

[英语错句]Friction make the work put into a machine be greater than the useful work accomplished by it.

(67)[汉语原句]瓶中的空气受热后就会膨胀。

[英语错句]On heating, the air in the bottle will be expanded.

(68)[汉语原句]接受机的许多原理也适用于发射机。

[英语错句]Many of principles of a receiver also apply for a transmitter.

(69)[汉语原句]最后对某加固计算机机箱在强迫风冷下的热特性进行了数值计算，获得了一些对电子设备热设计有价值的结果。

[英语错句]In the end, the thermal characteristics of a certain reinforced computer case under the forced air convection are calculated. Some valuable results for the thermal design of electronic equipment are obtained.

(70)[汉语原句]文中提出了一种使融合中心错误概率为最小的次佳判决融合方案，它包括融合中心的最小错误概率（MEP）检验和各种传感器的似然比检验。

[英语错句]A suboptimal decision fusion scheme that minimizes the probability of error at the fusion center is presented, it consists of a minimum-error-probability(MEP) test at the fusion center and likelihood ratio tests at the sensors.

(71)[汉语原句]本文引入所谓的网络"站级"概念，并基于此概念将网络中的所有结点在源一宿方向上划分成等级，从而构成不同等级的结点集。

[英语错句]A so-called "node-step" concept is introduced. Based on this concept, all nodes in the network are organized into steps on the source-to-destination direction so as to form several sets of stepped nodes.

(72)[汉语原句]空气把压力施加于四面八方。

[英语错句]The air exerts the pressure toward every direction.

(73)[汉语原句]这些窗子均经受不了这么大的力。

　　[英语错句]All these windows cannot withstand so large force.

(74)[汉语原句]物体越热，它辐射的能量就越多。

　　[英语错句]The hoter the body, the more the energy it radiates.

(75)[汉语原句]这是中国所曾制造的最大的飞机。

　　[英语错句]This is the largest aircraft which was ever manufactured in China.

(76)[汉语原句]半导体将在第二章加以讨论。

　　[英语错句]Semiconductor will be discussed in the chapter 2.

(77)[汉语原句]某些元素产生放射的能力被称为放射性。

　　[英语错句]The ability for some elements to give off radiations is referred as the radioactivity.

(78)[汉语原句]为了做到所有这一切，对计算机科学必须要有一个清晰的了解。

　　[英语错句] To do all these, sound knowledge of computer science is necessary.

(79)[汉语原句]不仅温度和光影响导电率，而且给半导体加杂质也会使导电率变化很大。

　　[英语错句]Not only temperature and light affect the conductivity, but the addition of impurities to semiconductors will also make it to change greatly.

(80)[汉语原句]人们经常发射各种卫星来获得有关太空的信息。

　　[英语错句]The various satellites are frequently launched to obtain informations about space.

(81)[汉语原句]我们的半导体工业是在20世纪50年代形成的。

　　[英语错句]Our semiconductor industry comes into being at the end of 1950s.

(82)[汉语原句]直流电总是朝一个方向流动。

　　[英语错句]The direct current always flow to one direction.

(83)[汉语原句]在这里必须使用一个8伏特的电池。

　　[英语错句]A 8-volts battery must be used here.

(84)[汉语原句]我和我的同事们愿对W.史密斯教授给予我们的大力帮助表示感谢。

[英语错句]I and my colleagues would like to express our thank to professor W. Smith for his great help.

(85)[汉语原句]结果表明，这两种方法其实质是一致的，只不过各有其应用的条件。

[英语错句]The results indicate that this two methods are consistent, they have only respective applied condition.

(86)[汉语原句]设计出了一种新的算法，它能自动地维持有用的副本的生存，从而大大地减少了网内的分组副本数。

[英语错句]A kind of new algorithm has been designed to be able to keep the life of useful copies. Thus the number of packet copies in a network will be decreased obviously.

(87)[汉语原句]已知电阻和电流，就能计算出电压来。

[英语错句]Giving resistance and current, voltage can be determined.

(88)[汉语原句]这台仪器的价格很昂贵。

[英语错句]The price for this instrument is expensive.

(89)[汉语原句]这个设备占地方太多。

[英语错句]This device takes too many places.

(90)[汉语原句]机器人是一种特殊的电子设备。

[英语错句]Robot is a kind of special electronic devices.

(91)[汉语原句]这位科学家说："电子是绕原子核旋转的"。

[英语错句]This scientist said "Electrons move round nucleus".

(92)[汉语原句]就在我们闭合电路的那一瞬间电流开始流动。

[英语错句]The current starts flowing on very moment we close circuit.

(93)[汉语原句]除了该电子外，氢原子还含有一个正质子。

[英语错句]Except the electron, hydrogen atom also contains a positive proton.

(94)[汉语原句]本规则有几个例外。

[英语错句]There is a few exceptions for this rule.

(95)[汉语原句]这六个月来他们一直在设计一种新型的计算机。

[英语错句]They have been designed a type of new computer since these six months.

(96)[汉语原句]本文应用场匹配方法分析和计算了这种结构的色散特性和

耦合阻抗，结果与Karp的实测值基本一致。

[英语错句]In this paper, a field-matching approach has been used, and have obtained dispersion characteristic and coupled impedance of this structure. Theory gives good agreement with experimental results obtained by Karp.

(97)[汉语原句]改进后的算法在位移矢量的估值精度上优于原算法。

[英语错句]The improved algorithm has an advantage compared with the original one in the accuracy of the estimation of the displacement vectors.

(98)[汉语原句]本文注意到该系统具有永久磁铁的特点，提出一种比较简易的方法，解决其磁路的计算问题。

[英语错句]This paper pays attention to having the characteristic of permanent ring magnet, and presents a kind of simple method of solving problem of calculation for the magnetic circuit.

(99)[汉语原句]格的最主要特点是将矢量空间R^n进行划分，这在矢量量化和编码理论中具有重要的现实意义。

[英语错句]The most important characteristic of lattices is that it divides the vector space R^n, and thus there is an important practical significance in the application of lattices to the vector quantization and coding theory.

2. The following paragraphs are extracted from articles submitted to a journal. Obviously it is a poor introductory paragraph with various mistakes like careless use of space, false use of run-on sentence, monotonous use of words, misuse of tense, and poor transition. Please revise them.

(1) The receptor activator of nuclear factor-κB ligand (RANKL) and its decoy receptor, osteoprotegerin (OPG), are important bone metabolism molecules, which directly control osteoclastogenesis. Many studies revealed that OPG-RANKL was expressed in human periodontal ligament cells (HPDL cells) and HPDL cells might regulate the alveolar bone metabolism through the RANKL/OPG system [1-3]. There are various factors acting on periodontal tissue in oral micro-environment which control the metabolism of local bone tissue through changing the concentration of OPG and RANKL.

(2) In this paper, in view of the randomness uncertainty and fuzziness uncertainty of meteorological parameters in ice disaster weather, we established a wind and ice loading risk analysis model, and proposed a fuzzy risk predictive

method. This paper aims to build basic model of risk assessment and provide warning information of the loading line to operator.

(3) In view of power systems lack load risk assessment and warning mechanism in facing extreme ice disaster weather, this paper established a wind and ice loading risk analysis model, and proposed a fuzzy risk predictive method. According to design standards of IEC60826-2003 and Q/GDW179-2008, we established wind and ice load curve and principle of state division, which are the basis of load calculation and risk identification. Furthermore, a transmission line reliability model is built, which considered the randomness uncertainty of line load. Pointing at the fuzzy characteristic of meteorological parameters and state division, this paper proposed a fuzzy prediction method, which provides a convenient tool for load forecast as well as deal with fuzziness uncertainty.

Teacher's Manual

Chapter One General Introduction to Research Paper Writing

1. (1) Rectification of this fault is achieved by insertion of a slash.
   (2) An improvement of its performance can be affected by the use super-heated steam.
   (3) The accuracy of the results is doubtful.
   (4) The addition or remove of heat may change the state of matter.
2. (1) The difference between the treated and untreated specimens can be clearly seen.
   (2) Significantly, even at this late date, Lautrec was considered somewhat conservative by his peers.
   (3) It focused on a subject that a great deal of the bourgeois and upper-class exhibition-going public is regarded as anti-social and anti-establishment.
   (4) Later Florey collaborated with Paul Fildes in an experimental study of the use of curare to relieve the intractable muscular spasms which occur in fully developed infection with tetanus or lockjaw.
   (5) When a patient is admitted to a psychiatric inpatient unit, the clinical team should avoid the temptation to commence specific treatments immediately.
   (6) Therefore after six months the dieter is behaving according to all twenty-six goals and she has achieved a considerable reduction in sugar intake.
   (7) Modern houses have so many labour-saving devices that it is difficult for the person at home to have adequate exercise by doing chores, cooking, and looking after a family.
   (8) Simply making the effort to reclaim this wasted material for fertilizer would have a positive effect on greenhouse releases.
   (9) It is difficult to imagine exactly what is meant by saying that such a classification is natural as any collection of objects could be classified in this way.
   (10) Unfortunately, since there are so many possible explanations, the correct one is most difficult to ascertain.
   (11) These exercises can easily be incorporated into an exercise routine, with each exercise repeated a number of times.
   (12) Fleming succeeded in isolating a streptococcus from the cerebrospinal fluid of the patient.
   (13) Effective vaccines prevent such hazards, but only if a social organization could ensure that all potential mothers are vaccinated in good time.
3. (1) A primary education system was established throughout Ireland as early as 1831.
   (2) This will reduce the amount of drug required and so the cost of treatment.
   (3) The material amenities of life have increased in Western society.
   (4) The press reflected the living culture of the people; it could influence opinion and reinforce existing attitudes but it did not create new forms of entertainment.

(5) Thus, he should have investigated how the patient has coped previously.

(6) The exchange rate fluctuated quite violently.

(7) In 1947 the Treasury raised the question of excluding South Africa (and India) from the sterling area.

(8) Dieters often feel that they should totally eliminate high-fat and high-sugar foods.

(9) Thus when a Gallic bishop in 576 converted the local Jewish community to Christianity, those who refused baptism were expelled from the city.

(10) Western scholars gradually produced a corpus of translations from the Arabic and studies of Islam.

(11) Ms. Tucker, Lord White's 29-year-old companion, has since retracted her statement.

(12) Discussion of the outcome of experiments that have used this method will be postponed until Chapter 7.

(13) They did not easily accept or tolerate differences in others.

(14) My high-school friend signed up for three years with the army so he could save enough money to go to university and study law.

(15) The solitary feeding of insectivores in forests was therefore attributed to a foraging strategy involving the pursuit of cryptic and easily disturbed prey by singletons.

(16) In style, the turn toward abstraction and simplification occurred earliest with Anquetin and Bernard and next with van Gogh.

(17) For Klein that cloudless day never arrived, but he never relinquished his hope for a just world.

(18) Eventually the Irish party was forced to return to Westminster.

(19) The court thinks it just and equitable to return the property.

(20) The English liked coal fires even though they do not always produce much heat.

(21) The story told by German propaganda, however, betrayed nothing of the mounting hopelessness of the 6th Army's position.

(22) These exercises can easily be incorporated into an exercise routine, with each exercise repeated a number of times.

(23) Marx took as one of his main tasks the understanding of how this system came into being in order to discover why this system had such power.

(24) This was before he had read the guidelines on how to conduct the research.

(25) The pressure to succeed as an individual made most women believe that the problems they encountered were probably of their own making.

4. Text 1: Most overdoses are taken when individuals are finding it difficult to sort out their life problems in a clear way. For this reason, the approach to treatment must, above all else, be a clear one; that is, one which helps the patient separate out each of his problems and plan ways of dealing with them.

Text 2: Wagner was what might be called a subjective artist in that his art had its source in his personality. His work seems virtually independent of the epoch in which he lived.

On the other hand, Bach can be considered an objective artist. He seems to have worked only with the forms and ideas that his time proffered him, feeling no inner compulsion to open out new paths.

5. (1) In spite of   (2) In the first place, In the second place
   (3) In the same way   (4) but   (5) As a result
   (6) thus   (7) For example   (8) usually
   (9) Naturally   (10) Unfortunately   (11) namely
   (12) also   (13) then,   (14) In fact
   (15) Indeed   (16) actually   (17) especially
   (18) namely

6. (1) The lives they chose seem overly ascetic and self-denying to most women today.
   (2) Weismann suggested that animals become old because, if they did not, there could be no successive replacement of individuals and hence no evolution.
   (3) By analogy, it may be possible to walk from one point in hilly country to another by a path which is always level or uphill, and yet a straight line between the points would cross a valley.
   (4) There are certainly cases where this would seem to have been the only possible method of transmission.

7. (1) correctly hedged   (2) not correctly hedged
   (3) not correctly hedged   (4) correctly hedged
   (5) correctly hedged   (6) correctly hedged
   (7) correctly hedged   (8) not correctly hedged
   (9) not correctly hedged   (10) not correctly hedged

8. Text 1 is more academic than Text 2.

9. Open

Chapter Two   Reading Strategies

1. (1) B   (2) A   (3) B   (4) A   (5) C
   (6) D   (7) A   (8) A   (9) A   (10) B

2. (1) D   (2) A   (3) B   (4) D

3. Paragraph 1: (1) B   (2) A   (3) A
   Paragraph 2: (1) D   (2) D   (3) D
   Paragraph 3: (1) B   (2) A   (3) C   (4) A   (5) B   (6) A   (7) C   (8) D

Chapter Three   Note-taking

1. [Version A] plagiarism
   [Version B] Improper paraphrase, plagiarism
   [Version C] appropriate paraphrase
   [Version D] not plagiarism

2. Paraphrase 2 has paraphrased using its one words, accurately reflecting and citing the author's idea.

Paraphrase 1 is plagiarism. It has combined copied pieces of the author's language without quotation marks or citations.

3. Passage 1: Jackson (1988) notes, "Buddhadasa's conception of human beings as active controllers of their own material and spiritual progress is most clearly presented in his view of work as integrating both social and spiritual activity."(p. 200)

   Passage 2: Contrary to many historians, Eric Foner argues that the Republican platform of 1860 should not be understood as an indication of Whig dominance of the party (175).

4. In "An Anthropologist on Mars", Sacks notes that although there is little disagreement on the chief characteristics of autism, researchers have differed considerably on its causes. As he points out, Asperger saw the condition as an innate defect in the child's ability to connect with the external world, whereas Kanner regarded it as a consequence of harmful childrearing practices.

5. (1) Deforestation increased markedly in the four southern states during 1987 and 1988. On account of this, it is heartening news that during the early part of the 1989 dry season the burning seemed to have been curtailed somewhat. The reason for this is a combination of policy changes, better controls on burning, and most important of all an exceptionally wet "dry" season.

   (2) In 1851, the average family size was 4.7, roughly the same as it had been in the Seventeenth century. However, the 1½ million couples who married during the 1860s, which the historian G. M. Young described as the best decade in English history to have been brought up in, raised the figure to 6.2.

   (3) Tropical forests are defined here as evergreen or partly evergreen forests, in areas receiving not less than 100 mm of precipitation in any month for two out of three years, with mean annual temperature of 24-plus degrees Celsius, and essentially frost-free.

   (4) The third National Government followed upon the resignation of the Liberal ministers and of the free trader, Snowden, in September 1932, after which it became little more than a Conservative government, with the addition of a few ex-Labour and Liberal politicians, all owing their seats to an electoral pact with the Conservatives.

6. (1) British weather is changeable.

   (2) Many learners find English pronunciation difficult.

   (3) The British drink a large amount of tea.

   (4) Big cities have growing traffic problems.

   (5) Most food nowadays contains additives.

   (6) Work can be organized to suit the capabilities of humans.

   (7) Most people in developing countries have to carry all their water.

7. Stoner and Wankel (1986) conclude that it is the view of Organizational Development practitioners that a better and more enjoyable team effort can result if the workplace environment encourages emotional openness.

8. Open

Chapter Four Title, Author/Affiliation, Keywords and Acknowledgements

1. (1) An Application of the Artificial Neural Network (ANN) in the Analysis of Structural Mechanics

   (2) Developing Computer Internet and Spreading Culture and Information

   (3) Monoclonal Antibodies in Nuclear Medicine

   (4) Mechanisms of Retinal Damage: Chronic Laser Radiation

   (5) Commercialization of the Natural Gas Vehicles

   (6) Prediction of Wash Load Rate by Bed Load Function?

   (7) a good title

   (8) Foreign Languages Learning and Cultural Background Teaching

   (9) Keywords: English, Vocabulary, Tendency

   (10) using larger space between words: Collocation Context Connotation

2. EEG and ECG assessment of mental fatigue in a driving simulator

Ding Xiaoguang[1]   Du Zhenzi[2]

1 **** University, Xi'an 710049, China 2 **** University, Xi'an 710049, China

Abstract: Driving Mental fatigue, which is a contributing factor to some serious transportation crashes, is measured by Electroencephalogram (EEG) and Electrocardiograph (ECG) in this study. Altogether, the ECG and multi-channel EEG of thirteen healthy subjects were recorded while they were performing a continuous simulated driving task for 90 minutes. The study investigated several important physiological parameters of the preprocessed ECG and EEG signals. The results shows that the possible indices for measuring simulated driving mental fatigue are significantly different before and after performing the driving task ($p<0.05$), involving the EEG alpha and beta, the relative power, the amplitude of P300, the approximated entropy of ECG, the low and high bands power of heart rate variability (HRV).

Key words: EEG; ECG; P300; HRV; driving mental fatigue

3. (1) The acceleration of gravity continually increases as the body approaches the earth, Air resistance being neglected.

   (2) Almost all metals are good conductors, silver being the best.

   (3) In Group 1, we have hydrogen and the alkali metals, all of low density.

   (4) There are many reasons for this, among them the fact that simulation allows the assessment of the potential performance before a newly designed system is operable.

   (5) Laser, its creation being thought to be one of today's wonders, is nothing more than a light that differs from ordinary lights.

4. Open

Chapter Five Abstract

1. Sentence 1: background information　　　Sentences 2-4: research aim
   Sentences 5-8: methodology　　　Sentences 9-10: results
   Sentence 11: conclusion

2. This study summarizes the results of a four-year project in science education conducted in a rural setting with English learners in grades K-6 in an elementary school district, southern California. Data were collected to measure student achievement in science, writing, reading, and mathematics for participating students. These data were analyzed relative to the number of years that students participated in inquiry-based science instruction that included the use of science notebooks. Results indicated that the achievement of English learners increased in relation to the number of years they participated in the project. The longer they were in the program, the higher their scores were in science, writing, reading and mathematics.

3. (1) c　　　(2) d　　　(3) b　　　(4) e　　　(5) a

4. Sentences 1-2 are concerned with background information and can be eliminated
   Sentences 3-4 represent purpose and method, and should therefore be combined.

5. Text 1: Worldwide, enrolments in higher education are increasing. In developed countries over half of all young people enter college, while similar trends are seen in China and South America. This growth has put financial strain on state university systems, so that many countries are asking students and parents to contribute. This leads to a debate about whether students or society benefit from tertiary education.

   Text 2: It is widely recognized that a university degree benefits the individual, since a graduate can expect to find a better job with a higher salary. In the USA the average graduate will earn $1 million more in a lifetime than a non-graduate. Many governments now expect students to pay a proportion of tuition costs, although it is argued that this discriminates against poorer students. Some countries give grants to students whose families have low incomes because their education is seen to be beneficial for the nation as a whole.

6. China is one developing country (but not the only one) which has imposed fees on students since 1997. The results have been surprising: enrolments, especially in the most expensive universities, have continued to rise steeply, growing 200% overall between 1997 and 2001. It seems in this case that higher fees attract rather than discourage students, who see them as a sign of a good education. They compete more fiercely for places, leading to the result that a place at a good college can cost $8000 per year for fees and maintenance.

7. Developing countries are under the greatest financial pressure. They may also experience difficulties in introducing loan schemes for students, since the lack of private capital markets restricts the source of borrowing for governments, which are often unable to raise sufficient cheap funds, while a further restraint has been the high default rates by students unable to repay their loans.

Chapter Six Introduction and Literature Review

1.

Establishing a Context	Reviewing previous research	Advancing to present research	Research purpose	Value/Finding/ Paper Structure
Sentences 1-5	Sentence 6	Sentence 7	Sentence 8	Sentences 9-12

2. students; a; /; /; /; evaluations; /; behaviors; students; The; the; relationships; /; perceptions; /; /; /; /; /; /; /; the; skills; perceptions; /; relationships; / ; teachers; students.

3. Is; prefers; are; attempt; maintains; are; lead; suggests; lead; is supported; have attempted; are; are; are; can be used; have; depict; might expect; would imitate; observed; have already been suggested; have yet been done; was; may help; is

4. Open

5. Text 1: general to specific

   Text 2: different approaches

   Text 3: time order

6. Open

Chapter Seven Methods

1. Open

2. Sentence 1: Overview

   Sentence 2: Sample

   Sentences 3-5: Restrictions

   Sentences 6-8: Sampling technique

   Sentences 9-11: Procedure

   Sentences 12-13: Materials,

   Sentences 14-16: Procedure,

   Sentence 17: Variable

   Sentence 18: Statistical treatment

3. Open

4. Open

Chapter Eight Results

1. were taught; displays; used; performed; scored; indicate; appears; is to be hoped

2.

	Verb(s)	Tense	Function
Sentence 1	shows	simple present tense	locate data
Sentence 2	were	simple past tense	describe data
Sentence 3	is indicated; explain	simple present tense	describe data
Sentence 4	show	simple present tense	presenting finding
Sentence 5	was; was	simple past tense	present findings
Sentence 6	would seem	modal	comment
Sentence 7	should be noted	modal	comment
Sentence 8	is; was	simple present tense	comment

3. Open

4. Open

5. Open

Chapter Nine Discussion

1. provide; was; pose; were; are; is; is; should be

2. Paragraph 2: B; A; C

   Paragraph 3: F; D; E

   Paragraph 4: G; I; J

3. Open

4. Open

5.

Patellofemoral disorders <u>are</u> amongst the <u>most</u> common clinical conditions encountered in the sporting and general population. Patellofemoral pain <u>is usually</u> described as diffuse, peripatellar, anterior knee pain. Symptoms <u>are typically</u> aggravated by activities such as ascending or descending stairs, squatting, kneeling, running and prolonged sitting.

A <u>wide</u> variety of disorders <u>may</u> fall under the umbrella term of patellofemoral pain. <u>As a result</u>, a thorough systematic evaluation of the patient's lower extremity alignment, patellar mobility and alignment, muscle flexibility, strength, co-ordination, soft tissue and articular pain <u>is</u> important in determining the <u>possible</u> causes of patellofemoral pain and prescribing an optimal rehabilitation programme. Management of patellofemoral pain syndrome <u>often</u> includes reduction of pain and inflammation through cryotherapy, heat therapy, massage therapy, muscle flexibility and strength training (<u>especially</u> quadriceps), patellar taping, bracing, orthotics, correction of abnormal biomechanics or other causative factors, acupuncture and surgery.

Chapter Ten Data Presentation

1. 1) grew slightly   2) rose steadily   3) fell sharply
   4) increased slightly   5) sharp rise   6) slight drop
2. 1) density   2) illustrates/shows   3) between
   4) emptier/less crowded   5) role/part   6) since/because
   7) tend
3. 1) table   2) range/variety   3) marriage
   4) Britain   5) rate   6) Iran
   7) half   8) proportion/figure   9) result/consequence
4. Open

Chapter Eleven Procedures of Paper Publication

1. Letter 1 is a cover letter and letter 2 is a query letter.
2. Open
3.

> Dear Editors,
>
> The attached files contain the manuscript A and manuscript B revised in accordance with the referees' comments. The revisions are highlight in blue.
>
> We did some additional experiments to see if the substrate and product remaining in the ionic liquid solvent could improve the reaction yield during the recycled runs. The experimental results revealed that 2%-3% N-acyl-a-amino acid remaining in the ionic liquid solvent did improve the recycling yields about 2%-3%. Meanwhile the isolation yield was slightly higher than extraction yield by 3%.
> Yours sincerely,
> Dawei Li
> Professor of Chemistry
> Department of Chemistry
> XZY University 31000
> P.R.China

Chapter Twelve Common Errors in Research Papers

1. (1) This new method has the advantages of high efficiency and easy adjustment.
   (2) This paper begins with the discussion of the features of this signal, followed by the description of its generation.
   (3) This device is characterized by easy operation and low price.
   (4) The sine law of the variation of the light intensity with the cylinder diameter has been emphasized.
   (5) Our method is different from those presented in the papers available.
   (6) Only through the study of the performance of the system, can we understand its advantages.

(7) If the self-bias circuit is not well designed, chopping oscillation will result in the LC oscillator.

(8) This paper provides a CAD method for increasing the printing speed and improving the printing quality.

(9) The mathematical description of and the full-compensation conditions for the 3-axis steady-tracking principle are also presented.

(10) A comparison of STM and ATM shows that ATM will be the basis of BISDN.

(11) A detail analysis is made of the ability of the components to bear loads.

(12) There are M polygons altogether, each of which has N vertexes.

(13) This is due to the fact that there exists a capacitance across the PN junction.

(14) This method requires accurate location, thus making its realization somewhat difficult.

(15) The recognition of A and the determination of B are the prerequisites for the use of this method.

16) Finally, we provide some problems that deserve to be noted in implementing this method and solutions.

(17)Because of the existence of the defect, the fatigue life of the components will be greatly decreased.

(18) A simple formula for calculate the charge distribution is derived and finally some examples are presented.

(19) The advantages of this method over the scanning methods have also been discussed.

(20) Given the constant K, one can be calculate C.

(21) Almost all of the periods of sequences generated by such generators are greater than any arbitrarily given value.

(22) This is too small a signal to make transistor Q4 on.

(23) Tin does not have a melting point as high as that of lead.

(24) The voltage across the resistor is a few tenths of a volt.

(25) This newly designed instrument is of good quality.

(26) This running machine will stop of itself in one or two minutes.

(27) All this illustrates that it is workable to prepare TiSi2 thin film using PECVD.

(28) In this case, neither the input nor the output does fall.

(29) The resistance of a conductor depends not only on the material of which the conductor is made, but also on the size and temperature of the conductor.

(30) Another comsat has launched on the morning of the 8th of October.

(31) This problem remains to be solved.

(32) There seem to be only two kinds of electric charge in the universe.

(33) This charge interacts with other charges present.

(34) The textbooks existing make no mention of this point.

(35) All values of x can't satisfy this equation.

(36) This voltage can hardly be measured.

(37) The conductivity of copper is higher than that of iron.

(38) In this laboratory, this instrument is more sensitive than any one else.

(39) The preface to this book is well written.

(40) To send out radio waves, high-frequency oscillations must be generated.

(41) Waves are able to bend around the edge of an obstacle in their path, a property called diffraction.

(42) The curve shows the variation of the current with the applied voltage in the circuit.

(43) They are very interested in this topic.

(44) Other types of electric motor are also widely used in industry.

(45) No student can solve this special kind of equation.

(46) Not until the invention of the microscope did the real study of bacteria become possible.

(47) It is necessary to know whether this material can stand so large a force or not.

(48) The machine will automatically start to operate again in two hours.

(49) The experiment began at eight o'clock.

(50) Voltage is measured in volts.

(51) These two engineers are busy designing a new type of software.

(52) Copper is a kind of matter and so is air.

(53) They will leave for Beijing to attend an international conference on communications.

(54) This material is very difficult to machine

(55) Substituting Eq.(7) in Eq.(8), we obtain a=b.

(56) Sound travels greatly less fast than light does.

(57) Work equals force multiplied by distance.

(58) This equipment has a few advantages all its own.

(59) We have defined mass units with which to measure m.

(60) The results obtained agree with the experimental values.

(61) The numerical computation of and the experiment on the steady-state flow and temperature fields in three dimensional multi-channels are discussed.

(62) An algorithm language for describing the solution of some engineering problems in the graph theory, which we call the Algorithm Language for the Graph Theory, is defined.

(63) One can see its therapeutic effect by observing the effect of a new drug on patient.

(64) Iron is almost as good a conductor as aluminum.

(65) It is easy to determine the weight of the body.

(66) Friction makes the work put into a machine greater than the useful work accomplished by it.

(67) Being heated, the air in the bottle will be expanded.

(68) Many of the principles of a receiver also apply to a transmitter.

(69) Finally, the thermal characteristics of a reinforced computer case under the forced air convection are calculated with some valuable results for the thermal design of electronic equipment obtained.

(70) A suboptimal decision fusion scheme for minimizing the probability of error at the fusion center is presented, which consists of a minimum-error-probability (MEP) test at the fusion center and likelihood ratio tests at the sensors.

(71) A concept of "node-step" is introduced, on the basis of which all nodes in the network are organized into steps in the source-to-destination direction so as to form several sets of stepped nodes.

(72) Air exerts the pressure in every direction.

(73)None of these windows can withstand so large force.

(74) The hotter the body, the more energy it radiates.

(75) This is the largest aircraft that has ever been manufactured in China.

(76) Semiconductors will be discussed in Chapter 2.

(77) The ability of some elements to give off radiations is referred to as radioactivity.

(78) To do all this, sound knowledge of computer science is necessary.

(79) Not only do temperature and light affect the conductivity, but the addition of impurities to semiconductors will also make it change greatly.

(80) Various satellites are frequently launched to obtain information about space.

(81) Our semiconductor industry came into being at the end of the 1950s.

(82) Direct current flow always in one direction.

(83) An 8-volts battery must be used here.

(84) My colleagues and I would like to express our thanks to Professor W. Smith for his great help.

(85) The results indicate that these two methods are consistent in essence, but they have their own applied conditions.

(86) A new algorithm has been designed which can maintain the survival of useful copies, thus greatly decreasing the number of packet copies in a network.

(87) Given resistance and current, voltage can be determined.

(88) The price for this instrument is high.

(89) This device takes up too much space.

(90) Robot is a special kind of electronic device.

(91) This scientist said, "Electrons move round the nucleus."

(92) Current starts flowing at the very moment we close circuit.

(93) In addition to the electron, a hydrogen atom also contains a positive proton.

(94) There are a few exceptions to this rule.

(95) They have been designing a new type of computer for the past six months.

(96) A field-matching approach has been used to analyze and calculate dispersion characteristic and coupled impedance of this structure. The results obtained are in good agreement with experimental ones obtained by Karp.

(97) The improved algorithm has an advantage over the original one in the accuracy

of the estimation of the displacement vectors.

(98) On the basis of the fact that this system has the property of permanent ring magnet, this paper presents a simple method for calculation of magnetic circuit.

(99) Lattices are mainly characterized by their division of the vector space Rn, which is practically important to the application of lattices to vector quantization and coding theory.

2. (1) The receptor activator of nuclear factor-κB ligand (RANKL) and its decoy receptor, osteoprotegerin (OPG) are important bone metabolism molecules, which directly regulate the process of osteoclastogenesis. Meanwhile, many studies have revealed that OPG-RANKL is expressed in human periodontal ligament cells (HPDL cells) which might regulate the alveolar bone metabolism through the RANKL/OPG system [1-3]. In fact, various factors act on periodontal tissue in oral micro-environment which modulates the metabolism of local bone tissue by changing the concentration of OPG and RANKL.

(2) To build a basic risk assessment model and to provide warning information of the loading line for operators, we established a wind and ice loading risk analysis model, and proposed a fuzzy risk predictive method based on the randomness uncertainty and fuzziness uncertainty of meteorological parameters in ice disaster weather.

(3) This paper established a wind and ice loading risk analysis model, and proposed a fuzzy risk predictive method based on power systems lack load risk assessment and warning mechanism in facing extreme ice disaster weather. According to the design standards of IEC60826-2003 and Q/GDW179-2008, we established wind and ice load curve and state division principle, which are the basis of load calculation and risk identification. Furthermore, we built a transmission line reliability model, considering the randomness uncertainty of line load. A fuzzy prediction method is proposed in view of the fuzzy characteristics of meteorological parameters and state division. This method is a convenient tool for load forecast and fuzziness uncertainty disposal.

References

Amanda Lourens. 2007. Scientific writing skills: guidelines for writing theses and dissertations[M]. Africa: SUN Press.

Anthony C. Winkler, Jo Ray McCuen-Metherell. Writing the research paper: a handbook[M]. Beijing: Peking University Press, 2008.

Ann M. Körner. 2007. Guide to Publishing a Scientific Paper[M]. Taylor & Francis e-Library.

Brooke Noel Moore, Richard Parker. 2003. Critical Thinking(7th ed) [M]. New York: Mcgraw-hill.

Carole Slade, 2007, Form and Style: Research Papers, Reports and Theses[M]. Houghton Mifflin Company.

Denzin, Norman K. & Lincoln, Yvonna S. (Eds.). 2005. The Sage Handbook of Qualitative Research (3rd ed.) [M]. Thousand Oaks, CA: Sage.

Gloria Origgi. 2010. Epistemic Vigilance and Epistemic Responsibility in the Liquid World of Scientific Publications[J]. Social Epistemology: A Journal of Knowledge, Culture and Policy, 14(6).

Karl Weber. 2007. Writing a Great Research Paper[M]. New York: Video Aided Instruction, Inc..

Janice R. Matthews, Robert W. Matthews. 2008. Successful scientific writing: a step-by-step guide for the biological and medical sciences[M]. New York: Cambridge University Press.

John Trzeciak and S.E. Mackay. 2005. Study Skills for Academic Writing[M]. New York: Phoenix ELT.

Pontille D., Torny D. 2010. The controversial policies of journal ratings: evaluating social sciences and humanities[J]. Research Evaluation, 19(5).

Rowena Murray, Sarah Moore. 2006. The handbook of academic writing: a fresh approach[M]. New York: Open University Press.

Stephen Bailey. 2006. Academic writing: a handbook for international students[M]. London:Routledge.

Swales, J. 1990. Genre Analysis: English in Academic and Research

Settings[M]. Cambridge: Cam bridge University Press.

Weissberg, R. & Buker, S. 1990. Writing up Research: Experimental Research Report Writing for Students of English [M]. New Jersey: Prentice Hall, Inc.

胡庚申. 2007.英语论文写作与发表[M].北京：高等教育出版社.

黄国文等. 2004.英语学术论文写作[M].重庆：重庆大学出版社.

刘振海. 2007.中英文科技论文写作教程[M].北京：高等教育出版社.

陈燕. 陈冠华. 2004.研究生学术论文写作方法与规范[M].北京：社会科学文献出版社.

任胜利. 2004.英语科技论文撰写与投稿[M]. 北京：科学出版社.

杨炳钧.2009.研究生英语学术论文写作基础[M].上海：复旦大学出版社.

学术论文写作与发表